The Cuban Missile Crisis

For thirteen days in October of 1962, a truly perilous flirtation with nuclear war developed between the United States and the USSR, as the superpowers argued over the installation of Soviet nuclear weapons in Cuba. Launched by rash judgment and concluded through circumspect leadership, the Cuban Missile Crisis acted as a catalyst for change during the Cold War. Resolved through back-channel negotiations, the moment is popularly remembered as the closest the world has ever come to full-scale nuclear war.

Using government memoranda, personal letters, and newspaper articles, *The Cuban Missile Crisis* details the actual events of the political history, while explaining widespread public response. In six concise chapters, Alice George introduces the history of Cold War America and contextualizes its political, social, and cultural legacy. This will be a must-read for anyone looking for an in-depth summary of these important events.

For additional resources please visit the companion website at: www.routledge.com/cw/criticalmoments.

Alice L. George is an independent historian. She is the author of *Awaiting Armageddon: How Americans Faced the Cuban Missile Crisis* and *The Assassination of John F. Kennedy: Political Trauma and American Memory* (Routledge 2012).

Critical Moments in American History

Edited by William Thomas Allison, Georgia Southern University

The Cuban Missile Crisis

The Threshold of Nuclear War

Alice L. George

Routledge
Taylor & Francis Group

NEW YORK AND LONDON

First published 2013
by Routledge
711 Third Avenue, New York, NY 10017

Simultaneously published in the UK
by Routledge
2 Park Square, Milton Park, Abingdon, Oxon OX14 4RN

Routledge is an imprint of the Taylor & Francis Group, an informa business

Library of Congress Cataloging in Publication Data
George, Alice L., 1952–.
  The Cuban missile crisis: the threshold of nuclear war/
  by Alice George.
  p. cm.
  Includes bibliographical references and index.
  1. Cuban Missile Crisis, 1962.   I. Title.
  E841.G395 2013
  972.9106′4—dc23
  2012035542

ISBN: 978-0-415-89971-0 (hbk)
ISBN: 978-0-415-89972-7 (pbk)
ISBN: 978-0-203-08149-5 (ebk)

Typeset in Bembo and Helvetica Neue
by Florence Production Ltd, Stoodleigh, Devon

Printed and bound in the United States of America by
Walsworth Publishing Company, Marceline, MO.

To Lou Oschmann, who supports me on the good days and the bad.

Contents

Series Introduction

Welcome to the Routledge *Critical Moments in American History* series. The purpose of this new series is to give students a window into the historian's craft through concise, readable books by leading scholars, who bring together the best scholarship and engaging primary sources to explore a critical moment in the American past. In discovering the principal points of the story in these books, gaining a sense of historiography, following a fresh trail of primary documents, and exploring suggested readings, students can then set out on their own journey, to debate the ideas presented, interpret primary sources, and reach their own conclusions—just like the historian.

A critical moment in history can be a range of things—a pivotal year, the pinnacle of a movement or trend, or an important event such as the passage of a piece of legislation, an election, a court decision, a battle. It can be social, cultural, political, or economic. It can be heroic or tragic. Whatever they are, such moments are by definition "game changers," momentous changes in the pattern of the American fabric, paradigm shifts in the American experience. Many of the critical moments explored in this series are familiar; some less so.

There is no ultimate list of critical moments in American history— any group of students, historians, or other scholars may come up with a different catalog of topics. These differences of view, however, are what make history itself and the study of history so important and so fascinating. Therein can be found the utility of historical inquiry—to explore, to challenge, to understand, and to realize the legacy of the past through its influence of the present. It is the hope of this series to help students realize this intrinsic value of our past and of studying our past.

William Thomas Allison
Georgia Southern University

List of Figures

Acknowledgments

I would like to express my appreciation to the helpful staffs at the John F. Kennedy Library, the Library of Congress, the National Archives, the Lyndon B. Johnson Library, the Dwight D. Eisenhower Library, the Rockefeller Archive Center, the Paley Center for Media in New York, the Martin Luther King Jr. Library and Archive, the Robert W. Woodruff Library, the Seeley G. Mudd Library, the Hoover Institution, the University of Rochester Rare Books Department, and the Wisconsin Historical Society. I also am indebted to William J. Allison and Rebecca Novack for their feedback in the editorial process, and to Elliot Blake for many errands on my behalf. I especially want to thank my life partner and proofreader Lou Oschmann for his patience and his diligence.

The Hoover Institution assisted in getting permission to use an interview with Ray S. Cline, who served in the CIA during the missile crisis era.

Timeline

July 26, 1953	Fidel Castro begins crusade to oust American ally Fulgencio Batista from Cuban leadership.
November 18, 1956	Nikita Khrushchev warns West: "We will bury you."
January 9, 1959	Fidel Castro takes power in Cuba after a long struggle against Batista.
January 8, 1960	Central Intelligence Agency begins planning means to overthrow Castro.
March 4, 1960	Belgium's *La Coubre* delivers arms to Cuba, explodes in Havana's harbor. More than 100 die in blast.
May 7, 1960	Soviet Union, Cuba establish diplomatic relations.
July 8, 1960	President Eisenhower slashes U.S. sugar imports from Cuba.
July 9, 1960	Soviet Union agrees to buy all Cuban sugar formerly purchased by United States; Khrushchev vows to protect Cuba from U.S. action.
August 28, 1960	United States places trade embargo on Cuba. Subsequently, Castro nationalizes around $1 billion in American investments.
Summer, 1960	Castro nationalizes $850 million in U.S.-owned assets in Cuba.
September 20, 1960	Khrushchev, Castro meet for first time at United Nations.
October 19, 1960	President Dwight D. Eisenhower announces partial U.S. trade embargo on Cuba.
November 8, 1960	John F. Kennedy defeats Richard Nixon in presidential election. Margin of victory among tiniest on record.
December 19, 1960	Cuba, Soviet Union announce alliance.
January 28, 1961	Kennedy receives first briefing on CIA plan to support exiles' invasion of Cuba.
April 4, 1961	Kennedy gives final approval to details of Bay of Pigs invasion.
April 9, 1961	JFK tells reporters U.S. military will not take part in attack on Cuba.
April 12, 1961	Kennedy rules out any U.S. military's role in refugee landing at Bay of Pigs.
April 14, 1961	Flying B-26 bombers, refugees fail to wipe out Castro's air force. Second round of bombing canceled to obscure U.S. involvement.
April 17–18, 1961	Roughly 1,400 refugees land near Bay of Pigs. Castro's remaining air force blocks attempts to establish a beachhead. Castro's forces kill 114, capture almost 1,200.

May 26, 1961	Khrushchev tells Presidium he is prepared to take tough action to push Western allies out of West Berlin.
June 3–4, 1961	JFK meets with Soviet Premier Nikita Khrushchev in Vienna. While browbeating JFK, Soviet leader threatens allied access to West Berlin.
July 25, 1961	Kennedy speaks to American people about Berlin Crisis, talks about calling up additional troops, encourages Americans to prepare home fallout shelters.
August 13, 1961	East German, Soviet troops build Berlin Wall, stopping flood of East Germans into West Berlin.
October 21, 1961	Deputy Secretary of Defense Roswell Gilpatric releases evidence United States has significant lead in nuclear arms race.
October 27, 1961	U.S., Soviet tanks square off at Checkpoint Charlie in Berlin.
October 30, 1961	Soviet Union tests most powerful nuclear weapon ever created—a 50-megaton device.
November 24, 1961	Inspector General's report blames CIA for misjudging Bay of Pigs issues.
Early 1962	Now under way is Operation MONGOOSE, a U.S. program to use sabotage, propaganda to undermine Castro.
January 21, 1962	Meeting in Uruguay, Organization of American States expels Cuba.
February 3, 1962	Kennedy announces near-total trade embargo on Cuba.
Late April–May, 1962	Khrushchev plans to put nuclear missiles in Cuba as counterweight to U.S. missiles in European nations, including Soviet Union's neighbor, Turkey.
May 20, 1962	Khrushchev unveils plan in Presidium presentation.
May 30, 1962	Castro agrees to accept Soviet missiles.
July 15, 1962	Soviet ships begin surreptitious shipments to Cuba.
August, 1962	U.S. intelligence agencies gather first reports of Soviet missiles in Cuba, wrongly assume weapons are conventional, not nuclear.
August 16, 1962	*Miami News* reports thousands of Soviet troops are in Cuba.
August 20, 1962	Maxwell Taylor tells JFK intensive study shows Castro cannot be toppled by Cuban forces alone.
August 23, 1962	Kennedy asks Pentagon to investigate removing Jupiter missiles from Turkey.
August 25, 1962	*Omsk* departs for Cuba with first of 67 foot medium-range missiles, 264 Soviet soldiers.
August 30, 1962	U.S. U-2 plane strays into Soviet air space.
August 31, 1962	Speaking on Senate floor, New York's Kenneth Keating claims to have evidence of nuclear missiles in Cuba.
September 2, 1962	Senators George Smathers, Homer Capehart, Strom Thurmond jointly call for action to halt Soviet buildup in Cuba.
September 4, 1962	JFK issues statement threatening grave consequences if Soviet Union puts offensive weapons in Cuba.
September 6, 1962	Khrushchev hosts Stewart Udall at Petsunda retreat, warns United States cannot dominate Soviet Union.
September 7, 1962	Kennedy asks Congress for authorization to call up 15,000 reservists.
September 8, 1962	Communist China shoots down U-2 plane over mainland.
September 12, 1962	TASS calls for end to U.S. provocation over Soviet deployments in Cuba.

September 13, 1962	In televised news conference, Kennedy states he does not believe Soviet personnel in Cuba represent threat; nevertheless, he repeats warning about offensive weapons.
September 15, 1962	First medium-range missiles reach island.
September 17, 1962	Khrushchev gives troops traveling on freighters permission to fire anti-aircraft guns; McGeorge Bundy tells senators only 2,700 Soviet "technicians" in Cuba.
September 20, 1962	U.S. Senate passes resolution authorizing use of force against Cuban aggression.
September 28, 1962	U.S. reconnaissance spots crates holding nearly obsolete, unassembled IL-28 bombers on Soviet ships bound for Cuba.
October 1, 1962	Cuban newspapers report Cubans will not bow to U.S. intimidation.
October 3, 1962	CIA Director John McCone, who believes nuclear missiles may be in Cuba, criticizes handling of Cuba by Secretary of Defense Robert McNamara, Secretary of State Dean Rusk. Congress passes joint resolution authorizing use of military force if offensive weapons in Cuba become threat to United States.
October 4, 1962	First Soviet nuclear warheads reach Cuba.
October 8, 1962	In House testimony Undersecretary of State George Ball confirms Soviet shipment of surface-to-air missiles to Cuba.
October 10, 1962	Keating alleges six medium-range missile sites in Cuba.
October 14, 1962	A U-2 flight over Cuba captures incriminating evidence on film. A Gallup Poll shows most Americans oppose military action against Cuba.
October 15, 1962	Photo analysts examine film, recognize signs of medium-range missile launch sites under construction.
October 16, 1962	JFK learns about missiles in Cuba, assembles key advisers in Ex Comm. He orders stepped-up reconnaissance of island. Ex Comm considers surgical airstrike to destroy missiles; air attack on missiles, other Cuban targets; air attacks tied to invasion; naval blockade of Cuba. Joint chiefs put pressure behind broad air attacks.
October 17, 1962	Military leaders bolster air defenses in southeastern United States. Soviet commander in Cuba, Issa Pliyev, becomes aware of increased U.S. overflights, suspects United States knows about missiles.
October 18, 1962	Reconnaissance update reveals existence of launch sites for intermediate-range nuclear missiles. Joint Chiefs of Staff recommend air strikes on missiles, other Cuban sites. JFK meets with Soviet Foreign Minister Andrei Gromyko, who dishonestly offers assurances Soviet arms in Cuba are purely defensive. Kennedy reads September 4 statement aloud.
October 19, 1962	Ex Comm establishes separate working groups to explore details of air strike or blockade. Within hours, blockade becomes favored option. Air Force General Curtis LeMay compares possible blockade to British Prime Minister Neville Chamberlain's appeasement in 1938 Munich meeting with Adolf Hitler.
October 20, 1962	Eight Soviet missiles become operational in Cuba. Most Ex Comm members support naval blockade; JFK affirms that decision. Navy alerts Guantanamo to prepare to evacuate civilians. Chinese troops attack Indian troops along shared border.
October 21, 1962	Commander of Tactical Air Command tells JFK destruction of all missiles unlikely in air strike. JFK calls publishers of *New York Times*, *Washington Post*, asks

that they withhold articles on crisis until he addresses nation. McNamara approves military's plans for blockade.

October 22, 1962   Military dependents leave Guantanamo. Strategic Air Command (SAC) puts more B-52s in air. JFK briefs former presidents and current leaders of Congress, who urge stronger action. Kennedy delivers nationally televised address. U.S. military raises alert level to Defense Condition, or DEFCON, 3. Khrushchev braces for military action. Castro announces island-wide mobilization.

October 23, 1962   Khrushchev responds with alarm to JFK's speech. At UN, Adlai Stevenson calls Cuba "accomplice" in Communist drive for world domination. Cuban ambassador Mario Garcia-Inchaustegui describes quarantine as "act of war," while Soviet Ambassador Valerian Zorin denies missiles in Cuba.

October 24, 1962   When quarantine takes effect, most large Soviet ships headed toward Cuba slow, stop, or reverse course. SAC raises alert status to DEFCON 2, just one step away from all-out war. Soviet tanker, *Bucharest*, crosses blockade line without challenge.

October 25, 1962   Khrushchev welcomes Acting UN Secretary General U Thant's proposal for temporary halt in arms shipments to Cuba, simultaneous suspension of U.S. quarantine line. Stevenson, Zorin engage in verbal warfare at UN.

October 26, 1962   Only ship to be stopped by quarantine line is Lebanese freighter, *Marucla*, which carries no weapons. Khrushchev seeks U.S. promise not to invade Cuba. Fearing imminent U.S. invasion, Castro appeals to Khrushchev in letter apparently endorsing nuclear attack on United States. Castro orders attacks on U.S. aircraft over Cuba.

October 27, 1962   Six missile sites reported operational. Khrushchev letter places new demand on United States—removal of missiles from Turkey. Soviets down U-2 plane over Cuba. U.S. plane mistakenly strays into Soviet air space, raising fears. JFK decides to offer Khrushchev public no-invasion pledge, private promise to remove missiles from Turkey, Italy. Robert Kennedy delivers deal to Ambassador Anatoly Dobrynin. JFK, Rusk pursue fallback plan, requiring UN assistance.

October 28, 1962   Khrushchev broadcasts a letter to Kennedy. In it, he agrees to withdraw missiles. Castro, who was not consulted, reacts angrily. In United States, sense of relief enwraps nation.

October 29, 1962   Under pressure from Khrushchev to spell out details of his promise to remove missiles from Turkey, JFK refuses to put anything on paper.

October 30, 1962   U Thant travels to Havana to work out UN inspection procedures for missile sites, but Castro refuses any inspection of missile removal.

October 31, 1962   President Kennedy orders renewal of low-level reconnaissance flights to monitor missile removal.

November 5, 1962   First ship leaves Cuba carrying missiles back to Soviet Union.

November 20, 1962   Khrushchev agrees to weeks-old U.S. request that IL-28 bombers be withdrawn as well as missiles.

January 7, 1963   Adlai Stevenson, Vasily Kuznetsov send U Thant message that Cuban crisis no longer requires United Nations input.

February 6, 1963   McNamara shows 400 aerial photographs in news briefing to prove presence of missiles in October, absence of missiles now.

June 10, 1963	JFK delivers speech at American University, seeking to end demonization of Soviet Union and to promote belief that two superpowers can coexist peacefully.
October 7, 1963	President Kennedy signs limited Nuclear Test Ban Treaty with Soviet Union, United Kingdom.
November 22, 1963	Sniper fire in Dallas kills Kennedy. Police quickly arrest Lee Harvey Oswald, who lived in Soviet Union for three years and has history of crusading on Cuba's behalf. Jack Ruby slays Oswald two days later. As conspiracy theories emerge about JFK's assassination, much speculation focuses on pro-Castro, anti-Castro Cubans.
October 15, 1964	Khrushchev ousted. Perceived defeat in missile crisis is one chink in armor that once protected his position.

CHAPTER 1

The Chill of the Nuclear Age

INTRODUCTION: THE COLD WAR

The Cuban Missile Crisis marks the world's closest brush with the Armageddon promised by the lethal combination of stark ideological differences and nuclear weapons. Its dangers were real, and the potential consequences were grave. After a week of stressful and sometimes-jumbled communications between the world's two most powerful nations, the crisis ended in compromises, both public and secret. By frightening American and Soviet leaders as well as their constituents, the missile crisis laid the groundwork for a more cautious approach to Cold War relations between the Soviet Union and the United States. The world never again allowed a confrontation to rise to the same level of peril. A product of the times in which it occurred, the crisis demonstrated American and Soviet willingness to risk a nuclear conflict to achieve superiority in the competition between East and West—an attitude that seems foolhardy in retrospect.

The specter of the Cold War overshadowed almost half of the twentieth century. It was a time when the global showdown between Communism and capitalism seemed to offer clear choices in black and white, with little space allowed for the shades of gray that typically color the political arena. Powered by postwar memories, newfound ambitions, and simplistic stereotypes, the Cold War shaped economic and political life in both the United States and the Union of Soviet Socialist Republics, commonly called the Soviet Union or USSR. And it drove Nikita Khrushchev and John F. Kennedy to a titanic near-disaster in the Cuban Missile Crisis. It was a faceoff in which the main combatants were not uniformed young men with guns slung over their shoulders: They were national leaders, middle-aged or older, sometimes working without a net.

Fortunately for mankind, both Khrushchev and Kennedy found a solution that went beyond the common black-and-white Cold War rhetoric and moved a step closer to embracing the gray.

At the close of World War II, as the Russian army swept across eastern Europe, solidifying an Allied triumph over Nazi Germany, the war's victors planted the roots of a Cold War that would divide them. Josef Stalin expanded his domain in the war's closing months, creating a sphere of influence that he planned to rule with an iron fist. Soviet power over Poland, Czechoslovakia, Hungary, East Germany, Romania, Bulgaria, and Yugoslavia led to the formation of Socialist governments throughout the region.[1] The Soviet Union itself was huge, and Stalin's imposition of his will on these satellites intensified the fear of Communism among Western nations. The United States, which rose to world leadership as Europe struggled to recover from the ravages of war, became a counter-balance to Stalin's dominion.

Anxiety about Communism had been a factor in American politics since the World War I era, when Marxists took control of the Soviet Union, setting off the first Red Scare in the United States. Stalin's efforts to consolidate his power only deepened those feelings. Consequently, historians have speculated that the United States undertook atomic bombings of Hiroshima and Nagasaki as much to intimidate its Soviet allies as to stop its Japanese enemies. The Soviet Union invaded Manchuria just a few days before the bombing of Hiroshima; therefore, pushing the Japanese toward a quick surrender represented a solid step toward limiting Stalin's ability to expand the area under Soviet control.

Fear of Communist expansion and world domination was an important element in what newspaper columnist Walter Lippmann dubbed "the Cold War" in 1946. In a confrontation powered by nuclear weapons, that trepidation sometimes escalated to outright terror. Consequently, one of the guiding principles of American and Western European foreign policy became "containment" of Communism.[2] The goal was to isolate Communist nations, accepting current holdings without allowing Stalin, his successor Khrushchev, or China's Mao Zedong to extend Communism into other nations. Communist leaders added to containment concerns by promoting wars of national liberation in developing countries within Latin America, Asia, and Africa, where instability reigned as European colonial powers withdrew. Khrushchev bragged that these smaller wars would combine to spread Communism around the globe.

Understanding the American conception of the Cold War requires consideration of Americans' view of their nation as it emerged from the "heroic" saga of World War II. Faced with the threat of an aggressive enemy, Americans sought to make their new adversary fit an established pattern. Although Communism and Nazism are located at opposite ends of the political spectrum, many Westerners sought to draw lessons from World War II and came to see Soviet totalitarianism as a reincarnation of Nazism. Thus, any Soviet leader became a stand-in for Hitler—and this was not an entirely fatuous notion. Stalin, like Hitler, ran death camps to eliminate his enemies and counted Jews among his chief targets.

In contrast, most Americans believed that the brave young men who stormed the beaches at Normandy—what would later be called "the greatest generation"—represented soldiers of freedom who stepped into the world arena to correct wrongs and to protect human rights. After the war, many Americans thought the United States' Marshall Plan to rebuild Europe demonstrated the nation's pious generosity by helping to rebuild Western Europe. The idealized United States worked to bring new life to areas destroyed by others. The destruction that atomic bombs had brought to Japan became an unfortunate side effect of the drive to topple tyranny. Once a frontier to be conquered, the United States now stood tall. Both righteous and ambitious, this was a nation ready to claim a century.

Writing during World War II in *And Keep Your Powder Dry*, anthropologist Margaret Mead challenged U.S. citizens to follow in their ancestors' footsteps and tap into American character:

> If we are to give our utmost effort and skill and enthusiasm, we must believe in ourselves, which means believing in our past and in our future, in our parents and in our children, in that peculiar blend of moral purpose and practical inventiveness which is the American character.[3]

In July 1962 when President Kennedy wrote an article for *Sports Illustrated*, he reflected Americans' view of their nation and its history. Promoting his national program for physical fitness among the nation's youngsters, Kennedy wrote, "It was men who possessed vigor and strength as well as courage and vision who first settled these shores and over more than three centuries, subdued a continent and wrested a civilization from the wilderness."[4]

Theologian Reinhold Niebuhr noted in 1959 that Americans "are still inclined to pretend that our power is exercised by a peculiarly virtuous nation. The uniqueness of our virtue is questioned both by our friends and our enemies."[5] In another analysis, foreign affairs specialist Alton Frye wrote, "It is a familiar critique of nationalism in general, and Americanism in particular, that it tends to veer toward a secular religiosity that is incapable of compromise with others."[6]

Several scholars have noted that American nationalism and anti-Communism seemed to be grounded in a sense of destiny and "chosenness." Many Americans believed their nation had been selected by God to provide a model for the rest of the world. As Niebuhr argued, the view from the outside differed. The Soviet Union, its allies, and many other nations saw the United States as an imperialistic and expansionistic nation trying to spread its own political and economic systems around the world.

Late in the Cold War, historian John L. Gaddis concluded that self-doubt affected America's acceptance of its position as a world leader. He contended that the United States sometimes failed to use its power because

> we are not wholly comfortable in the role of a great power, that we tend to worry more about it than other great powers have in the past and that we tend to look, more actively than most other great powers do or have done, for ways to justify the power we have not in terms of power itself, but of some very different end.[7]

Moral superiority, not military might, explained the United States' position of dominance in the minds of many.

During the 1950s a new force began coloring American attitudes. At odds with citizens' belief in the nation's special nature, this new feeling created a stifling sense of foreboding without totally extinguishing American exceptionalism. Creeping into the American psyche was apprehension about the possibility that Communism's restrictions on freedom might yield a regimented society that could tackle twentieth century technological advancement more efficiently than a capitalist democracy. This idea gained momentum after the Soviet Union's launch of the first artificial satellite *Sputnik* in 1957 and was reinforced four years later when Yuri Gagarin became the first human to orbit the Earth. These achievements in rocket technology received added psychological heft from Soviet claims of massive increases in industrial production. Another blow to the American feeling of technological and moral ascendancy occurred in 1960 when a sophisticated and secret American spy plane known as a U-2 was shot down over the Soviet Union. This incident suggested that the Soviet Union could defend itself well against a bomber attack, and at the same time, the plane's downing became a source of embarrassment because America's World War II hero, President and retired General Dwight D. Eisenhower, lied about the existence of the spy plane until the Soviet Union presented evidence that both the plane and the pilot, Francis Gary Powers, had been recovered.

All of these factors combined to create a barely submerged and growing inferiority complex jockeying for a position within the American consciousness. While American exceptionalism suggested that the United States was unique and excelled over any other nation, Americans quietly began to question this conclusion. Khrushchev perpetuated U.S. insecurity in the 1950s when he said, "Whether you like it or not, history is on our side." Shortly after the Soviet Union pulverized rebellion in Hungary in November 1956, he told a group of Western ambassadors: "We will bury you."[8] When Kennedy ran for president in 1960, one of his campaign themes—the missile gap—assumed Soviet dominance in the arms race. After he became president, he learned that the Soviet Union was far behind the United States in production of missiles and warheads. However, in 1960, he and many other Americans had accepted Khrushchev's claims of Soviet supremacy.

Eighty-four percent of Americans believed that the United States was losing ground in the worldwide struggle against Communism, according to a 1962 Harris Poll, and among the hands that rocked the cradle, pessimism was greatest: Ninety-two percent of mothers of children 10 or younger believed that Communism was gaining the upper hand in its competition with the United States.[9] At the same time, 40 percent of Americans taking part in a Gallup Poll believed that the Soviet Union was winning the propaganda war; only 33 percent saw the U.S. government as the victor on that battlefront.[10]

Despite his claims, Khrushchev knew that his nation was outgunned, and he was alarmed to realize that American U-2s would enable the United States to pre-empt his bragging rights by photographically capturing images of his small Soviet strategic missile force. Furthermore, Khrushchev realized that the United States gave its citizens a quality of life unavailable to Soviet citizens. To minimize evidence of that problem, he needed to maintain belief in his nation's military and technological dominance.

Because of the Cold War, Eisenhower felt that the military had too much influence on American policymaking. He attempted to reduce the military's ability to affect decisions, and in a 1960 farewell address he warned Americans about the rising power of the "military-industrial complex" that profited from Cold War fears. He urged voters not to give the military or armament manufacturers the ability to guide the United States away from peace and toward war because it was, in essence, good for business. Eisenhower emphasized that both the existence of a large military force in peacetime and the ongoing drive to produce new weapons systems could create an imbalance in the nation's policies. When Kennedy became president and learned that the United States dominated the Soviet Union in the nuclear arms race, he asked Deputy Secretary of Defense Roswell Gilpatric to reveal the truth: Taking a page from Eisenhower's book, JFK wanted to counter military scare tactics intended to generate greater expenditures on bigger and better weapons. However, as crises occurred around the globe, Kennedy expanded military spending.

On American soil, the arms race was propelled by a tendency to see Communism as a monolithic force despite evidence to the contrary. A great split developed between China and the Soviet Union during the Khrushchev era. China felt that the Soviet Union should encourage violence to establish Communist regimes in newly emerging Third World nations.[11] In 1959, the Soviet Union reneged on a pledge to help China develop nuclear weapons, and Khrushchev issued an announcement in July 1960 that his nation was recalling all advisers from China.[12]

Cold War espionage yielded many secrets during these years; however, sophisticated spying did not correct the fact that the United States and the USSR failed to understand one another. Each viewed the other through a fixed set of stereotypes that predicted behavior falling within narrow and well-precedented boundaries. Actions that fell outside those cozy cubbyholes were shocking and mysterious—and that made them dangerous. Moreover, each side doubted that it would be feasible to establish a rational dialogue with the other. A January 1962 Gallup Poll in the United States, Canada, and Great Britain showed that more than a third of respondents were convinced that it would be impossible to live peacefully with the Soviet Union.[13]

VISIONS OF NUCLEAR WAR

Beginning with the Soviet Union's first tests of atomic weapons at the close of the 1940s, the Cold War and the Nuclear Age became intertwined entities. While the United States produced the first working atomic bombs in 1945 and the first hydrogen bomb in 1952, the Soviet Union was never far behind, detonating an atomic bomb in 1949 and a hydrogen bomb in 1953. Much of this era's terror reflected the new human ability to cause massive devastation with nuclear weapons. The same power that heightened tensions seemed to lower the odds of direct conflict, discouraging the two leading combatants from engaging in battle beyond skirmishes over contested ground in the human mind. The Cold War opened up the possibility of a conflagration propelled by fear of "the other," whether that adversary was shaped to fit into the mold of a "godless Communist" or a "capitalist imperialist."

Until the early 1960s, the destructive power of nuclear weapons seemed to define the limits of the Cold War, relegating it to a war of ideas rather than a bloodbath fed by the deaths of American and Soviet soldiers. The unique nature of these weapons contorted the public policy of civilian leaders, but military chiefs on both sides sometimes spoke about nuclear weapons as if they were routine additions to their arsenals. To discourage this viewpoint, JFK gathered several foreign policy aides early in his administration to spend an afternoon learning from experts about the possible effects of nuclear war. After hearing a description of blast effects, resulting firestorms, and painful deaths from radiation sickness, JFK beckoned Secretary of State Dean Rusk into his office and said, "And we call ourselves the human race!"[14]

Because troops from the United States and the Soviet Union never faced one another on a bloody battlefield, the Cold War often seemed more like an elaborate psychological construction than a true war. However, it did spin off real-life, smaller conflicts, often fought by proxies representing the two sides. By the time of the Cuban Missile Crisis, the competition between Communists and capitalists had sparked one full-fledged war, when the United States and its allies supported South Korea after an invasion by Communist-controlled North Korea in 1950. Chinese troops entered the conflict, backing North Korea. President Harry Truman, who had made the difficult decision to obliterate Hiroshima and Nagasaki, steered clear of using atomic bombs against North Korea, and the war ended in a stalemate three years later. In other trouble spots, the world's most powerful nations offered military assistance to competing sides and sometimes sent troops as military advisers or combatants.

Even without head-to-head battles, this "war" was costly and dangerous. Each side felt pressure to maintain readiness and a need to douse grass fires that might threaten the status quo. Over the course of the Cold War, blood was spent in Korea, Vietnam, and many lesser-known trouble spots; however, between the two superpowers, this was primarily a war of words, a conflict in which rhetoric had the potential to become deadly if events spiraled out of control. Cold Warriors often struggled more intensely to win hearts and minds than to capture physical resources in an age that devalued every square foot of the planet by making it destructible. The Nuclear Age dispelled the promise of planetary permanence that once had framed human existence.

During the brief period when the United States had a monopoly in atomic weaponry, it was able to twice use atomic bombs without the threat of comparable retaliation. However, the existence of adversary nations, each with these powerful weapons, raised the question of whether either nation could launch a first strike with impunity or whether any nuclear attack would become a form of national suicide. These realities led to the belief espoused by Eisenhower and others that ownership of nuclear weapons alone served as a deterrent to war. Especially as the weapons offered more devastating results, the likelihood of using them seemed to decline—unless a nation chose the ultimate form of defense, staging a pre-emptive, offensive attack to riddle an enemy's forces before it could launch a counterstrike. The United States tended to disavow a first strike as "contrary to our historical national values."[15] However, many Americans believed that Communism was an insane belief system and feared that men who embraced this alien ideology might be willing to use weapons of mass destruction despite their horrible cost.

When Kennedy became president in 1961, the United States had about 18,000 nuclear weapons, ranging in power from a ten-megaton warhead with great destructive power to a warhead small enough to serve as a battlefield weapon. Estimates suggest that these weapons probably carried a gross yield that was a million times as high as the destructive power that leveled Hiroshima.[16] During the months between the fall of 1961 and the spring of 1962, the number of American intercontinental ballistic missiles (ICBMs) increased by more than 100 percent, climbing from thirty to seventy-five—and by the end of 1962, that total exceeded 200, including more powerful, solid-fueled Minuteman missiles.[17]

The Strategic Air Command's Single Integrated Operations Plan (SIOP), the nation's blueprint for nuclear war with the Soviet Union, called for using 2,500 thermonuclear weapons and possibly causing 350 million deaths. This strategy involved hitting both the USSR and its allies, and it accepted that radioactive fallout would threaten American allies, neutral nations, and the United States itself.[18] Eisenhower reportedly "expressed his concern that there might be nothing left of the Northern Hemisphere."[19] A paper produced at Johns Hopkins University in 1956 noted that because the Western allies used a "maximum violence" strategy in World War II, "the dominant conviction in the U.S. during the last decade has been that if war comes it will be total and that consequently it is unrealistic to make preparations to fit it in any other way."[20]

Political scientist Michael Mandelbaum believes that Americans were especially focused on the threat of nuclear war during what he calls the "nuclear epoch"—a period beginning with the launch of *Sputnik* in 1957 and ending in late 1963 with the signing of the Limited Test Ban Treaty. A 1961 Gallup Poll of Americans showed that 59 percent described themselves as very worried or fairly worried about a third world war in June 1961.[21] No nuclear war occurred during those years, but the world's inhabitants were not free from the effects of nuclear weapons. Test detonations produced fallout in the form of the carcinogenic strontium 90, which found its way into the milk supply after cows ate contaminated grass.[22] Nevertheless, when asked in early 1962 whether the United States should resume atmospheric nuclear testing after a voluntary moratorium shared with the Soviet Union, 66 percent of Americans favored reinitiating tests.[23] First the Soviet Union and then the United States resumed atmospheric nuclear testing in the autumn of 1961.

The Soviet Union

The Soviet Union, also known as the Union of Soviet Socialist Republics or USSR, was an important nation in the events of the twentieth century. For much of the century it was the world's largest nation in geographical area. It also was the most powerful Communist nation and was an active competitor in the nuclear arms race and the space race.

The nation evolved after revolutionaries toppled the despotic Tsarist Russian empire in 1917 at a time when the Tsar's power had been weakened by World War I. The initial revolution that ousted Tsar Nicholas II offered the people only chaos under a provisional government that represented a weak alliance of forces. In November 1917, the Bolsheviks, who wanted to install a purely Socialist state, managed a coup d'état under the leadership of Vladimir Ilyich Lenin, who had spent much of the war in the neutral nation of Switzerland. Germans aided Lenin's return to his homeland because they wanted to eliminate Russia as an enemy in the war, which pitted the Axis Powers—Germany, Austria-Hungary, and Turkey—against the Allies—Britain, France, Italy, Russia, Japan, and the United States. This gamble paid off: Lenin's triumph brought Russia's withdrawal from the war. Soon after Lenin's ascension, he and his confederates acted to eliminate private property by nationalizing industrial plants and transportation operations. In the early years, the Bolsheviks struggled to feed the population and sometimes resorted to a reign of terror to silence dissidents. The rationalization for one bloody crackdown was an unsuccessful assassination attempt against Lenin, but the estimated casualties of 140,000 went far beyond punishing failed assassins. There was a civil war between the Bolsheviks' "peasant army" and their opponents, known as white armies. Estimates of the death toll in the civil war range from 10 million to 30 million. The Bolsheviks triumphed in 1919, and 1.5 million members of the opposition emigrated to other nations. By the end of 1920, the Red Army had recaptured all of the non-Russian-speaking nations that had once been part of the Russian empire, and Lenin greatly limited the freedom of non-Russian-speaking states. In 1922, the government announced the union of Russia, Belorussia [now Belarus], the Ukraine, and the Transcaucasian Federation (Armenia, Azerbaijan, and Georgia) to form the Union of Soviet Socialist Republics, an authoritarian state. By its end almost seventy years later, the Soviet Union had grown to encompass fifteen supposedly autonomous Soviet Socialist Republics.

Lenin sought to use the USSR as a prototype to launch a worldwide Bolshevik revolution, and he began supporting dissidents across Europe. While seeking to establish stability at home, the government initially identified itself as the sole purchaser of all grain. This created turmoil among the peasants and eventually was refined, allowing the peasants to maintain subsistence farming. Repression of individual rights was increased to maintain the Bolsheviks' power. As the government bureaucracy grew, it failed to provide the kind of input originally assigned to local Bolshevik organizations.

Lenin became ill in 1921–2 and suffered several strokes. His illness led to a power struggle between Josef Stalin and Leon Trotsky. Lenin lived until 1924, and three years later Stalin rose to power as dictator, while Trotsky was exiled. Stalin's efforts to impose a system of collectivism in agriculture led to millions of deaths; however, his drive to expand industrialization was more successful. During the 1930s, Stalin engineered the "Great Terror," which eliminated many citizens identified by Stalin as "enemies of the people." Thousands suffered execution, while millions were forced to serve in slave work camps, known as gulags, which were typically located outside Russia. These purges weakened the Red Army. Consequently, when short-time ally, Adolf Hitler, turned on Stalin in World War II, the Soviet leader was ill prepared to overcome the invading Nazi army. It took years, but the Soviet Union eventually mustered the strength to conquer the Nazis, drive them out of the USSR, and spread the Red Army across Eastern Europe as the Nazis retreated.

Under Stalin's leadership, the postwar Soviet Union was able to develop the atomic bomb in 1949 and begin work on the hydrogen bomb, first successfully tested in late 1953. Stalin died in March of that year with no definite successor. In 1955, the Soviet Union and its eastern European satellites officially formed an alliance against aggression from outside the Soviet sphere. Albania, Bulgaria, Czechoslovakia, East Germany, Hungary, Poland, Romania, and the Soviet Union signed the Warsaw Pact.

After a power struggle that included the assassination of one contender, Nikita Khrushchev ascended to become the nation's leader in the mid-1950s. Khrushchev pushed the nation to compete with the United States in the nuclear arms race and the space race, which produced rockets and simultaneously bolstered Soviet efforts to produce missiles that could deliver nuclear warheads around the world. He led the USSR through the most perilous moments of the Cold War, vying for power with the United States on issues related to West Berlin and Cuba. (See Khrushchev biography page 28.)

Foes ousted Khrushchev in 1964. He was immediately replaced by Leonid Brezhnev as party first secretary and Alexei Kosygin as prime minister. In 1965, Nikolai Podgorny joined the leadership as president. Initially, Kosygin had the upper hand in leading economic reform; however, Brezhnev soon consolidated his power by leading operations such as the 1968 move to extinguish the rebellious "Prague Spring" in Czechoslovakia. By the early 1970s, Brezhnev had amassed more power than Kosygin and grasped the reins, pushing for technological advancement, which he acknowledged would temporarily award higher status to those with specific skills rather than providing the equality promised by pure Communism. Under his leadership, Soviet relations with China declined; however, he reached agreement with President Richard Nixon on the first major arms control measure, the Anti-Ballistic Missile Treaty in 1972. Within the Soviet Union, Brezhnev was known for suppressing creativity in the arts and literature. The Soviet government had long been guilty of oppressive actions toward its Jewish minority, and under Brezhnev, steps were taken to allow more Jewish emigration.

Yuri Andropov, a former leader of the Soviet secret police, or KGB, assumed leadership of the party when Brezhnev died in 1982. He promoted several reformers, including future leader Mikhail Gorbachev. Andropov is perhaps best remembered for his defense of the Soviet military's downing of a South Korean airliner in 1983. He served only two years before dying and being replaced by the 72-year-old and ill Konstantin Chernenko, who died in 1985. Gorbachev, a man only in his early fifties, took over the party's leadership shortly afterward.

Gorbachev saw himself as an agent of change. From the beginning, he made it clear that he wanted to cause economic restructuring—Perestroika—and social reform—Glasnost. Perestroika immediately ran into trouble as Gorbachev sought to place machine building above production of consumer goods. He backed cooperatives and allowed the establishment of family farms if the families paid to lease the land. These initiatives ran into opposition from the bureaucracy, which feared change. Perestroika's failure led to a shortage of consumer goods and agriculture woes. The USSR's long and entrenched war in Afghanistan also drained the treasury, leaving Gorbachev under difficult conditions with little flexibility, although he did oversee the final troop withdrawal in 1989. The budget deficit rose to unprecedented highs as Gorbachev struggled to make his plans work, and the economy underwent a catastrophic collapse.

The openness implied in Glasnost was challenged in 1986 when a reactor at the Chernobyl nuclear plant exploded. Gorbachev suppressed information about the accident for more than two weeks despite large-scale evacuation of the immediate area. Afterwards, he became more determined to promote government openness and sought to win over members of the intelligentsia by bringing dissident physicist Andrei Sakharov and his wife Yelena Bonner back from exile. Gorbachev allowed non-Russian minorities to voice complaints publicly, and this unsettled many of his colleagues.

Gorbachev's reforms lacked broad support among party officials, and though many active party members endorsed reform, they rejected Perestroika and increasingly gave their support to another reformer, Boris Yeltsin. In 1989, Gorbachev and Yeltsin began a power struggle that helped to bring about the disintegration of the Soviet Union and its sphere of influence. In August 1991, the KGB, the military, and other conservatives attempted to oust Gorbachev from office, and though the coup failed, it destroyed Gorbachev's political career and led to the dissolution of the Soviet Union, which began with the secession of Baltic states in the following months. Russia alone took over the Soviet Union's place on the United Nations Security Council, although the Ukraine, Belarus, and Kazakhstan also became nuclear powers after the demise of the USSR. Missiles in all three nations were dismantled during the 1990s, leaving Russia as the sole surviving nuclear power in the former Soviet Union.

An additional facet of the Nuclear Age was the prospect of deadly accidents. More than once, mistaken readings and false alarms had threatened to spark nuclear war. Pentagon records show that there were twenty American nuclear accidents between 1950 and 1962. The most alarming incident occurred January 24, 1961, when the pilot of a crashing B-52 jettisoned two hydrogen bombs in rural North Carolina.[24] The weapons had a destructive force 500 times greater than the bomb that leveled Hiroshima. One bomb landed softly with a parachute and was easily extracted where it landed near Goldsboro. The other impacted in a swamp and parts of it were never found.[25] Five of the six interlocking safety guards on one bomb failed.[26]

Civil defense operations became a part of preparing for nuclear war. To make the public accept possible use of nuclear weapons, it was essential to offer some hope of survival. However, training children in the 1950s to duck under their desks to avoid the monsters known as atomic bombs made civil defense a joke to some of the youngest Americans. With the development of ever-more-powerful hydrogen bombs, even deep bunkers did not guarantee survival among those near a blast site, so the United States tried to provide the only kind of defense that seemed likely to save lives—protection from the radioactive fallout that would blanket a blast area and then flow with eastward-moving weather patterns, causing radiation sickness in neighboring regions.

Eisenhower supported civil defense because he saw it as a way to maintain citizens' morale. He participated in Operation Alert, an annual nationwide drill. Readiness was an appealing idea, especially for a former military planner like Eisenhower, but he had doubts about civil defense. In his diary, he speculated that all-out war for thirty to sixty days could achieve "a mutual destruction of terrifying proportions" and leave behind a disjointed nation "wholly dependent upon reserve supplies for a matter of several years."[27] A National Security Council report estimated that an intense non-surprise attack against the United States in 1959 would take 58 million lives, 12 million from blast and heat, and 46 million from fallout. A surprise strike would kill 91 million out of a national population of 177 million.[28] To be effective, a civil defense program had to be expensive— and the United States was spending far too much on arms to make that kind of investment in saving civilians. (Such programs existed in neutral countries without big military budgets. Switzerland and Sweden both had effective plans to safeguard civilians.)[29] In a 1957 National Security Council meeting, Secretary of State John Foster Dulles argued that it would be reasonable to tell the public there was no defense against a massive nuclear attack; however, Eisenhower hesitated to embrace that level of brutal honesty. He contended that even a weak civil defense program could contribute to the nation's survival.[30] After a nuclear assault, he believed, the nation would be run "as one big camp."[31] A 1956 report predicted that "a massive nuclear attack on the United States . . . without drastically improved preparation of the people, would jeopardize support of the National Government and of the war effort, and might well result in national disintegration."[32]

JFK gave civil defense a push in the summer of 1961 when the Soviet Union threatened West Berlin's continued existence. In a July 25, 1961 speech, he created a panic among some Americans by urging establishment of family fallout shelters. The $1,000+ shelters for sale were beyond the reach of most Americans, although approximately 20,000 families built fallout shelters during that era.[33] Basements in homes could be used as makeshift shelters but there would be a great variance in fallout protection. And while such shelters represented a viable option in 80 percent of northern homes, only 10 percent of houses in the south featured basements.[34] After Kennedy's speech, the White House received more civil defense inquiries in a single August day than it had amassed in the entire month of January.[35] Sales of survival goods surged, too.[36] Nonetheless, only 7 percent of Americans had made civil defense preparations in their homes by October 1961.[37] This represented a rise of 2 percentage points since July.[38] A November 1961 Gallup Poll showed that 58 percent of Americans favored public facilities over family shelters, and a month later, another survey indicated that 60 percent of Americans had given some thought to what life would be like in a fallout shelter.[39] A 1961 *U.S. News & World Report* survey found that most Americans expressed fatalism about nuclear war, and the interviewers discovered "no mass movement toward preparedness." A journal article in *Social Problems* found a similar "widespread sense of futility on the part of most Americans who feel that nuclear war is not something they can help avert. . . . They tend to retreat into fatalistic lethargy."[40] What public officials seldom addressed was the likelihood that nuclear war would kill domesticated and wild animals and contaminate crops, placing added stress on the food supply. While insects would thrive, their natural predators would die.

As governments struggled to prepare for the worst, nuclear war was best conceived within the human imagination. No nuclear war had ever been fought, and Americans tended to avoid dwelling on the devastation that struck Japan in 1945. Like doomsday novels and films, government scenarios for nuclear war and civil defense had little basis in fact because the events they anticipated had no place in history. Theories about nuclear war ranged from cool-headed analyses drawn from studies of Hiroshima and Nagasaki to the sometimes-wild speculation of science fiction.

Although Khrushchev's memoirs make it clear that he found the prospect of nuclear war terrifying, it is difficult to tap into his typical constituent's feelings, given the closed nature of Soviet society. However, nuclear war became a part of popular culture in the United States and other western cultures. As such, it promised a future of misery and fear— or simply a void characterized by the absence of existence, a man-made nothingness. In some visions, future human life consisted of claustrophobia-induced insanity generated by life in fallout shelters; in others, it was a lonely tale, with few survivors and little hope for re-establishing human civilization.

British-Australian novelist Nevil Shute produced one of the most enduring nuclear war narratives in 1957. *On the Beach*, which was turned into a film in 1959, paints a grim image of life after nuclear warfare. The Northern Hemisphere is a vast wasteland where blasts, firestorms, and radioactive fallout have eliminated the last traces of human life. The Southern Hemisphere, primarily unaffected by the bombs' immediate effects, is dying, too, as a cloud of fallout drifts southward, carrying the promise of a painful death. Most of the book's action occurs in Australia, where the only surviving U.S. submarine has taken refuge. All that is left of the United States is a great wasteland, and Australia's population is preparing to ease into death with the assistance of government-provided suicide pills. The last to die are accidental casualties of other people's wars. Within the Eisenhower administration, the film version of *On the Beach* created anxiety. A United States Information Agency "Infoguide," which remained classified until 1994, urged officials to reassure Americans that a nuclear war would never eliminate all human life—an assertion that could not be proven because of unknown environmental effects.[41] In addition, an official of the Office of Defense and Civil Mobilization[42] condemned the film as creating a sense of hopelessness about nuclear war.[43] However, more memorable than any government statement was the film's epitaph for mankind: "The war started when people accepted the idiotic principle that peace could be maintained by arranging to defend themselves with weapons they couldn't possibly use without committing suicide. . . . The devices outgrew us. We couldn't control them."[44]

While the missile crisis was unfolding, many Americans read excerpts from *Fail-Safe* in the *Saturday Evening Post*. Eugene Burdick and Harvey Wheeler's thriller, which was later turned into a film, spotlights the possibility of accidental war. One of the book's characters compares nuclear weapons to pagan gods toying with humanity. "And like the gods of Greek tragedy," he concludes, "they know only how to destroy, not how to save."[45] As the story unfolds, U.S. bomber pilots act as automatons, mechanically following mistaken orders to destroy the Soviet capital, and as Moscow lies in ruins the American president makes a desperate effort to avert war by ordering another U.S. bomber to decimate New York City, killing thousands, including the president's wife and the bomber pilot's family. Like Burdick and Wheeler's bomber pilots, the weapons operators in Mordecai Roshwald's 1959 novel, *Level 7*, push the buttons to launch a war without considering the consequences. Other books, such as Walter M. Miller Jr.'s *A Canticle for Leibowitz* and Pat Frank's *Alas, Babylon*, both published in 1959, picture primitive worlds in the aftermath of nuclear war.

Riding the No. 2 spot on the *New York Times* Best-Seller List at the beginning of the crisis was *Seven Days in May*, a novel that envisioned a different kind of threat: a military coup precipitated by an American president's quest for peace with the USSR. In this novel, too, the potential danger is amplified by the existence of nuclear weapons. "Civilization can go with a moan and a whimper overnight," the president concludes. "But how can an individual feel anything but helpless? He can't grab a rifle and rush out to defend his country."[46] Within weeks of the crisis, Kennedy had read both *Fail-Safe* and *Seven Days in May*.[47] He believed that an American military coup could overthrow an inexperienced leader.[48] The existence of nuclear weapons raised the ante on that kind of gamble.[49]

TV series of this era also considered nuclear war. Two episodes of Rod Serling's *The Twilight Zone* examined different aspects of this unthinkable future. In one, the sole survivor of a nuclear holocaust finds delight in discovering books from a flattened library, but before he can take refuge in the pages of literature, his reading glasses break, forever separating him from the potential companionship offered by the printed word.[50] In another episode, neighbors prompted by a civil defense warning come to blows over access to a family's fallout shelter. Later, the alarm proves to be false, while destruction of the neighbors' mutual trust is painfully true.[51]

Thus, as Americans in 1962 headed toward the most perilous showdown of the nuclear era, they had disturbing images of what to expect, and government civil defense information offered little more hope than doomsday fiction. Most Americans expected an unwelcome opportunity to experience the real thing. The percentage of Americans who expected a third world war rose from 32 percent to 73 percent between 1945 and 1948.[52] And in the year of the missile crisis, a pilot study found that most residents of a small midwestern town believed that nuclear war would destroy civilization.[53] We do not know what ordinary Russians, Ukrainians, Hungarians, or Poles expected from nuclear war, but on the American side, eerie shadows darkened daily life.

THE UNITED STATES AND CUBA: A HISTORY

The relationship between the United States and Cuba began to take shape long before the Cold War. Early in the nineteenth century, acquisition of the island, which lies just ninety miles from Florida, became a part of America's yearning for expansion. As early as 1823, Secretary of State John Quincy Adams commented that the "laws of political gravitation" made America's acquisition of the island inevitable, given its proximity and its crucial location in the Gulf of Mexico.[54] Twenty-five years later, President James K. Polk attempted to buy Cuba from Spain. William McKinley, who took office in 1897, considered purchasing the island, but he dropped the idea and instead pressured Spain to end a two-year-old rebellion humanely. Since the revolt had begun, the island's Spanish governor Valeriano Weyler had relocated 300,000 civilians, placing them in camps as he tried to separate rebels from the benign population. Weyler, who was known to Cubans as "The Butcher," called establishment of these camps "reconcentration." In 1898 after the U.S. consul general reported new anxieties sparked by rioting in Havana, McKinley sent an armored cruiser, the *Maine*, to the city as a visible manifestation of U.S. concerns. When the *Maine* was destroyed on February 15 in a series of explosions that killed 266 sailors, Americans blamed Spain. McKinley insisted that Spain end relocations, establish an armistice, and negotiate to grant independence to Cuba. Spain agreed to the first two conditions but rejected the third. On April 25, after a preliminary investigation found that a mine had shattered the *Maine*, the United States declared war on Spain and in the Teller Amendment, Congress committed the nation to securing Cuban independence. In a war that lasted only months, the United States captured Cuba, the Philippines, and Puerto Rico from Spain and began establishing its own reputation as an imperialist power.[55]

Championing Cuban rights had been a powerful rationale for the war. Allying U.S. interests with the rebels provided what appeared to be a re-enactment of the American colonies' own battle to expel a European power; however, Americans did not view Cubans as equals. In fact, Cuba, Puerto Rico, and the Philippines were characterized by many Americans as wayward children who found sanctuary in the arms of the virtuous and wise United States.[56] In 1903, the Platt Amendment stated

The cause of the *Maine*'s destruction remains unsettled. While Americans suspected that Spain ordered sabotage, some observers speculated that the United States may have destroyed its own ship to provide an excuse for war. More recently, there has been speculation that a mechanical problem caused the explosion.

that Cuba recognized U.S. rights to intervene at any time to protect the island's independence. After more than ten years of American oversight, Cuba gained formal independence in 1909. The United States did not relinquish its "rights" under the Platt Amendment until 1934, and over the coming decades, American leaders bolstered a series of corrupt Cuban leaders whose trade policies were favorable to American companies. Most Cubans remained poor and clearly, expulsion of Spanish governors did not carry the promised democracy.

After leading a successful revolution against the repressive U.S.-backed regime of Fulgencio Batista, Fidel Castro stormed into Havana in early 1959. Initially, many Americans saw Castro as a romantic figure—a young, handsome revolutionary who had overcome terrific odds to topple an entrenched and corrupt dictator; however, when Castro later moved to nationalize property held by U.S. citizens and began castigating the United States as an imperialist marauder, Americans became suspicious and feared that he would fall under Khrushchev's spell.

In 1960, when JFK ran for president, he warned, "For the first time in history, an enemy stands at the throat of the United States." Cuban novelist José Soler Puig described Americans' feelings toward a potentially hostile regime in Cuba similarly by saying, "We are inside them, we live in their throat."[57] Castro became an intimate enemy. In a study of U.S. language referring to Cuba, Louis A. Peréz Jr. found repeated use of the term "cancer" to describe Castro's Cuba. This term implies evil and the possibility of poisoning healthy tissue—in this case, the American domain. Kennedy used this metaphor in 1960; his Republican opponent, Richard Nixon, picked up the language in his 1962 book, *Six Crises*. In Peréz's *Cuba in the American Imagination*, he cites at least nine such references from a variety of sources.[58] American speakers also discussed the "loss" of Cuba as if it had recently belonged to the United States.

For Khrushchev, Castro and his followers embodied an appealing image: Cuba's unshaven rebels represented passionate Communism in a way that the Soviet Union's bleak, totalitarian bureaucracy never could. U.S. antipathy toward Castro grew as his friendship with the Soviet Union mushroomed. When Castro asked for arms, Khrushchev allowed two Soviet bloc nations—Poland and Czechoslovakia—to supply tanks, artillery, fighter planes, and antiaircraft guns. Along with the weapons came advisers to serve as trainers. When a Belgian shipment of armaments aboard *La Coubre* reached Havana's harbor in March 1960, the ship was wrecked by blasts that took more than 100 lives. At a service for those killed, Castro drew parallels between *La Coubre* and the *Maine* and asserted that the United States had sabotaged both vessels to provide an excuse to invade Cuba.[59] No evidence ever tied the United States to the sinking of

La Coubre; however, U.S. leaders found ways to devastate Cuba, none-theless. In 1960, shortly after Castro's first meeting with a high-ranking Soviet emissary, the United States eliminated Cuba's supply of oil, a vital resource powering Cuban industry. In July, the Eisenhower administration went further, cutting off all sugar purchases from the island, and the administration initiated a partial trade embargo against Cuba a month later. The United States also welcomed more than 160,000 Cubans who fled Castro's regime.[60] By 1962, Cuba's cash-poor economy was almost entirely oriented toward trade with the Soviet bloc.[61]

In late 1959 and early 1960, the Central Intelligence Agency began planning to overthrow Castro. At a March 1960 meeting, CIA officials told Eisenhower that the United States should bolster political opposition within Cuba, broadcast anti-Castro propaganda from a CIA post in the Caribbean, establish sources in Cuba to provide information and undermine the government, and train a paramilitary force off the island.[62] In the summer of 1960, Khrushchev first stated that the USSR would take action to protect Castro's regime from any American military action. The Soviet Union also attempted to bolster the island's economy with $100 million in trade credits and a promise to buy five million tons of sugar over a three-year period.[63] Despite their close ties, Khrushchev had two concerns about Cuba's leader, according to authors Aleksandr Fursenko and Timothy Naftali: that Castro, under the influence of his co-revolutionary Che Guevara, might embrace the "permanent revolution" strategy espoused by China's Mao or that he might establish a more independent Communist regime like Marshal Josip Broz Tito's Yugoslavia.[64] In mid-1960, Castro and Khrushchev first met in New York, while attending the United Nations General Assembly. Khrushchev spoke for more than two hours, and Castro applauded enthusiastically. Around the same time, the Soviet Union assumed the job of arming Cuba—and within two years, more than $250 million in war materiel had been delivered to the island.[65] In 1960, Castro announced that the Cuban government was taking possession of 382 privately operated companies and banks, some of which were held by American investors.[66]

A major factor in Castro's relatively quick adoption of an alliance with the Soviet Union was his fear of an American-backed invasion. He knew that American investors were angry about losing money, and he also realized that the Cuban exile community in the United States was led by wealthy and conservative Cubans likely to attract American political support. Moreover, Castro was aware that CIA instructors in Guatemala were training a team of exiles who later would undertake the Bay of Pigs invasion.

The CIA, with Eisenhower's permission, had started preparing a paramilitary force of about 300 Cuban exiles who were expected to invade

Cuba and lead a citizens' revolution. Later, the CIA decided that supplying an ongoing revolution would be too difficult to handle surreptitiously, so the agency expanded the number of men needed and decided to launch a visible landing near the city of Trinidad with the hope that this $13 million operation would encourage other Cubans to rebel. On the

Figure 1.1 Nikita Khrushchev and Fidel Castro make their way through a New York City crowd during a 1960 visit to the United Nations in New York. Herman Hiller photo. *New York World-Telegram* Collection, Library of Congress.

day before Kennedy's inauguration, he and his foreign policy team met with Eisenhower and his key advisers. When Kennedy asked whether the United States should support a guerrilla campaign in Cuba, Eisenhower voiced his unqualified support. He also told Kennedy: "We cannot have the present government there go on."[67]

Kennedy's first official meeting about the planned invasion occurred eight days after his inauguration. By then, preparations were swiftly moving toward implementation. Given the potential embarrassment of being tied to an unsuccessful assault, leaders of the military assumed a surprisingly small role in the scheme and were not involved at all until late in 1960. They opposed the CIA's plan to launch a military assault; however, they were unable to give Kennedy a clear reason to scuttle the plan. General Lyman Lemnitzer, chairman of the Joint Chiefs of Staff, did say that he would be surprised if such a small force achieved as much as the CIA expected. Military leaders also stressed that the element of surprise was crucial. With the Cuban exiles already training in Guatemala, Kennedy became swept away by the project's apparent momentum. Backing down, he apparently thought, might seem like a hypocritical rejection of his own campaign stance: During the 1960 presidential race, Kennedy had called for a similar operation. Roger Hilsman, director of the State Department's Bureau of Intelligence and Research, later argued that if JFK had rejected an Eisenhower administration plan to overthrow Castro, "the fact of his saying 'no' would promptly leak to the Republicans—and his administration, plastered with a label of 'weakness,' would never get off the ground in the great enterprises he had set for it."[68] Another factor was Kennedy's slim margin of victory in 1960. Without a national mandate, he probably felt that he was in no position to abandon plans that had been hatched under Eisenhower, who was a respected military leader.

In April 1961, Khrushchev wrote a letter to Kennedy affirming that the Soviet Union would act to protect Cuba from American attack.[69] Because he feared the broader implications of a U.S.-backed invasion, JFK insisted that the attack be "an unspectacular landing at night in an area where there was a minimum likelihood of opposition," and he said that if tactical air support was needed, the aircraft should appear to be defectors from the Cuban air force. These restrictions forced planners to move the landing away from mountains that could have served as a refuge if the invaders met an overwhelming hostile force.[70] No one, however, clearly explained this to Kennedy. Instead, the CIA hoped that he ultimately would change his mind and order a U.S. military air strike to prevent the invasion's failure.

Within the administration, the plan's only vocal opponent was Chester Bowles at the State Department. Kennedy's closest aides viewed Bowles as an Adlai Stevenson-style intellectual, and therefore, his concerns were dismissed. (Although Adlai Stevenson was Kennedy's ambassador to the United Nations, the president and his intimates distanced themselves from the 1952 and 1956 Democratic presidential nominee. They viewed him as unrealistically idealistic and overly inclined to negotiate instead of taking tough action.)

Senator J. William Fulbright, chairman of the Senate Foreign Relations Committee, told Kennedy that he, too, thought any U.S. participation in the plan was a bad idea: He believed that a U.S.-backed invasion would be a disaster for relations with developing nations because it would indicate that the United States was willing to overthrow a Third World nation's government to install a more friendly regime.[71] In an April 4 meeting to mobilize the operation, JFK asked each of the civilian and military leaders around the table to state his opinion about whether the plot should go forward; his advisers unanimously gave their support. Two days later, reporter Ted Szulc of the *New York Times* learned enough about the clandestine mission to write an article describing it. Kennedy heard about the story and called *Times* publisher Orvil Dryfoos to complain. Dryfoos let the front-page story run, but he ordered editors to remove the word "imminent" from a description of the invasion and to delete any mention of the CIA.[72] Nevertheless, the essential element of surprise, deemed so vital by the military, now clearly had been lost. At a televised news conference April 9, Kennedy deepened his commitment not to involve U.S. troops when he stated that there would be no intervention in Cuba by the United States military.

Once set into motion, the Bay of Pigs operation almost immediately foundered. The first action was a bombing raid on Cuba's air force. The CIA arranged for the exiles to fly planes from Nicaragua, and those aircraft were made to look like Cuban air force planes. According to CIA plans, the attacking planes would wipe out Castro's airpower, and no one would tie the assault to the United States. In reality, the strike left 40 percent of Castro's planes undamaged. In addition, one exiled pilot pretended to have engine trouble and flew to Miami, where he unsuccessfully claimed to be a defecting member of Castro's air force: At least one reporter noticed that his plane was slightly different from the B-26s used by the Cuban military. Almost immediately, Cubans accused the United States of being responsible for the attack, and Kennedy canceled a second strike scheduled to coincide with the April 17 landing. Without the second air strike, Castro's air force, which was stronger than the CIA believed, was able to trap invaders on the beach at the Bay of Pigs where they had disembarked from the six ships. The Cuban military response prevented invaders from establishing a beachhead. The CIA begged for military air attacks to rout Castro's troops. Kennedy refused but assigned six unmarked Navy planes to fly over the beach early on April 18 and disperse Castro's planes so that a supply drop could be made to the invaders. As it turned out, even that small effort failed because of a timing issue. There were other foul-ups, too. Pilots for the exile brigade became confused and dropped paratroopers into a swamp rather than on dry land. When the hopelessness of the situation became clear on April 19, the U.S. Navy rescued fourteen exiles. Castro's forces had easily defeated the invaders, killing 114 and capturing 1,189.

Although Kennedy had tried to divorce the United States from the action, hiding the government's involvement was impossible. Kennedy, who had never lost an election, was shocked by this unexpected defeat. Almost blindly, he had accepted predictions about the likelihood of its success. CIA officials may have failed to alert him to the dangers because they assumed he could not, or would not, allow the mission to fail. "Everyone around him thought he had the Midas touch and could not lose," wrote Arthur M. Schlesinger Jr.[73] Kennedy had been riding high with a 73 percent approval rating in the latest Gallup Poll.[74] Theodore Sorensen wrote that "the Bay of Pigs had been—and would be—the worst defeat of his career, the kind of outright failure to which he was not accustomed. He knew that he had handed his critics a stick with which they would forever beat him." Kennedy himself questioned his decision-making process. "How could I have been so far off base?" he asked. "How could I have been so stupid to let them [the experts] go ahead?"[75]

The failure cast gloom over his bright, young administration. "Responsible world opinion was, to say the least, somewhat shocked by this episode," Senate Majority Leader Mike Mansfield wrote to Kennedy weeks after the fiasco.[76] The *New York Times'* C.L. Sulzberger argued in print that "we look like fools to our friends, rascals to our enemies, and incompetents to the rest."[77] Speaking at a news conference, Kennedy accepted responsibility for this failure. "I am the responsible officer of the Government–and that is quite obvious," he said.[78] American voters rewarded his honesty by giving him the highest approval rating of his presidency: 82 percent. "The worse I do, the more popular I get," he remarked ironically.[79] Kennedy held CIA leaders responsible, but he also blamed himself: Things like this were not supposed to happen to him. James Reston wrote in the *New York Times*: "For the first time in his life, John F. Kennedy has taken a public licking. . . . [D]efeat is something new to him, and Cuba was a clumsy and humiliating one, which makes it worse."[80]

The Bay of Pigs intensified the Kennedy administration's antipathy toward Castro's regime, creating an atmosphere in which Cuba became an almost-obsessive issue within the White House. "We were hysterical about Castro," Secretary of Defense Robert McNamara later recalled.[81]

Kennedy learned from his mistakes. The failure at the Bay of Pigs clarified how important it was to have the correct decision-making apparatus in place. This significantly affected whom he chose to include in discussions of the missile crisis and how he made decisions—by moving trusted advisers toward a consensus rather than simply voting yes or no on a pre-existing plan. In practical terms, the mission's failure also reduced rebel activities within Cuba, where the invading exiles had generated no sympathetic revolt among the island's population.[82]

In the mission's aftermath, JFK asked retired general Maxwell Taylor to investigate what happened. Taylor found that the Joint Chiefs felt no responsibility for the failure in Cuba and that the CIA had failed to communicate adequately with Kennedy. An inspector-general's report delivered on November 24, 1961 took a tougher look at the CIA's role and found that the agency had failed on many fronts: It had underestimated Castro's popularity, his military force, and the amount of training and equipment necessary to make such a landing successful. By this time, Kennedy had cleaned house at the CIA, forcing Director Allen Dulles and his deputies to resign in September. The United States was not alone in drawing lessons from the failed invasion: Although Castro's forces had won, Soviet leaders considered it a close call and increased their involvement in Cuban security.

After failure at the Bay of Pigs, the United States followed several strategies to hold Castro in check. One approach was to isolate Cuba from other Latin American states. A National Security Council memo just days after the invasion stressed the importance of a unified stand by the United States and its Latin American allies through the Rio Treaty, which declared that an attack on any American republic "shall be considered an attack against all."[83] At an Organization of American States conference in Uruguay in January 1962, member nations characterized Cuba's Communist government as being incompatible with the organization. The group refused to allow Cuba's membership, blocked all member nations from providing weapons to Castro, and approved plans for a unified defense against Communist infiltration.[84] Castro responded to the OAS's action by issuing the Second Declaration of Havana. In it, he attacked U.S. economic and political exploitation of Latin America. Reaching beyond the OAS, Kennedy used the Alliance for Progress as another means of cementing ties with southern neighbors. The aid program encouraged economic cooperation between the United States and Latin America. In February 1962, JFK expanded the U.S. trade embargo against Cuba, ending virtually all trade between the two nations.

Almost a year after the failure at the Bay of Pigs, a Cuban tribunal sentenced the captured invaders to thirty years of hard labor, with the possibility of winning their freedom through "indemnification" payments. The price tag for some men's freedom ran as high as $100,000.[85] The last of the men were freed on Christmas Eve 1962 after large payoffs by Americans. The Central Intelligence Agency concluded that the prisoner trade was made so that Cuba could obtain much-needed foreign currency.[86]

After the Bay of Pigs, the United States did not completely abandon invasion planning. The military prepared a number of contingency plans to seize control of Cuba. OPLAN 312 outlined an air attack with many options ranging from an assault on a single target to widespread strikes on multiple objectives; OPLAN 314 described an invasion on land that would accompany an air strike; OPLAN 316 mapped out a land invasion with less time to assemble the invasion force.[87] Just such an invasion was rehearsed in two Marine landings during the spring of 1962 on Vieques, an island municipality in Puerto Rico.

A different approach to the Cuban problem could be found in Operation MONGOOSE, a surreptitious operation intended to undermine Castro's government. Brigadier General Edward Lansdale, widely recognized for his successful support of the Philippine government's efforts to overcome Communist insurgents, supervised MONGOOSE. He reported to the Special Group (Augmented) chaired by Taylor under the watchful eyes of the president's brother, Attorney General Robert Kennedy. Other members of the SGA were CIA Director John McCone, National Security Adviser McGeorge Bundy, Undersecretary of State U. Alexis Johnson, Lemnitzer, and Gilpatric. In November 1961, JFK instructed the CIA to "use our available assets to help Cuba overthrow the Communist regime."[88] A key factor in the operation's strategy was the unproven belief that there was at least an undercurrent of rebellion already existing in Cuba.

In a February 1962 report, Lansdale called for the beginning of covert action in March, with continued buildup running through July. He recommended a final policy decision in August followed by the beginnings of guerrilla operations in Cuba through December. He hoped to set off an open revolt and the overthrow of Castro's government in October 1962. Lansdale's plans generally involved small acts of sabotage or other mischief that could bolster a rebellion only if a significant number of would-be rebels truly existed in Cuba. The pettiness of MONGOOSE operations can be seen in one plot: Lansdale asked the Pentagon to develop a program

By October 1962 when the missile crisis occurred, General Lemnitzer was no longer a member of the SGA; Taylor had replaced him as chairman of the Joint Chiefs; and Robert Kennedy was acting chairman of the SGA.

that would lead to prayers among U.S. military units with Cuban personnel. The plan was to take photos and leak them to Cuba to create concern about a U.S. invasion.[89]

Because it fell short of being a well-orchestrated program, Bundy called Operation MONGOOSE "a psychological salve for inaction."[90] McCone summed up MONGOOSE's mission in an October 4 meeting when he said that high-level officials wanted the operations to continue with "a low noise level."[91] On at least one occasion, Robert Kennedy reported that the president was dissatisfied with the operation's record.[92] Two government studies reported no internal uprising in Cuba and determined that there was no real hope of toppling Castro without large-scale U.S. involvement.[93] And still MONGOOSE, which seemed more and more like a prankster's game, continued. More than forty years later, McNamara categorized the operation as "reprehensible."[94]

Taking a more studied approach, the State Department recommended techniques for sabotaging Cuba's economy, while the Pentagon suggested a wave of bombings in the United States that could be blamed on Castro. Exiled opponents of Castro received CIA help to return to their homeland where they hoped to stockpile weapons and encourage rebellion. The CIA had a variety of other plans, including assassination plots against Castro, exploitation of the Mafia to sneak guns onto the island, and use of chemicals to eradicate Castro's beard, which was expected to be a public relations disaster for the Cuban leader.[95] JFK once shocked *New York Times* reporter Szulc by asking, "What would you think if I ordered Castro to be assassinated?"[96] We now know that assassination plots were not unusual in this era when the CIA plotted in 1960 to kill Castro, Patrice Lumumba of the Congo, and Rafael Trujillo of the Dominican Republic. Furthermore, use of the Mafia to aid in these activities in Cuba made a certain amount of sense: Mobsters suffered big financial losses when Castro's policy ended Havana's role as a playground for wealthy Western tourists who wanted to gamble.

U.S. actions toward Castro's Cuba nudged it closer to the Soviet Union, and created further estrangement between the United States and his regime. It became a vicious circle. Because Castro expected U.S. opposition, he embraced the Soviet Union. Because he developed ties to the Soviet Union, the United States encouraged other Latin American countries to condemn him. Because the OAS rejected him, Castro leaned more heavily on the Soviet bloc and became open to the idea of accepting missiles from Khrushchev. Because he allowed the Soviet Union to place missiles on Cuban soil, the United States opposed him more fervently.

CHAPTER 2

Kennedy and Khrushchev

SETTING THE STAGE FOR DISASTER

John F. Kennedy and Nikita Khrushchev entered 1962 without a clear channel of communication. Their relationship had suffered a rocky start. During the 1960 presidential campaign, Khrushchev thought that Kennedy took a more adversarial stance toward the Soviet Union than his opponent, Richard Nixon. This was especially true on two of the most important issues to the Soviet leader: disarmament and Berlin. Consequently, he was wary about Kennedy's election. The Soviet Foreign Ministry labeled the president-elect as "unlikely to possess the qualities of an outstanding person."[1]

Neither man truly understood the other. As the unelected leader of a totalitarian regime, Khrushchev was susceptible to the idea that the president alone governed the United States. The Soviet leader received little feedback from his advisers, who typically gave unanimous support to whatever action he proposed. As a result, he had complete power over his nation's nuclear forces and held the fate of millions—or perhaps even billions—in his hands. In the United States, at a time when American cynicism toward leaders was about to skyrocket, the man in the White House wielded the relatively new and growing power to destroy nations and bring devastation to his own land without the voters' consent.[2] However, unlike Khrushchev, Kennedy worked within a system of checks and balances that forced him to consider opposing views within his own Democratic Party and the opposing Republican Party.

Because he was facing difficulties at home, Khrushchev was strongly motivated to maintain the appearance of success in the Cold War without placing a further drain on Soviet resources. His seven-year initiative to improve living conditions in the Soviet Union was clearly failing just two years after its launch. Consequently, when the Bay of Pigs invasion occurred, Khrushchev expressed mixed reactions. Publicly, he sent Kennedy a vituperative letter of protest. More quietly, he asked Foreign Minister Andrei Gromyko to communicate his desire for better relations with the United States. Khrushchev believed that Kennedy might have been led astray by hardliners, and he saw benefits in reaching out to him. In many ways, this reaction reflected Khrushchev's often-contradictory behavior toward the United States.

As Kennedy prepared to meet the Soviet leader for the first time at a June 1961 summit in Vienna, he hoped to make progress on a nuclear test ban treaty, and to achieve that he wanted to get agreement from Khrushchev for a limited number of inspections to verify compliance. In addition, he was eager to formalize an agreement designating the Southeast Asian nation of Laos as a neutral entity. Khrushchev had no interest in finalizing a test ban; in fact, his top military advisers were urging him to end the two-year voluntary moratorium. He was open to discussion on Laos; however, the top item on his agenda was the divided city of Berlin.

Just as the roots of the Cold War lie in World War II, one of the era's hottest issues arose from the resolution of that war. When the fighting ended in Europe, the Allies split Germany into pieces. The Soviet Union took control of what would become East Germany, while the Western powers guided the area that would exist as West Germany for more than forty years. Berlin, which fell within the Soviet sector, was similarly divided into a Soviet zone, a U.S. zone, a British zone, and a French zone. It had been Hitler's capital, and each of the Allies wanted a chunk of it. Over time, the Western powers united their zones to form West Berlin, while the Soviets kept East Berlin. Repeatedly during the Cold War, the USSR threatened the future of West Berlin. In 1948, the Soviet Union implemented a land blockade of the city, which could be reached only by traveling through East Germany. The Western allies responded by airlifting goods to West Berlin. Ten years later, the Soviet Union precipitated another crisis by insisting that the three Western Allies must withdraw all troops from West Berlin within six months—and though no Allied troops withdrew, the threat led to the departure of many East Germans, who fled into West Berlin. The refugee flood was a big problem for East Germany, and in 1961, Khrushchev threatened West Berlin's existence as a means of stopping the stampede of refugees. East Germany's leader, Walter Ulbricht, had told Khrushchev that he could not wait much longer to end the flight of East Germans into West Berlin. Consequently, Khrushchev advocated tough action at a May 26 meeting of the Presidium, the executive board of the Central Committee of the Communist Party. Because of the dangers inherent in nuclear war, he doubted that the United

Nikita Khrushchev Biography

Born into a Russian peasant family in 1894, Nikita Sergeyevich Khrushchev received only four years of formal education before becoming a metal worker in the Ukraine. After the Bolshevik revolution of 1917, he rose steadily through the hierarchy of the Communist Party and claimed a place in Moscow's party structure by 1929. He became a member of the Central Committee of the Communist Party in 1934. Recognizing Khrushchev's loyalty and ingenuity, Soviet leader Josef Stalin assigned him to oversee the Ukraine in 1938. After the Nazi German invasion in 1941, Khrushchev took responsibility for preserving and evacuating Ukrainian industry. When Germany seized complete control of the Ukraine, Khrushchev was given the rank of lieutenant general in the Soviet army, and he was assigned to stimulate civilian resistance. He was an adviser during the defense of Stalingrad (now Volgograd) and when the Soviet Union expelled the Germans from the Ukraine, he returned to his duties there as first secretary of the Ukrainian party. Stalin gave Khrushchev a position in the Kremlin in 1949. He served as Moscow party chief, was a member of the Politburo or Presidium of the Communist Party, and became one of Stalin's closest allies.

Stalin's death in 1953 after years of physical decline was no surprise; however, the tyrannical leader had made no effort to prepare a successor to lead the USSR. Initially, he was replaced by a four-man group that included Khrushchev as first secretary of the Communist Party. One member of that quartet, KGB chief Lavrenti Beria, inspired fear in the others, and Khrushchev joined a conspiracy to kill Beria just months after Stalin's death. In 1956, Khrushchev, who was emerging as the most powerful man in the Soviet Union, startled the Communist Party's twentieth congress by delivering a six-hour attack on Stalin's methods of maintaining absolute control through brutality. In the following year, Khrushchev became the undisputed leader of the Soviet Union.

Both a showman and a politician, Khrushchev attracted international attention through his often-flamboyant public behavior, which included pounding his shoe on a desk at the United Nations in 1960. He ruled the Soviet bloc with a firm hand, having already crushed a rebellion in Hungary in 1956. Under his bold leadership, the Soviet Union proudly became the first nation to send a satellite into orbit in 1957 and sent the first man into orbit just four years later. Khrushchev's often-overblown, fist-swinging speeches about the scientific advancements of the USSR enabled him to convince much of the world, including many Americans, that the ruthlessly ordered Soviet system might have advantages.

A true believer in Communism, Khrushchev tried to spread his nation's economic philosophy around the world, especially in the developing nations of Latin America, Asia, and Africa. Cuba became his first clear ally outside Europe. While rejecting the purges of the Stalin era, Khrushchev maintained a totalitarian government at home. In 1960, he made a show of canceling a Paris meeting with Eisenhower after the president and his administration lied about the existence of high-altitude spy planes over the Soviet Union. When Khrushchev revealed that he had downed a U-2 and captured its pilot, Eisenhower refused to apologize, and Khrushchev dramatically called off their scheduled summit. Nevertheless, in the long run, the combative little man improved relations with the United States.

One recurrent theme in Khrushchev's relations with the United States was East Germany's right to take control of West Berlin. Recognizing the emotions that led the Soviet Union, the United States, Great Britain, and France to divide the city into four sectors at the end of the war, Khrushchev felt that the agreement's time had passed. When he consolidated his power, the postwar era was more than a decade old, and he argued forcefully that West Berlin should become part of Communist East Germany rather than remaining a pocket of democracy and capitalism within the Eastern bloc.

Khrushchev's loud, bullying mannerisms stunned John F. Kennedy in their 1961 Vienna summit. Through letters, especially during the Cuban Missile Crisis, the two men ultimately achieved a polite and productive relationship. They shared a belief that Communism and capitalism could coexist peacefully. Khrushchev's commitment to Cuba and his apparent defeat in the missile crisis caused him to lose prestige at a time when his domestic policies also were coming under fire. In October 1964, the Central Committee of the Communist Party forced him to resign. He died in 1971.

States would go to war, even if he launched a nuclear strike on West Germany, France, and England.[3] What he planned was to sign a treaty giving the East German government control of all access routes to West Berlin—road, rail, and air. Although he hoped to avoid direct action against West Berlin, he believed this move would force the Western powers to abandon their sector of the city. He planned to make maintenance of West Berlin as difficult as possible. Westerners seeking to reach West Berlin would be required to fly into East German airports and to face all of the difficulties experienced by Westerners visiting the Soviet bloc. As on other issues before the Presidium, Anastas Mikoyan was the only member to question Khrushchev's strategy. Mikoyan thought Kennedy might stand up to Khrushchev's efforts at intimidation. Provoked by Mikoyan's opposition, Khrushchev decided on even stronger action: a promise to shoot down any allied plane that attempted to land in West Berlin. Khrushchev challenged the United States, knowing that nuclear war was a possibility. His son, Sergei, has said that his father's trick was to intimidate the United States by threatening to attack with "weapons we didn't have."[4]

When Kennedy and Khrushchev met in Vienna, the Soviet leader attempted to bully the younger and less experienced JFK. In the early going, he lectured Kennedy about American shortcomings, such as alliances with right-wing dictators in Spain and Iran. On the second day, Kennedy sought to establish some rapport by telling Khrushchev about his youth, but Khrushchev, whose difficult childhood bore no resemblance to Kennedy's privileged youth, refused to make the discussion personal. Instead, he silenced Kennedy by ranting about the Soviet Union's wealth of iron ore deposits. When Kennedy led the conversation to the topic of Laos, where the two men shared common ground, Khrushchev again tried to avoid engaging in a true dialogue by criticizing U.S. policy on Thailand and Taiwan. Nevertheless, they did reach an oral agreement on neutralization of Laos before moving on to less agreeable topics, such as disarmament, a test ban, and Berlin. Khrushchev told Kennedy that he wanted destruction of weapons, not an end to testing. A test ban carried no guarantee of reduced military expenses. However, for the already-outgunned Soviet Union, disarmament offered the prospect of escape from an unending, costly arms race. While Kennedy had hoped that Khrushchev might agree to a test ban with ten inspections a year, Khrushchev would agree to only three.

When the conversation turned to Berlin, Khrushchev explained his plan to block access routes to West Berlin and added that Western troops could remain there only if Soviet troops also could have a place in that part of the city. He promised continued free communication between West Berlin and Allied nations, but stood firm on limiting physical access to the city. Kennedy rejected the whole idea. Khrushchev concluded by declaring that the East German treaty must be signed by December, and Kennedy predicted, "It will be a cold winter."[5] The summit ended with Kennedy feeling battered and dejected. He told *New York Times* correspondent James Reston that the Soviet leader had "just beat hell out of me."[6] Robert Kennedy later remarked that "this was the first time the president had ever really come across somebody with whom he couldn't exchange ideas in a meaningful way."[7] Kennedy's much-vaunted charm had failed him.

In a July 8 address to graduates of Soviet military academies, Khrushchev revealed a 33 percent increase in the Soviet defense budget and suspension of cuts in military forces that had been planned for 1961. At home, Kennedy felt heat from conservative leaders who believed he should clearly demonstrate America's commitment to its European allies and declare a national emergency over Berlin. On July 25, in a national address, he announced that he would ask Congress for a $3.25 billion hike in the defense budget and that he would call up reservists and National Guardsmen. He also made his biggest push ever for civil defense preparedness. Faced with Kennedy's speech and with KGB reports that the North Atlantic Treaty Organization (NATO) was preparing for possible military action, Khrushchev decided in August to follow an earlier recommendation from Ulbricht and close the border between West Berlin and East Germany by building a wall on all sides of West Berlin. Installation of the concrete and barbed wire barrier shocked citizens in the United States and other Allied countries; however, this action had the advantage of confirming West Berlin's boundary—and its continued existence. It also stopped short of a direct head-to-head conflict between the two superpowers. Shortly after the wall's construction, Kennedy ordered 1,500 troops and a convoy of armored vehicles to proceed to West Berlin via the autobahn as a show of force. In September, Khrushchev decided to abandon plans for a treaty with East Germany.

American leaders saw Berlin as a symbolic island within a Communist state and used the city as a shining representation of Western values. Khrushchev told his inner circle, "Berlin is the tail of imperialism, and we can yank it when they do something wrong to us."[8] The whole 1961 dispute was like a chess game that reached a stalemate—and then ended unceremoniously. Ulbricht, like Castro a year later, felt betrayed by Khrushchev's unilateral decision to resign from the game.

After the United States revealed that its nuclear weaponry greatly exceeded the Soviet Union's arms, Khrushchev decided to demonstrate Soviet power through the October 30, 1961 detonation of the most powerful nuclear device ever tested. The fifty-megaton bomb was not viable as a weapon: It was so large that only the Soviet Union's TU-95 Bear bomber could carry it. These slow planes easily could be shot down by American defenses. In addition, using the bomb in Western Europe was not an option because fallout would have drifted into the nations of the Soviet bloc.[9]

Neither Khrushchev's decision to back down in Berlin nor news of U.S. missile superiority lessened many Americans' fear of the Soviet Union—a terror that would provide much of the context for the nation's reaction to the Cuban Missile Crisis. "What brought critics of widely divergent political persuasions to similar conclusions was a shared image, born of *Sputnik*, of the ten-foot-tall Russians who rarely do anything wrong," Arnold L. Horelick wrote in a Rand Corporation analysis of the crisis that was commissioned by the Air Force. "And a complementary, equally erroneous image, fostered by the U-2 and the Bay of Pigs debacles, of U.S. administrations that rarely do anything right."[10]

KHRUSHCHEV'S GAMBIT

Blustery and bombastic, boastful and boisterous, Khrushchev was a man with a rich imagination and a willingness to embrace risk when he believed the odds were in his favor. He bragged about a Soviet drive for world domination, but that was a bluff: His realistic goal in 1962 was to attain something close to equal footing with the United States in the nuclear arms race. To accomplish that, he was willing to make a big gamble—until it became clear that he should fold his cards and accept the limited winnings on the table before him.

The Soviet leader first seriously considered placing offensive nuclear missiles in Cuba during the spring of 1962 when he was traveling through Bulgaria. The charm of his cunning plot was its ability to accomplish multiple goals in a single daring move. Khrushchev reasoned that his plan would protect the island and achieve far more. On the soil of the Soviet Union, Khrushchev had relatively few missiles that could reach the United States, and his nation had no missiles in other lands. Engineering ballistic weapons capable of traveling such great distances was expensive and technologically challenging. Placing Soviet missiles in Cuba would put most of the United States easily within range of less expensive weapons—medium- and intermediate-range missiles—and that would reduce the United States' dominance in a head-to-head conflict.

These missiles were expected to double or triple the number of warheads targeting the United States. At that time, the Soviet bloc had no more than thirty-six intercontinental missiles[11] and 138 long-range bombers.[12] The United States possessed 203 intercontinental ballistic missiles[13] and 144 submarine-launchable *Polaris* missiles[14] as well as 1,595 bombers.[15] The Soviet Union also was far behind in the production of nuclear warheads. The United States had a stockpile of about 7,211 strategic warheads and 20,085 non-strategic (lower-yield) warheads,[16] while the Soviet Union owned only 522 strategic warheads and 2,800 non-strategic warheads.[17] Overall, the United States was estimated to have a 17-to-1 advantage in strategic weapons.[18] Adding to the American military's advantage was the simple fact that the United States could launch a long-range missile with only a few minutes' warning, while Soviet weapons required hours to prepare.

Even if the United States destroyed some of the missiles in Cuba, Khrushchev contended that "if a quarter or even a tenth of our missiles survived—even if only one or two big ones were left—we could still hit New York, and there wouldn't be much of New York left."[19] At a time when Americans tended to think of Soviet leaders as something just short of alien life forms, Khrushchev understood, perhaps more clearly than his American counterparts, that even a nuclear strike that destroyed only one American metropolis would be psychologically devastating to the United States. The other advantage that the missiles in Cuba gave the Soviets was the ability to launch a first strike with less warning time. The difference would be only a matter of ten minutes or so, but the United States' ability to disperse targeted planes and get bombers into the air would be shortened.

Khrushchev also thought placement of missiles in Cuba would outrage Americans so much that it would generate negotiations about U.S. missiles aimed at the Soviet Union from America's European allies. "The Americans had surrounded our country with military bases and threatened us with nuclear weapons, and now they would learn just what it feels like to have enemy missiles pointing at you," Khrushchev wrote in his memoirs.[20] The Soviet leader was particularly perturbed by the admittedly outdated Jupiter missiles in one of the Soviet Union's next-door neighbors—Turkey—a NATO ally of the United States.

Looking at the big picture, Khrushchev believed that implantation of missiles in Cuba could solidify the Soviet Union's position in world leadership at a time when his nation was squabbling with the other Communist giant—China. With this bold maneuver, he hoped to quash criticism throughout Socialist nations, silencing both his rivals in Communist China and hard-liners in his own country. Sergei Khrushchev later explained what his father wanted: "If not leader of the world, a role for which the Soviet Union did not qualify at all—it was unable to catch up to the United States even in per capita consumption of meat and milk—then at least leader of the Socialist segment of the globe."[21]

Moreover, Khrushchev sincerely wanted to protect Cuba from a U.S. invasion, which he feared was imminent. The expectation of an American attack on Cuba was a logical outgrowth of the Bay of Pigs invasion and of the American government's tendencies to loudly make exhaustive plans for all military contingencies and to engage in harsh rhetoric to pacify conservative forces in American politics. When speaking in December 1962 about his rationale for placing missiles in Cuba, Khrushchev cited only the desire to protect Cuba; however, this could have been accomplished with fewer missiles targeting only the southeastern United States where a U.S. military invasion force logically would form.[22] At a 1989 meeting of missile crisis participants in Moscow, Sergei Khrushchev said that his father "regarded the question of the defense of Cuba as seriously as the question of the defense of the border of the Soviet Union, not distinguishing between them."[23]

In the view of highly placed General Anatoli I. Gribkov, the missile plan fit perfectly into Khrushchev's world view. Relying heavily on missiles, submarines, and thorough civil defense planning, Khrushchev had announced his intention to slash ground forces as well as the Soviet Union's surface navy in 1958. He had begun demobilizing more than a million officers and enlisted men in January 1960, although he put this troop cutback on hold a year later. He also demolished or simply scrapped planes, ships, and tanks.[24] He saw missiles as the nation's military future—a future that warranted greater attention.

Americans feared that Soviet leaders might one day start a nuclear war, but Khrushchev had reason to worry about American aggression, too. In a *Saturday Evening Post* interview, Kennedy told Stewart Alsop that the United States could not and would not rule out initiating a nuclear war despite repeated statements that making a first strike would violate American moral standards. As Alsop interpreted Kennedy's position: "Khrushchev must not be certain that, where its vital interests are threatened, the United States will not strike first."[25] Beyond that, the United States continued to talk with leaders of NATO allies about placing missiles in their countries. On October 16, 1962, shortly after the United States' discovery of the missiles, German Minister of Foreign Affairs Gerhard Schröder was meeting with American officials to talk about placing medium-range nuclear missiles in additional NATO nations, including Schröder's West Germany, which abutted the Warsaw Pact nations.[26]

Khrushchev formally unveiled his Cuban missile plan on May 20, 1962, when he presented it to the Soviet Presidium. Khrushchev did not have to deal with outspoken debate from advisers. In the words of Sergei Khrushchev, "In the Kremlin everyone always agreed with him."[27] Despite the boldness of Khrushchev's plan, only Mikoyan expressed reservations. He argued that this strategy might instigate a nuclear war, but Khrushchev brashly rejected the idea of allowing fear of nuclear war to govern policy decisions. Just a few days later, the Presidium unanimously approved the plan. Khrushchev probably welcomed the almost-total absence of challenges to his ideas; however, in the long run, thoughtful criticism might have helped him to anticipate the likely American response.

Khrushchev soon encountered a possible obstacle to his plan. The KGB's Aleksandr Alekseyev, working undercover in Havana as a Tass correspondent, knew Castro and doubted that Castro would accept the weapons. Knowing Castro's outspoken independence, Alekseyev argued that, whenever possible, the Cuban leader wanted to stand alone against the United States.[28] He also suggested that Castro might "be scared" about the danger of a nuclear attack on Cuba.[29]

To Khrushchev's delight, Alekseyev was wrong: Castro told Soviet officials that he was flattered by the plan. He agreed to accept it without any serious reservations. Military strategists estimated that Soviet personnel would need four months to install the weapons. Khrushchev proceeded eagerly and hoped to keep the missiles a secret until sometime after the November 6 congressional elections in the United States so that the American response would not be guided by the politics of the moment. In all, there would be twenty-four launch sites for thirty-six medium-range missiles, known as R–12s, and sixteen sites for twenty-four intermediate-range missiles, known as R–14s. Soviet R–12s had a range of about 1,100 miles, while the intermediate-range missiles could travel twice as far and carry warheads twice as powerful. In Cuba, each missile would carry a one-megaton warhead.[30] Because of the need to install the missiles quickly, workers would place them on launch pads rather than anchoring them in fortified bunkers. Soviet military leaders assured Khrushchev that there was little chance of American discovery before the installations were complete. The missiles, they implausibly told him, could be disguised as coconut palms, or they could be hidden within natural camouflage provided by Cuba's trees. The Soviet Union also planned to send crates holding unassembled and somewhat outdated bombers. These Ilyushin 28 (IL-28) planes were light bombers capable of traveling 1,500 nautical miles, putting a significant portion of the United States within reach of Cuban bombers.

Militarily, this plan offered multiple challenges. Because this technology was new to Cuba,[31] the military proposed sending more than 50,000 troops to the island. About 230,000 tons of supplies and hardware would be necessary to support the missiles and the men. Included would be two tank battalions, four motorized regiments, and a MiG-21 fighter wing. The Soviet Union never planned to integrate Cuban soldiers into the missile operation.

Transportation was the most daunting problem. All of the troops and cargo had to be shipped 7,000 miles.[32] With the exception of a few amphibious attacks during World War II, the Soviet military had little experience of staging complex naval operations, even at much shorter distances and with much less cargo.[33] Transporting missiles by airplane would have been impossible because of their size, and adding flights from Moscow to Havana to move the troops would have attracted unwanted attention.

As Khrushchev worked out the details of his military venture, he was struggling to cope with quality-of-life issues at home. On June 11, he appeared on television to explain a 30 percent increase in meat prices and a 25 percent hike in butter prices. The cost of producing these products had long exceeded sales prices, but the government had subsidized farmers to suppress costs. Khrushchev had resisted raising consumer prices, but economic advisers convinced him that higher prices would give farmers a profit and spur increased production. This strategy, although logical in a market economy, failed to work in a centralized, Socialist nation: While their leader was making a massive spending commitment to place missiles in a tiny nation on the other side of the world, Soviet citizens were struggling to put food on the table.[34]

In July, Castro's brother Raul, who was Cuba's armed forces minister, arrived in the USSR to finalize a military deployment agreement. Shipments would begin almost immediately, and the Soviet military planned to complete the installations in autumn. Khrushchev's plot was given the code name Operation Anadyr.[35] His government maintained such tight secrecy that no typewritten documents on the subject were circulated.

As the project was mobilizing, Khrushchev maintained his verbal assault upon the United States. He wrote to Kennedy demanding a 30 percent reduction in the number of Western soldiers in West Berlin. He wanted to see those troops replaced by soldiers from Warsaw Pact or neutral nations. By 1966, he argued, the entire contingent of foreign troops should be eliminated. Claiming that he wanted to help JFK, Khrushchev asked U.S. Ambassador Llewellyn "Tommy" Thompson whether Kennedy wanted Berlin to become a crisis before or after the November elections that threatened to increase Republican representation in Congress.[36] He ordered Georgi Bolshakov, a representative of the Soviet armed forces' foreign policy directorate known as the GRU, to convince Kennedy to stop conducting reconnaissance of Soviet ships in international waters, and when JFK agreed, the president asked that the Berlin issue be sidelined for a while. Khrushchev accepted Kennedy's concession but was unwilling to forgo his demands on Berlin. In late July, the United States and the Soviet Union were able to finalize a formal agreement to neutralize Laos, but this pact promised no improvement in U.S.–Soviet relations. In early September, Khrushchev hosted Kennedy's Secretary of the Interior, Stewart Udall, at his Petsunda retreat in Georgia, and Khrushchev warned Udall that "it's been a long time since you could spank us like a little boy—now we can swat your ass."[37] By varying between cooperation and bellicosity, Khrushchev kept America's leadership off balance. Particularly since their unproductive 1961 meeting in Vienna, Kennedy was unsure about how to interpret Khrushchev's words or his actions— and Khrushchev may have hoped to make himself a distraction at a moment when the Soviet Union desperately hoped for a lapse in U.S. security operations.

Managing to transport the missiles without raising American suspicions was a big job. First, Soviet planners directed innocuous cargoes to foreign ships, thus freeing space on Soviet vessels, where secrecy could be maintained more effectively. In July, a large armada of Soviet ships began sailing to Cuba. There was a virtual traffic jam in the Dardanelles and Bosporus with so many Soviet freighters leaving the Black and Baltic seas. In many cases, these vessels were loaded in isolated locations so that prying eyes could not see the cargo. Use of radios and telephone lines was prohibited in communications between Moscow and the ports; instead,

Soviet leaders used couriers to exchange information with the ships preparing to transport military materiel. As another measure to prevent leaks, troops were denied outside communication after reaching their ports of departure. Throughout implementation of the plan, high-ranking military officials led their underlings to believe that Operation Anadyr was simply a military exercise.[38]

While much of the Soviet mobilization and mammoth transport effort went surprisingly well, the leader of the Soviet force in Cuba, a World War I cavalry officer named General Issa Pliyev, struggled to make things work. An old cavalryman seemed like an odd choice to supervise a corps of rocket command officers. In some fairly twisted logic, Khrushchev reportedly thought that choosing Pliyev would reinforce the idea that the missiles were being installed to defend Cuba and not to start a nuclear war. However, Pliyev had difficulty leading unfamiliar officers who were specialists in a field outside his own expertise. Over time, deployments began to fall behind schedule. Pliyev also lacked diplomatic skills, which made it difficult to negotiate a potentially prickly relationship with Castro. Even before he boarded the *Tupolev 114* for Cuba, a comical scene set the stage for his Cuban performance. The longtime military officer initially refused to board a ship carrying a passport that bore a pseudonym, Ivan Aleksandrovich Pavlov, a false identity intelligence officers considered necessary to guard the project's secrecy.[39]

Khrushchev often was brazen in conversation with Americans, but in the Cuban operation, he counseled his underlings to be circumspect so that the operation could maintain a low profile. In September, Soviet leaders slashed the number of men and the amount of equipment needed by excluding a squadron of surface ships and eleven submarines with a total complement of 5,640 naval officers and men. The surface ships, in particular, seemed likely to garner more attention than a clandestine operation could bear. Also, eliminating these vessels made it easier to stretch supplies.[40]

For those who did make the trip to Cuba aboard a freighter, the voyage was difficult. On ships carrying missile-related equipment, it was typical to place agricultural machinery on the deck to avoid generating suspicion. This required finding room for missiles and soldiers below decks. The first missiles arrived in Cuba in mid-September aboard the *Omsk*. With the 67-foot medium-range missiles stacked diagonally against a wall, 264 men each had a living space of just 16 square feet when the ship departed August 25. Official orders about the route to be taken were kept in sealed envelopes and opened jointly by the ship's captain and a KGB officer. The ship was directed first to the Bosporus. The next envelope dispatched it to Gibraltar, and the third revealed its final destination—Cuba. The last instructions included an order to destroy the paper on which they were written. The ship's hatches were shut whenever the *Omsk* approached land or passed foreign ships. Most soldiers sweltered below decks as the sun baked the ship's metal surfaces. At night, small numbers of soldiers took turns enjoying fresh air on the deck. The effects of seasickness and heat combined to cause the average soldier to lose 22 pounds during the voyage, according to author Michael Dobbs. Some troops traveled to Cuba in much greater luxury as make-believe tourists aboard a passenger liner, the *Admiral Nakhimov*.[41] Each ship carried Defense Ministry folders filled with information about nations friendly to the USSR. Among them, of course, was Cuba. Commanders' study papers were hidden within public relations materials so that if a ship was captured, its destination would not be apparent.[42]

The most precious cargoes were the caches of nuclear warheads. Within the Soviet Union, passenger trains, rather than freight trains, transported them to ports. Once placed on ships, they became vulnerable to seizure at sea. The dueling needs for security and secrecy led to debates about patrolling the ships' routes with Soviet bombers or warships. Eventually, both ideas were rejected as threats to the mission's secrecy. However, four submarines were dispatched toward Cuba and while one had to return to its home base because of mechanical problems, the other three successfully evaded American submarine defenses in the Atlantic. The first warheads arrived in Cuba October 4.

The number of Soviet bloc dry cargo ships arriving in Cuba rose significantly in August–October 1962. While the monthly average in the first half of 1962 was fifteen ships per month, thirty-seven ships transported dry cargo in August.[43] In all, eighty-five ships participated in Operation Anadyr, and those ships made 243 trips between the Soviet Union and Cuba.[44] In mid-September a TASS statement carried the headline "Put an End to the Provocation" and called for cessation of U.S. speculation about the meaning of these shipments.

When the ships reached Cuba, agricultural equipment was unloaded in the daytime, but all military cargoes had to be off-loaded under the cover of darkness and delivered to their destination on remote roads. Some soldiers were required to wear civilian clothes in Cuba, while others wore Cuban military uniforms. Many also sported facial hair to blend more effectively with the native population. Officers forbade speaking Russian in public.

Although the Soviet military initially argued that hiding missiles among Cuba's tropical forests would be easy, they discovered that Cuba is thinly wooded in places. Also, the long shapes of the missiles and the rows of auxiliary vehicles, ranging from tanks to fuel trucks, would eventually become impossible to hide from U.S. spy planes. As the weapons arrived, all military officers had strict orders that no missiles were to be fired without authorization from Moscow. Khrushchev wavered but eventually gave Pliyev authority to use the less powerful tactical weapons only if he could not communicate with his superiors in Moscow.

Meanwhile, Cuba's leaders developed their own strategy for dealing with a possible U.S. invasion. The Cuban General Staff planned to divide the island into three zones—eastern, central, and western. Each would have its own independent command so that armed resistance could continue even if one zone was isolated from the others.

By early October, missile site construction was well under way. Workers laid concrete to serve as missile launch platforms, assembled parts warehouses, and excavated a bunker to house warheads, which were to be held in depots near the missile sites. There was a central nuclear depot in Bejucal that housed fifty-five warheads slated to be used on weapons within a forty-mile radius. In other areas, it was necessary for a single depot to contain both warheads for missiles and bombs for the IL–28 squadron.[45] Pliyev told Khrushchev that the first medium-range missiles would be operational before the month's end. The intermediate-range missiles appeared to be headed toward completion in November. Hundreds of Cuban families were relocated to make way for the deadly hardware. U.S. intelligence estimates later suggested that several million Cubans knew about the missiles while the American government remained unaware of them.[46]

When faced with a moral question about whether the secret installation of the weapons was acceptable policy, Khrushchev justified his actions by citing the United States' clandestine use of U-2 planes to spy on Communist nations. He noted Eisenhower's initial dishonesty about the planes' existence. Khrushchev continued to believe in the wisdom of his policy. He doubted that the Kennedy administration would move swiftly to oust the missiles once they stood on launching pads. In making these judgments, he correctly reasoned that Eisenhower had been as capable of deception as he was, but he underestimated the effect of the secret missiles on Kennedy as the head of a democratic nation. JFK had no Presidium of yes-men to rubber-stamp his policies; instead, he faced the prospect of political opposition both inside and outside of his own political party. Moreover, the United States had been traumatized just twenty-one years earlier by a Japanese sneak attack on Pearl Harbor. The prospect of a surprise assault by Soviet missiles from Cuba raised memories of that day and kindled an almost primal response from a generation of American leaders who keenly recalled World War II and attempted to use its lessons as a road map in establishing future policy.

KENNEDY'S PREDICAMENT

Although American intelligence did not reflect much concern about growing Soviet involvement in Cuba, the shipping boom did not go unnoticed. Wary of creating a panic and sparking demands for military action, the Kennedy administration initially accepted the Soviet Union's assurances that only defensive weapons were being transported to Cuba. However, this optimistic appraisal became increasingly difficult to maintain.

> The administration's public labeling of weapons as defensive and offensive was problematic. The distinction often lay in the eye of the beholder, especially among people who believed that a large arsenal of offensive weapons represented a deterrent to attack. From that perspective, all missiles could be seen as defensive.

Beginning on August 31, Sen. Kenneth Keating, a New York Republican, issued repeated public statements about the dangerous nature of the Soviet cargo shipments. Over the following weeks, he warned Americans that the Soviet Union might be planting offensive weapons in Cuba. His calls for caution resonated with fellow politicians, who saw Cuba as a hot-button issue among voters. The senator, who apparently had sources in the Cuban refugee community, first warned that surface-to-air missiles (SAMs) were being unloaded in Cuba, and he later asserted quite accurately that unassembled IL-28 bombers could be found among the crates of Soviet materiel.[47]

Accurate and false reports about the Soviet buildup in Cuba quickly began popping up in the media, especially in Florida. The *Miami News* reported August 16 that thousands of Soviet military personnel had landed in Cuba over the previous two weeks.[48] On August 25, the *Washington Daily News* editorialized that Castro, like Adolf Hitler, intended to destroy neighboring nations.[49] On September 19, the *Tampa Tribune* quoted so-called Cuban expert Carlos Todd as saying that Communist forces would divide the island into three zones, with one dominated by Chinese, one by Russians, and one by African Communists.[50] (Even after fifty years of study, no one has found evidence of Chinese or African Communists in Cuba in 1962.)

Perhaps in response to growing chatter about nuclear weapons placement, Kennedy asked the Department of Defense on August 23 to investigate "what action can be taken to get Jupiter missiles out of Turkey." In National Security Action Memorandum 181, Kennedy also requested an investigation of the possible impact of SAMs and surface-to-surface missiles in Cuba.[51] While his staff argued that there were no offensive

John F. Kennedy Biography

Born into a wealthy, politically oriented Massachusetts family, John F. Kennedy first was elected to political office in 1946, when he successfully ran as a World War II hero and won a seat in the House of Representatives representing his home state at the age of 29. After serving three terms in the House, he captured a Senate seat in 1952 and served there through 1960, when he captured the Democratic presidential nomination and later became the youngest man and the first Roman Catholic to be elected to the American presidency.

The handsome and photogenic president led the nation during a time of crises, both domestic and international. Kennedy, known to friends as Jack, served as American commander-in-chief during a dangerous era when nuclear war seemed to be a genuine possibility. In 1961, he experienced a gargantuan failure when he endorsed the doomed CIA-backed Bay of Pigs invasion carried out by Cuban refugees. During the rest of that first year in office, he struggled through his first summit meeting with Nikita Khrushchev in Vienna, reached a formal agreement on the neutrality of Laos, and stood firm on the sovereignty of West Berlin. However, on the international front, he is best remembered for bringing 1962's Cuban Missile Crisis to a peaceful conclusion. In June 1963, he delivered a bold foreign policy address at American University in Washington. In that speech, he abandoned Cold War rhetoric and proclaimed that peaceful coexistence with the Soviet Union was possible. Over the course of his presidency, Kennedy sent a growing number of military advisers to South Vietnam, but he sent no combat troops. In the autumn of 1963, his administration tacitly accepted plans to overthrow the regime of South Vietnamese President Ngo Dinh Diem, although Kennedy was shocked to hear that Diem had been assassinated. Months before his own assassination on November 22, 1963, JFK successfully completed a limited test ban treaty with the Soviet Union and the United Kingdom. This agreement banned all nuclear testing except underground experiments. Both the American University speech and approval of the Test Ban Treaty had their roots in the missile crisis.

On the domestic front, he had a lackluster record in Congress, but his term was quite eventful, especially in the field of civil rights as African Americans protested legal restrictions facing them in the south. Initially, Kennedy handled each civil rights crisis separately without adopting a strong overarching philosophy about the rights of black Americans. When protesters encountered violence after challenging southern segregation on Trailways buses, Kennedy dispatched 400 federal marshals to protect them. The following year, he ordered federal marshals, National Guardsmen, and federal troops to Mississippi to enable James Meredith, a black veteran, to become the first African-American student at the University of Mississippi. In the spring of 1963, after witnessing TV footage of police violence against peaceful black demonstrators in Birmingham, Alabama, Kennedy spoke to the nation about the need for civil rights legislation that attacked the moral issue of racial discrimination. Also in that year, he federalized the National Guard to integrate the University of Alabama and met with black leaders of the March on Washington, where Martin Luther King Jr. spoke eloquently in his "I Have a Dream" speech.

After Kennedy's assassination in Dallas on November 22, 1963, he became a symbol of civil rights progress. Although he had been slow to join that fight, his memory was venerated by many in the movement because he was the first president since Andrew Johnson to push strong civil rights legislation.[52] In death, he also was identified as a strong Cold Warrior who helped his nation—and the world—to avoid nuclear war without bowing to Communism. We know today that his behind-the-scenes efforts to protect the peace may have carried more weight than his Cold War brinkmanship.

weapons in Cuba and that the Soviet men arriving there were technicians rather than soldiers, the president prepared for trouble. By this time, he knew that McCone suspected the Soviets might be preparing to place nuclear missiles there.

On September 2, Florida's Senator George Smathers, a Democrat and a Kennedy intimate, joined then-Democratic (and future Republican) Senator Strom Thurmond of South Carolina and Republican Senator Homer Capehart of Indiana in raising a battle cry over the need to stop the Soviet Union's arming of Cuba. Two days later, Kennedy issued a statement belittling the Soviet presence on the island, but also declaring "that the United States in conjunction with other [Western] Hemisphere countries, will make sure that while increased Cuban armaments will be a heavy burden to the unhappy people of Cuba themselves, they will be nothing more."[53]

Tellingly, on the same day that JFK declared there were no offensive weapons in Cuba, he wrote a secret memo ordering McNamara to take responsibility for increasing surveillance of shipments to Cuba and for maintaining the U.S. naval base at Guantanamo.[54] In addition, Robert Kennedy delivered a document from the president to Soviet Ambassador Anatoly Dobrynin. It voiced U.S. discomfort with the activity in Cuba and with the possibility that Cubans might get control of technologically advanced weapons such as nuclear missiles. On September 7, JFK asked Congress to give its approval to mobilization of 15,000 military reservists, a plea that lawmakers swiftly heeded. McCone cabled the CIA on September 10 while on his honeymoon, saying, "Appears to me quite possible [Soviet] measures now being taken are for purpose of ensuring secrecy of some offensive capability such as MRBM's [medium-range ballistic missiles] to be installed by Soviets after present phase completed and country secured from over-flights."[55]

The next day, the Soviet Union warned that U.S. action against Cuba could ignite nuclear war, and on September 13 Kennedy opened a news conference with another statement on Cuba. In it, he rejected the idea of "unilateral military intervention on the part of the United States," but he declared that the United States would respond militarily if weapons in Cuba became a threat to American citizens.[56] In part, the assumption that the Soviet Union would not put offensive weapons in Cuba may have been the product of wishful thinking, but it also was based on a CIA Board of Estimates report that Soviet placement of offensive ballistic missiles in Cuba "would be incompatible with Soviet practice to date and with Soviet policy as we presently estimate it. It would indicate a far greater willingness to increase the level of risk in U.S.–Soviet relations than the USSR has displayed thus far."[57]

Testifying before the Senate Committees on Foreign Relations and Armed Services on September 17, McGeorge Bundy downplayed the significance of the Soviet shipments, telling lawmakers that a total of 2,700 military technicians had arrived in Cuba during July and August. Three days later, the Senate approved a resolution supporting allocation of military force in Cuba "to prevent the creation or use of an externally supported offensive military capability endangering the security of the U.S"—an authorization Kennedy had not sought. The House supported the Senate action by a vote of 384–7, and the joint resolution received final approval on October 3. In a meeting on that day, McCone criticized both McNamara and Rusk because the Pentagon and State Department continued to state unequivocally that there were no offensive weapons in Cuba.[58]

On October 8, Undersecretary of State George Ball testified before the House Select Committee on Export Control about the Soviet Union's arming of Cuba. He told lawmakers that the military equipment arriving on the island included fifteen SAMs as well as missiles generally used by the Soviet Union for coastal defense. Journalist Walter Lippmann summed up Ball's testimony, saying, "The United States, using only conventional weapons, would dispose of Cuba in a few hours. . . . The present Cuban military buildup is not only not capable of offensive action, but also it is not capable of defensive action against the United States."[59] Early October U-2 photos showed crated-up pieces of the IL 28 bombers, but the White House was not alarmed. In an October 10 speech on the Senate floor, Keating claimed for the first time that six intermediate-range ballistic missile sites were under construction in Cuba. Despite the administration's efforts to limit speculation, anxiety was growing among the American people. Castro made no effort to lessen those fears. On October 1, newspapers carried a statement from the Cuban Revolutionary Government entitled "The Cuban People Will Not Be Crushed."

While White House spokesmen were pooh-poohing the danger attached to the Soviet shipments, the U.S. military was making plans— just in case. On October 1, McNamara met with the Joint Chiefs of Staff, and it was agreed that Admiral Robert L. Dennison, commander-in-chief of the Atlantic Fleet, would begin planning a blockade of Cuba. Two days later, Dennison started moving naval assets under the cover of PHIBRIGLEX62, a large-scale amphibious assault exercise set for October 15–20. An F4 squadron was relocated to the Naval Air Station at Key West on October 8 to bolster air defenses in the Caribbean.[60]

Cruise missiles were tactical weapons ideal for relatively short-range strikes on targets at sea or on land. One could hit a target more than 100 miles away. That put Florida's southern coast within range of the cruise missiles in Cuba.

As the military planned, American spy resources quietly sought to clarify what was happening in Cuba. An August 29 U-2 flight photographed much of the western portion of the island and spotted eight SAM sites under construction. This heightened worries about the safety of U.S. spy planes. At the same time, there was growing concern, voiced by Rusk, that the U-2 program might heighten danger on the international scene. One U-2 had strayed over Sakhalin in the Soviet Union on August 30, and a Nationalist Chinese U-2 had been downed September 8 over the Chinese mainland. After the August 29 flight, the Committee on Overhead Reconnaissance recommended that the next flight cover the eastern and central regions of the island. On September 5, a flight over Cuba located three additional surface-to-air missile sites in the island's central area, but cloud cover prevented a clear view of the east. By September 14, a previously unidentified construction area at Banes in eastern Cuba had been labeled as the site of cruise missiles. One of the worst hurricane seasons in years limited the number of U-2 flights during the three-week period of September 5–26: Only one U-2 flew over Cuba during those weeks, and it returned with no usable photos. There was no startling evidence in photos captured by flights on September 26, September 29, October 5, and October 7.[61] Weather again prevented flights between October 7 and 14.[62] The United States remained unaware of a looming conundrum.

CHAPTER 3

The Ticking Clock

MONDAY, OCTOBER 15

It began like any other day in 1962. On the radio, Elvis Presley's twangy baritone bellowed "Return to Sender" and the falsetto voices of the Four Seasons harmonized to profess belief in the false idea that "Big Girls Don't Cry." TV fans could look forward to an evening episode of *Ben Casey* or *The Lucy Show*. The United States had a president who looked like a movie star, and a first lady who was even more beautiful. America was a prosperous, gadget-crazy behemoth and, for the moment, peace reigned.

However, at the CIA's National Photographic Interpretation Center, anxiety filled the air. Comparing what they saw in new U-2 photos with file photos of Soviet weapons systems, analysts pored over the images. Just the day before, two pilots—Rudolf Anderson Jr. and Richard S. Heyser— had soared high above Cuba and the automatic cameras on their planes had captured secrets neither pilot could have seen from 70,000 feet above the ground. What the photo interpreters found was shocking: medium- range Soviet missiles and construction projects to make them operable. With these missiles, the Soviet Union could easily hit the American southeast with devastating nuclear force. Millions of Americans would soon be living in the crosshairs of Soviet weapons at the nation's back door.

Late in the day, information about the missiles' discovery began to proliferate through the Central Intelligence Agency, the Department of State, and the Pentagon, largely via a series of veiled conversations on phone lines that were not secure. Roger Hilsman of the State Department alerted Rusk during a State Department event honoring German Foreign Minister Schröder. Rather than interrupting in a way that might attract attention, Hilsman called and asked a waiter to surreptitiously pass a note to Rusk. The waiter complied. After reading the message in his lap, Rusk called Hilsman at home. Without going into details because they were on an unsecured line, Hilsman reported that his suspicions had been confirmed and that evidence would be available the following morning. Kennedy's advisers decided not to burden him with the news on this night.[1] He was in New York campaigning for Democratic candidates and was scheduled to return to the White House after midnight.

TUESDAY, OCTOBER 16

Still in his bedroom and just starting his day by scanning the morning newspapers, President Kennedy received a visit from Bundy shortly before 9 a.m. Bundy quickly reported the medium-range missiles in Cuba. One of JFK's first reactions was a personal one: "He can't do that to me!"[2]

Though the Cuban Missile Crisis came as a shock to Kennedy and much of America's leadership, the Soviet Union's action should not have been entirely unexpected. The Communist giant made no secret of its desire to attain dominance in nuclear weaponry. Through a combination of shameless bluster and gruff steeliness, Khrushchev already had falsely convinced many world citizens that the Soviet Union held the lead in the nuclear arms race. By making a series of threats to seize West Berlin, Khrushchev had revealed himself to be a gambler—and placing missiles in Cuba required the boldness of exactly that sort of risk taker.

Probably more than contemporary American leaders knew, Khrushchev also felt an emotional attachment to Cuba, which he saw as a microcosm of successful Communist insurgency. "Nikita loved Cuba very much," Castro later said. "He had a weakness for Cuba."[3] Khrushchev saw Castro's revolution as proof that Communism was the wave of the future. "He is a genuine revolutionary, completely like us," said Mikoyan, when he became the first Soviet leader to meet Castro in 1960.[4] Khrushchev called Cuba's revolutionary-in-chief a "heroic man."[5]

The missile installations surprised the Kennedy White House for several reasons. Just as Khrushchev had wrongly accepted his advisers' assurances that missiles could be camouflaged as coconut palms, Kennedy had fallen victim to experts' reliance on Cold War assumptions that proved to be untrue. At bottom, Kennedy's advisers held an entrenched and erroneous belief that Khrushchev's future behavior could be predicted simply by examining his past behavior. Cold War stereotypes contributed to the administration's failure to recognize Khrushchev's abilities as a careful strategist and an audacious schemer. Also, clearly, the Kennedy administration did not want to believe that Soviet missiles were in Cuba: Accepting the truth created all kinds of problems, not limited to national defense issues. Kennedy knew that if he did not act boldly, he would come under attack from hard-core conservatives in both parties. Even without confirmation of the missiles' presence in Cuba, many Americans were upset about Cuba. "The fact is the country's blood pressure is up, and they are fearful, and they're insecure," Lyndon Johnson observed.[6]

To tackle the crisis, Kennedy pulled together a relatively large group of advisers known as "the Ex Comm," or Executive Committee of the National Security Council. In reality, membership in this group had more to do with the president's trust in specific individuals than with job assignments. Some, like Johnson, McNamara, McCone, and Rusk, logically belonged in this body because of the nature of their jobs. Others, such as Attorney General Robert Kennedy, Secretary of the Treasury Douglas Dillon (a Republican and an undersecretary of state under Eisenhower), JFK's Special Counsel Theodore C. Sorensen, and Appointments Secretary Kenneth O'Donnell found seats at the table because of the president's belief in their judgment. Additional members included four more representatives from the State Department, former Ambassador to the Soviet Union Llewellyn "Tommy" Thompson, and administrators George Ball, Edwin Martin, and U. Alexis Johnson; and three more representatives of the Pentagon, Assistant Secretary of Defense for International Security Affairs Paul Nitze, Deputy Secretary of Defense Roswell Gilpatric, and General Maxwell Taylor, who chaired the Joint Chiefs. This group, along with intermittent participants such as former Secretary of State Dean Acheson

Faulty Soviet Assumptions

The United States was actively planning to invade Cuba. Although contingency plans for an invasion had been compiled, the Kennedy administration had no immediate plans to invade.

Cubans might not want nuclear missiles. Castro was more than happy to receive the missiles and extremely angry to lose them at the crisis's end.

Soviet specialists could plant missiles on the island without attracting American suspicion. In fact, heavy Soviet shipping to Cuba raised concerns even before U-2 planes captured images of the launch sites. Furthermore, when photographed on clear days, the missile sites were obvious to analysts.

The United States would accept the presence of missiles in Cuba without taking aggressive action. When Kennedy and his aides gathered to discuss the missiles' presence, they considered only aggressive action.

and United Nations Ambassador Adlai Stevenson, met repeatedly in secret over the succeeding days. Kennedy's decision to surround himself with a diverse committee of advisers had its roots in the disaster at the Bay of Pigs. At that time, he had accepted the guidance of a handful of intelligence and military representatives—advice that led to defeat and embarrassment. To provide himself with time to think, Kennedy wanted to conceal U.S. awareness of the missiles until he had explored the available options with his advisers and made a decision about appropriate U.S. action.

Rather than offering hints of a brewing crisis, Kennedy maintained scheduled appointments. He welcomed astronaut Wally Schirra and his family to the White House, showing off daughter Caroline's pony Macaroni. He met with a panel studying mental retardation and attended a luncheon in honor of His Royal Highness Hasan al-Rida al-Sanusi of Libya.

Between previously scheduled events, he learned what the nation was facing. In late morning, Kennedy waited in the Cabinet Room for the Ex Comm's first meeting. As the members arrived, 4-year-old Caroline ran into the room. Her father escorted her out, asking, "Caroline, have you been eating candy?" When he got no reply, he said, "Answer me. Yes, no, or maybe." The president disappeared briefly, and when he returned, he wore a grave expression.[7]

Art Lundahl, director of the National Photographic Interpretation Center, briefed the group on two medium-range ballistic missile sites visible in U-2 photos. Lundahl also identified another apparent launch site with unidentified weaponry. Images revealed an island speckled with signs of military activity.

For the Ex Comm, the biggest mystery was Khrushchev's intent: Knowing the risks, why would he take the chance of putting missiles in Cuba? At first, many suspected his action was just a feint turning American attention southward to win an advantage in what they considered to be the more important dispute over the fate of West Berlin.[8] Others thought Khrushchev was preparing to barter and wanted something valuable on his side of the table. Some believed that he was attempting to raise his nation's standing in the nuclear arms race. Within the Ex Comm, there was little belief that the placement of missiles in Cuba had anything to do with Cuba itself.

Regardless of Khrushchev's motives, the committee quickly concluded that an American response must be chosen carefully. Doing nothing and sending a protest note were the first options to be discarded. Just as quickly, the group concluded that any response must avoid triggering nuclear war. The other possibilities—a bombing raid on the missile sites; a broader air strike against airfields and SAM sites as well as missiles; a naval blockade; and a full-scale invasion of Cuba—required research and debate.

Kennedy, who saw the missiles as primarily a psychological impedi-
ment, argued that leaving them in Cuba was politically unacceptable.[9] He
believed the missiles gave Khrushchev a dangerous reservoir of diplomatic
leverage.[10] McNamara contended that the missiles did not change the
strategic nuclear balance because a missile fired from Russia was just as
deadly as one discharged from Cuba. In so doing, he failed to acknowledge
that the closeness of Cuba caused a quantifiable change in American
vulnerability because the Soviet Union could use less powerful missiles to
hit American targets.

In that first meeting, the group leaned toward direct military action.
One of the first orders to emerge from the Ex Comm was a demand for
more high-altitude U-2 flights as well as low-level reconnaissance. With
SAMs and other anti-aircraft weapons in Cuba, these missions would be
dangerous. Rusk, who saw only two alternatives—an immediate air strike
or an air strike after consultation with allies—also foresaw troubling
consequences: "I think we'll be facing a situation that could well lead to
general war." McNamara thought that the United States' options really
depended on two unknowns: whether missiles could be made operational
swiftly and whether warheads had reached Cuba.

Kennedy had one overriding concern about an air strike: In the face
of a U.S. attack that failed to destroy all of the missiles, the Soviets might
choose to use whatever missiles were left, and that could launch nuclear
war. Standing in for the voice of realism, Taylor warned Kennedy, "It'll
never be 100 percent, Mr. President."[11] As the Ex Comm considered its
options, the general spurred military preparations.

> The decision can be made as we're mobilizing, with the air strike,
> as to whether we invade or not. I think that's the hardest question
> militarily in the whole business, and one which we should look at
> very closely before we get our feet in that deep mud in Cuba.[12]

Taylor proposed an invasion by 90,000 men over eleven days.[13]

In a memo distributed on this day but probably written before
discovery of the missiles, the CIA's Deputy Director Marshall S. Carter
reported that the agency was seeking permission from the Special Group
(Augmented) for nine proposed acts of sabotage that would serve the panel's
top goal: to oust Castro. Among the Operation MONGOOSE plots were
demolition of a railroad bridge, underwater destruction of port facilities,
a grenade assault on the Chinese embassy in Havana, a demolition operation
at the Matanzas power plant, a hit-and-run mortar assault on a SAM site,
and incendiary attacks on tankers and oil refineries.[14] MONGOOSE's
agents sought to irritate the Cuban government like a ravenous mosquito

on a hot summer day. Leaders in Washington hoped these pesky attacks might spur similar action by dissident Cubans. That afternoon, at a MONGOOSE meeting, Robert Kennedy expressed discouragement with the program, and set up daily meetings with the Special Group (Augmented) to begin immediately.[15]

Late in the day, JFK spoke at a foreign policy conference for newspaper and TV editors. After a downbeat speech about the nation's survival, Kennedy recited a verse that may have encapsulated how he felt on this day. He said:

> Bullfight critics row on row
> Crowd the enormous plaza full
> But only one is there who knows
> And he is the one who fights the bull.[16]

In that day's second Ex Comm meeting, McNamara reported that the Joint Chiefs favored a broad air strike. Taylor estimated that it would take at least a day to mobilize an air strike by 400 pilots in at least 100 sorties. Some committee members began seriously considering the prospect of a naval blockade, which was less likely to draw a hair-trigger violent response but might qualify legally as an act of war. Others turned their attention to how worldwide opinion might respond to a surprise U.S. invasion. At a dinner party that night, Kennedy surprised his companions by estimating that the "odds are even on an H-bomb war within ten years."[17]

At the Pentagon, officials began updating contingency plans for Cuba. In a meeting of the Joint Chiefs of Staff, the top military leaders agreed that the recommended sequence would be: "get additional intelligence; make surprise attacks on missiles, airfields, PT boats, SAMs, and tanks; concurrently, reinforce Guantanamo; prepare to initiate an invasion." When McNamara told the chiefs that he opposed attacking if the weapons were operational, they unanimously opposed his position.[18] Invasion plans called for using one Marine Division, one Army Airborne Division, and one Army Infantry Division.[19] Military leaders predicted that an invasion could be launched within seven days. Decades later, it would become clear that these men were trying to see the light while standing in the dark. Instead of the anticipated 10,000 Soviet troops in Cuba, there were about 42,000.[20] Furthermore, American strategists did not know that nuclear warheads for the medium-range missiles had reached Cuba. And they had no evidence that Soviet troops had short-range tactical nuclear weapons or that their initial orders gave them the authority to use those weapons without direct consultation with Moscow.[21] This equipment included Lunas—battlefield weapons with a range of about thirty-one miles and a payload close to one-seventh of the bomb that had flattened Hiroshima. When fired, a Luna would create a firestorm, destroying any tank or armored personnel carrier within a 500-yard radius of the blast.[22] Other tactical weapons included cruise missiles and nuclear mines. In all 102 tactical nuclear warheads had been shipped to Cuba.[23] Revamping contingency plans without so much vital information was dangerous, but because policymakers were unaware of how much they did not know, they believed that they were methodically addressing the facts.

WEDNESDAY, OCTOBER 17

Members of the Ex Comm devoted a lot of attention to the idea of a surgical strike on the missiles and warheads alone. They wondered whether U.S. attackers could get all of the missiles without costly collateral damage, such as the deaths of Cuban civilians. Questions also arose about whether an air assault should target Soviet planes, and less destructive weapons, such as SAMs, cruise missiles, and tanks. In this day's two unrecorded meetings, Kennedy's advisers increasingly edged away from supporting a surprise attack, with George Ball arguing most strenuously for a diplomatic solution rather than armed assault. (Coincidentally, a Gallup Poll released October 14 had found that 65 percent of Americans opposed sending U.S. troops to Cuba.[24] Of course, the poll respondents had no idea that Soviet nuclear missiles were in Cuba.) Estimates on this day were that the missiles spotted so far could kill eighty million Americans if fired at the nation's cities.[25]

In a memo for the Ex Comm, Sorensen noted that

> it is generally agreed that these missiles, even when fully operational, do not significantly alter the balance of power—i.e., they do not significantly increase the potential megatonnage capable of being unleashed on American soil. . . . The Soviet purpose in making this move is not understood—whether it is for purposes of diversion, harassment, provocation or bargaining.[26]

This comment reflects how little America's leaders comprehended Soviet motives and how they allowed a numbers game about the two nations' total stockpiles to cloud their vision of Khrushchev's intentions. By looking for a more convoluted explanation, they were overlooking the Soviet leader's strongest motivations.

On this day, the ExComm discussed five specific diplomatic or military options:

- JFK, who had a previously scheduled meeting with Soviet Foreign Minister Andrei Gromyko the following day, could confront him with the evidence.
- The United States could dispatch an envoy to speak to Khrushchev privately about U.S. demands for the missiles' withdrawal.
- In the United Nations Security Council, the United States could ask representatives from the USSR and Cuba to explain the secret installations.
- The United States could establish a naval and air blockade to stop the arrival of offensive weapons in Cuba.
- A surprise surgical air strike could attempt to eliminate the missile installations with pinpoint bombing.[27]

The Joint Chiefs dispatched orders to the Continental Air Defense Command to bolster air defenses in the southeast. Admiral George W. Anderson, chief of naval operations, alerted all fleet commanders to have as many ships as possible ready to sail on twenty-four hours' notice. Military leaders were confident that they could launch an invasion of Cuba without setting off a full-scale war, and because they feared that an air strike might fail, they opposed being locked into planning for an air strike alone.[28] Meanwhile, more than forty U.S. warships approached Puerto Rico for the latest Caribbean military drill, PHIBRIGLEX, at the island of Vieques. As they had in the spring, Marines were scheduled to make an amphibious landing to overthrow an imaginary dictator. Some irreverent Pentagon planners began calling the exercise Operation ORTSAC—a backward spelling of Castro's name. Knowing this, it seems unbelievable that U.S. leaders were later surprised to learn that Castro feared a U.S. invasion.

The new U.S. ambassador to France, C.E. Bohlen, who happened to be a former ambassador to Moscow, wrote a memo for the Ex Comm on likely Soviet reactions to various strategies. He believed that a quick, successful surgical strike would bring only political grumbling from Soviet leaders. Direct communication with Khrushchev, in Bohlen's estimation, could generate a denial followed by removal of the missiles, or it could lead to bartering over Soviet missiles in Cuba vs. U.S. missiles in Turkey and Italy. He contended that an unannounced, broader air strike plus an invasion would create the greatest possibility of general war. He saw the fourth option as "a political communication to Khrushchev follow-ing in the event of a negative reply, by a declaration of war and the institution of U.S. blockade of Cuba." He believed that a bold U.S. declaration plus a blockade would prompt a diplomatic response from the Soviet Union.[29]

In Cuba, Pliyev received reports of multiplying American overflights and realized that his operation probably had lost its "secret" status. He anxiously reported this news to the General Staff in Moscow. SAM missiles were capable of downing a U-2 and lower-flying planes were certainly within reach of available weapons, but orders from Moscow told SAM commanders that they did not have authority to fire on American planes unless an invasion seemed imminent.[30]

THURSDAY, OCTOBER 18

Lundahl showed the Ex Comm more missile launching sites and crates apparently holding parts for Soviet IL-28 bombers. New photo analysis provided greater details about the medium-range missile sites and for the first time spotted launch sites for intermediate-range missiles, which could reach targets as far away as California. McCone reported the findings of the Guided Missile and Astronautics Intelligence Committee: Between sixteen and thirty-two missiles would be functional within a week. Rusk reviewed the negative effects that a unilateral attack might have on American allies and the equally contentious response likely if the United States took no action. In a discussion about maintaining support from the Organization of American States, Kennedy addressed the difficulty in winning Latin American support on any issue involving Cuba "because they think that we're slightly demented on this subject."[31]

On this afternoon, Kennedy's diplomatic demeanor was put to the test when he met with Gromyko, Rusk, and Thompson for more than two hours. The Soviet foreign minister offered assurances that no offensive weapons were in Cuba. Kennedy, in turn, read aloud his statement declaring that the installation of offensive weapons in Cuba would spur a U.S. response. Kennedy saw Gromyko as a liar, but the Soviet foreign minister was equally struck by what he saw as American arrogance. He recalled Kennedy saying that the current regime in Cuba was unacceptable, and he remembered asking the president why the United States felt it had a right to decide what was appropriate for another nation. Gromyko later recalled that Kennedy "was nervous, though he tried not to show it, and kept contradicting himself."[32] A State Department summary of the meeting indicated that although he did not mention the missiles, Kennedy did send Khrushchev a pointed message, saying that "neither he nor Mr. Khrushchev must take actions leading to a confrontation of our two countries.[33] Television reporter Elie Abel later recalled Gromyko "leaving the White House that evening in a mood of unwonted joviality."[34] That night, to avoid arousing curiosity, nine Ex Comm members piled into a single car to reach a White House meeting. Robert Kennedy, Taylor, and McCone rode in front, while six others crowded into the back, an arrangement that required some presidential advisers to sit on one another's laps.

As the crisis proceeded, the members of the Ex Comm found themselves increasingly split into two camps—the hawks, who favored strong military action, and the doves, who counseled against rashness. On the first day, almost everyone was a hawk, but as the implications of military actions became clearer, several drifted into the dove camp. The hawks, led by Nitze, Dillon, Bundy, and Taylor, argued that a dramatic Soviet threat necessitated an equally impressive American show of strength; the doves, who included Robert Kennedy, Rusk, Ball, and McNamara, voiced greater wariness about stumbling into nuclear war by failing to give Soviet leaders a respectable means of retreat. On this day, Ball repeated his opposition to a surprise air strike, noting that "we tried Japanese as war criminals because of the sneak attack on Pearl Harbor."[35] Both hawks and doves made strong arguments. As Ball later commented, "I was scared to death that Nitze, Dillon, and Taylor, would wear the president down."[36]

With every passing hour, military planning progressed. Key West, the closest base to Cuba, was being cleared of all utility and support aircraft to make room for operations to organize reconnaissance missions, mount a possible air strike, and direct coastal defense aircraft. The Marine Air Corps sent a squadron to Puerto Rico to reinforce that island's defense status. Military personnel and materiel received top priority on trucks, trains, and planes.[37] Aboard one train, a young private later remembered seeing a frightened officer weeping. "Damn it, lieutenant, don't cry in front of the private," a higher-ranking officer reportedly declared.[38] The Joint Chiefs decided to postpone PHIBRIGLEX and keep troops aboard the ships originally scheduled to participate. They concluded that the earliest feasible date for an air strike was October 21, but the optimum date was October 23. The earliest date for invasion was October 28; the optimum date, October 30.[39]

Over the years, the terminology categorizing "hawks" and "doves" has been adopted broadly to describe those who favor aggressive use of military power to protect American interests vs. those who lean toward negotiation to achieve peace. The Vietnam War became a particularly divisive topic for these opposing viewpoints. During the missile crisis, JFK began the decision-making process halfway between the two camps. Ultimately, he embraced the doves' viewpoint but continued making preparations to follow the hawks' advice if Khrushchev failed to respond as he hoped.

FRIDAY, OCTOBER 19

While Kennedy's team studied alternatives, the military moved toward implementation of all options, from surgical air strikes to a full-scale invasion. Emotions were running high among some military leaders who were beginning to bridle at the direction of civilian leaders. In a Friday morning meeting of the Joint Chiefs, Air Force General Curtis LeMay said that simply implementing a blockade "would be a pure disaster"; however, he joined the other chiefs in agreeing that an air strike could be delayed twenty-four hours to allow consultation with allies.[40] Later, when the joint chiefs met with Kennedy in the Cabinet Room, LeMay became exasperated with resistance to his calls for bold military action. "It will lead right into war: This is almost as bad as the appeasement at Munich!" he declared.[41]

JFK was leery of military logic, which often amounted to a citation of U.S. nuclear superiority. Because even the best estimates suggested that a nuclear war could kill 70 million Americans, Kennedy beseeched the joint chiefs to consider the ultimate outcome: "You're talking about the destruction of a country!"[44] Reflecting later on the military's position, Ball asserted, "The military really wanted war—an airstrike, an invasion, the works."[45] Kennedy himself later spoke to the U.S. ambassador to India, economist John Kenneth Galbraith, about military advice. Galbraith later described "Kennedy's deep mistrust of the advice he was getting, particularly from the military and from some of the more militarily disposed civilians who felt, some of them, that it was their duty to outdo the generals."[46] In fairness, a U.S. Marine Corps memo expressed doubts about an invasion. Even if three Marine divisions participated instead of the one currently designated to take part in an invasion, the report predicted that it could take "several years" to establish a stable government.[47]

At a meeting of the United States Civil Defense Council in Knoxville, Steuart L. Pittman, assistant secretary of defense for civil defense, reported that thirty-five American cities, including New York and Washington, had enough fallout shelters to serve the population. This optimistic appraisal

> Curtis LeMay, often caricatured as a gung-ho general who welcomed nuclear war, hated what he labeled as "so-called thinkers." At the outbreak of the Korean War, he had urged that the United States attack North Korea "immediately with incendiaries and delete four or five of their largest towns."[42] As chief of staff for the Air Force and an integral player in the development of the Strategic Air Command, he once told SAC crews that "there are only two things in this world, SAC bases and SAC targets."[43]

would crumble within a week when federal, state, and local officials dusted off existing plans and looked at civil defense preparedness through the eyes of human beings anticipating imminent nuclear war. The United States was not at all prepared.

Military planning moved ahead. Two Marine units—one in Cherry Point, North Carolina, and one at Camp Del Mar in southern California—received orders to prepare to move out. The following day, both units departed without knowing their destination.[48]

The Office of National Estimates issued what it called a "crash" estimate entitled "Soviet Reactions in Certain US Courses of Action on Cuba." The report indicated that a key Soviet motive was to achieve an appearance of a balance of nuclear forces between East and West. It also noted the new missiles' key role in any Soviet first strike.[49]

Hours after meeting with the joint chiefs, JFK left Washington for a previously scheduled campaign swing that would take him to Cleveland; Springfield, Illinois; and Chicago. While the president was out of the

Figure 3.1 A reconnaissance photo taken October 14, 1962 shows a medium-range ballistic missile launch site in San Cristobal, Cuba. John F. Kennedy Library.

capital, meetings continued at the State Department. The Ex Comm divided into two groups: the air strike committee—Robert Kennedy, Dillon, Bundy, McCone, and Acheson; and the blockade panel—McNamara, Rusk, Thompson, and Ball.[50] In a meeting of the air strike panel, Bundy made a strong stand for an assault and claimed the backing of Acheson, McCone, Dillon, and Taylor. Robert Kennedy, now clearly in the dove camp, responded by telling the group with a smile that he had spoken to the president and both had concluded that a Pearl Harbor-like surprise attack was "not in our traditions."[51] By the end of the day Robert Kennedy went even further, firmly rejecting the idea of an unannounced air attack. "If we make a surprise attack, we will be accused of another Pearl Harbor," he told working group members.[52] Meanwhile, State Department and Justice Department lawyers assured the other working group that a blockade could be executed without a declaration of war, especially if the United States convinced the Organization of American States to support it. Late in the day, the results of a new intelligence analysis concluded that "the missile deployment appears calculated to achieve quick operational status and then to complete site construction." Bundy left a message for Kennedy in Chicago. He indicated that the situation was "so hairy" that he thought the president ought "to come home."[53]

SATURDAY, OCTOBER 20

On Saturday morning, after reviewing a proposed presidential address drafted by Sorensen, Robert Kennedy called his brother and endorsed the president's immediate return to the White House. Kennedy's press office told journalists that the president was abbreviating his campaign trip because he had a cold. When the Ex Comm next met to brief the president, members presented four options: an air strike, a blockade as a first step that might lead to more direct military action, a blockade aimed at freezing the missile implantation but not eliminating those weapons already in place, and a blockade as the opening step in achieving a diplomatic solution, possibly through a superpower summit. As a guest at this day's Ex Comm meeting, UN Ambassador Stevenson opposed all of the options, arguing for negotiation as the primary strategy. He rejected military action and declared that the United States should be prepared to abandon all foreign bases in return for adoption of the same policy by the Soviet Union. Stevenson was pummeled by doves as well as hawks for his opposition to what they viewed as an inevitable military challenge. With the majority of the Ex Comm now leaning toward a blockade,

McNamara pointed out that in any negotiation, the United States must be prepared to surrender something in return for Soviet dismantling of the missiles. Possible options, he suggested, were removal of U.S. missiles from Turkey and/or Italy and setting a time limit on the United States' continued use of the Guantanamo naval base. The president also received an update on the missile sites, some of which appeared to be almost operational, although U-2 photos could not provide conclusive evidence about whether nuclear warheads had arrived in Cuba. Intelligence experts estimated that perhaps as many as eight missiles could already be operational. (The first regiment of eight launchers was operable on this day.)[54] At 4:30 p.m., Kennedy voiced his support for a blockade. McGeorge Bundy later concluded that Kennedy chose the blockade because "of all the courses available this was the one which came nearest to a balance between the requirement of putting effective political pressure upon the other side and the requirement that that pressure be placed on them in such a way as to leave an opening for peaceful settlement in which the missiles would come out of Cuba."[55]

The president's decision to establish a blockade did not rule out eventual use of other approaches, and Kennedy did not want to formalize his decision until he spoke with General Walter C. Sweeney, the man who would execute any air assault. Keeping all options open, the Ex Comm produced a draft statement to the Cuban government to be sent in advance of an air assault.[56] Unsigned handwritten notes from this day's Ex Comm meeting address questions about how the blockade would be implemented and how the crisis might affect Berlin.[57] In a landscape crowded by question marks, Kennedy and his advisers sought to answer the unanswerable.

The federal bureaucracy continued to produce reports on the crisis. The Office of National Estimates produced another "crash" report: "Major Consequences of Certain US Course of Action on Cuba." It stated, "We believe that the Soviets would be somewhat less likely to retaliate with military force in areas outside Cuba in response to a speedy, effective invasion than in response to more limited forms of military action against Cuba."[58] A new CIA report acknowledged that the weapons in Cuba significantly increased "Soviet gross capabilities for initial attack on US military and civilian targets." Nevertheless, the report concluded that "these missiles in Cuba will probably not, in the Soviet judgment, insure destruction of US second strike capability to a degree which would eliminate an unacceptably heavy retaliatory attack on the USSR."[59] William P. Bundy, an assistant to Nitze and brother to McGeorge Bundy, issued a document entitled "Possible Soviet Courses of Action against Overseas Bases and their Vulnerability to Such Actions." He concluded

Faulty American Assumptions

The Soviet Union's history of keeping nuclear weapons on its own soil proved that no missiles would be implanted in Cuba. This turned out to be untrue. Khrushchev had never placed nuclear missiles in Eastern European satellite nations, probably because their locations did not offer a strategic advantage. However, he had provided tactical nuclear weapons to East Germany.[60]

Because the Soviet Union had sold surface-to-air missiles in Egypt, Indonesia, and Tanzania without supplying offensive weapons, identification of SAM missiles in Cuba was not a precursor to the installation of offensive weapons. The SAMs in Cuba were there for a specific reason: to keep surveillance planes from discovering signs of missile base construction.

Berlin represented the biggest Cold War hot spot, and whatever was happening in Cuba was merely a pretext for action in Berlin. Khrushchev treated Berlin and Cuba as two different Cold War battlefields, and the missile implantations in Cuba carried more immediate danger for the United States than his ongoing threats to take action against West Berlin. However, for days, Ex Comm members dwelled on possible ties to Berlin.

The monolithic nature of Communism suggested that China's attack on India might be related to the missile crisis. Despite frequent Kennedy administration references to "Sino-Soviet" activity, the Soviet Union and Communist China did not enjoy good relations at this time and would not have acted in concert.

Because the missiles in Cuba did not add enough weapons to overcome the United States' dominance in the nuclear arms tally, there was no added danger. This position, embraced by McNamara and others, failed to consider how many more weapons were aimed at the United States. Raymond Garthoff, who worked in the State Department's Bureau of Political/Military Affairs, issued a paper to the Ex Comm reporting that with missiles in Cuba, a surprise attack by the Soviet Union would reduce U.S. missiles by 30 percent more than previously estimated, leaving the nation with just 15 percent of its missiles still capable of making a retaliatory strike.[61]

that "the Soviets are probably playing their cards on Cuba for leverage on two situations, Berlin and the overseas bases of the US and its key allies." He identified seven different categories of locations serving as homes to U.S. bases. Within the seven categories were twenty-eight nations, three colonies, five "former colonies with residual rights," Guantanamo, and Berlin. Depending on the nature of the bases, he anticipated different levels of resistance to a possible imposition of a general rule that countries could not place bases on foreign soil. In some cases, he expected Soviet efforts to "scare the local government, via its opposition, to abrogate US base rights."[62]

McNamara ordered Anderson to present several papers on a blockade, and Dennison contacted the base commander at Guantanamo, telling him to prepare for evacuation of all military dependents. Round-the-clock planning sessions set the tone at the Pentagon. "This brought forth almost a panic in the building because things started to happen. People started to worry about moving divisions," recalled General Horace M. Wade who was the Air Force's assistant deputy chief of staff for planning and programs.

> They started to worry about preparing plans for an invasion,
> mobilizing the forces, Reserve forces, the Guard forces,
> were they going to get congressional support, and they knew
> they couldn't mobilize the Guard and the Reserve without
> congressional support. They didn't want to reveal a lot of
> this information that they had from photography to the people
> on the Hill because they knew it would be in the newspapers
> the next day. . . . It made a real tense situation around there
> for several days.[63]

Continuing preparations for a possible air strike now envisioned an attack composed of 800 sorties.[64]

Rumors of a Cuban crisis were muted in the press. The White House told reporters that Kennedy's fever and cold were improving.[65] The day's biggest news was a heavy battle between Communist Chinese troops and Indian soldiers along their shared border. The Chinese had launched a two-pronged assault along the mountainous boundary. Officials in Washington hoped but were not sure that the Chinese invasion and the Soviet missile project were unconnected. Galbraith, then operating from the U.S. Embassy in India, exulted in the pleasant surprise he experienced over "how much license [he had] in handling the Chinese attack." At the time, he was unaware that his supervisors were preoccupied with Cuba.[66]

SUNDAY, OCTOBER 21

At midday, Kennedy met with the man responsible for organizing an air assault on Cuba. He asked Sweeney about the likelihood of success. Sweeney explained how planes would be allocated to strike the missile sites as well as airplanes on the ground. He assured the president that an air assault would be "successful," but Taylor pointed out that "the best we can offer is to destroy 90 percent of the known missiles." At the time, the military guessed it had identified about 60 percent of the missiles, which meant that about 46 percent of the Soviet missiles likely would survive an attack.[67] This briefing helped to solidify Kennedy's judgment that a blockade was the correct first step. However, he told the military to be prepared to make an air strike anytime over the coming week.[68]

With the president's speech now scheduled for Monday evening, the State Department began drafting letters to all allies explaining the United States' plan of action. In Ex Comm meetings over the last week, Acheson had argued strenuously that the White House should provide high-level briefings for key European heads of state, and as a result Kennedy dispatched Acheson himself to confer with French President Charles De Gaulle on the day of Kennedy's address. Equipped with photos of missile sites, Acheson flew on Air Force One with one ambassador, three CIA employees, and three armed guards. The plane first landed at a Strategic Air Command base in England, where U.S. Ambassador to Great Britain David Bruce met the delegation. Upon greeting them, Bruce told the men that he had two interesting things in his raincoat pockets. One obviously held a bottle of something alcoholic. Acheson stuck his hand in the other pocket and was shocked to feel a revolver. He asked why Bruce was armed. Bruce said that the State Department had ordered him to carry the weapon. The ambassador, who had not yet been briefed on the crisis, admitted that he was not sure why. "There was nothing said about shooting me, was there?" Acheson asked. Bruce assured the elder statesman that his life was safe, and Acheson soon told Bruce why the State Department was resorting to cloak-and-dagger tactics.[69] An armed escort had been recommended for Acheson and Sherman Kent of the CIA because they were transporting highly classified material.

At the CIA, McCone made sure that agency files held a history of his often-disregarded warnings about Soviet actions in Cuba. The memo tracked his speculation, beginning in early August and continuing up to the day when U-2 photos confirmed the missiles' presence.[70] In the evening, under JFK's orders, McCone went to Johnson's Washington home, The Elms, to brief the vice president on developments. Johnson had just returned from a campaign swing through Hawaii. The long-scheduled political jaunt served as camouflage to hinder the media's discovery of the growing crisis. After receiving the update, Johnson asked what would happen if Khrushchev did not reply favorably to Kennedy's ultimatum. McCone replied, "Then blood will flow."[71]

At this point, several news sources had begun asking questions about ship and troop movements. Among them were Norfolk's *Virginia News-Pilot*, the Associated Press, the *New York Herald Tribune*, the *Washington*

Post, CBS News, and the *New York Times*. Worried about a leak before his speech, Kennedy called the *Washington Post's* publisher Philip Graham and *New York Times's* publisher Orvil Dryfoos. He asked both men not to reveal the details of the crisis in Monday's publications.[72] As a result, news reports included only vague references to a crisis atmosphere in Washington. There was some speculation about the nature of the crisis but no firm information about the missiles. Sorensen later noted that JFK "considered it the best kept secret in government."[73] To confuse reporters, Averell Harriman, assistant secretary of state for Far Eastern affairs, spent much of this day working in an empty White House office where he could be seen by journalists.

Speaking about the Ex Comm's decision against an immediate air strike, Taylor told the other members of the Joint Chiefs of Staff that "the Pearl Harbor complex has affected the good people at the White House. . . . There will be no air strike, but it is in the offing."[74] Within the military, rules were confirmed for operation of a blockade, and McNamara approved them. The guidelines reflected a basic desire to block the arrival of new weapons while holding the use of force to a minimum. Planning was guided by the mandate that all critical decisions would be made in Washington.[75] In three meetings of the joint chiefs, the military's leaders decided that limited reconnaissance flights should be flown tomorrow, the day of Kennedy's speech. They also received approval from McNamara to disperse fighter aircraft and Strategic Air Command B-47s on Monday. The chiefs planned some movement of troops to Florida, both to form a possible invasion force and to provide additional defense of the Florida coast to be used in the event of a Cuban attack using conventional weapons.[76] Pentagon officials adopted a new habit: sleeping in their offices. On this night, McNamara's rest was interrupted by a visit from Anderson. The secretary of defense donned a robe over his pajamas and consulted with Anderson for an hour before returning to sleep. An elaborate countdown document established the order of actions in the Departments of Defense, State, and Justice as well as the White House, beginning twenty-four hours before Kennedy's 7 p.m. speech. The goal was to leave nothing to chance.

By now, the Soviet Union had begun to detect unusual American military activity. There was a noticeable increase in the number of Strategic Air Command bombers on duty, and naval activity in the Caribbean seemed to go beyond the previously scheduled exercises in Puerto Rico. Soviet leaders also heard reports that McNamara had asked top officials to stay near the Pentagon.[77] At the State Department, Hilsman analyzed recent conversations between American and Soviet officials and wrote a memo noting the Soviet Union's obvious effort to avoid conflict over

Cuba. Hilsman assumed that all of the cited Soviet officials were aware of the missiles; however, at least one Soviet source, Dobrynin, knew nothing about them. Based on his assumptions and his analysis, Hilsman argued that the United States should avoid directing its complaints toward the USSR. "Our public statements," he contended, "should be keyed to Cuban irresponsibility in obtaining offensive weapons rather than to the Soviet role in providing them."[78]

In Norfolk, Captain G.E. Miller of the *USS Wrangell* got word that he should sail to the Caribbean immediately. That night, he departed Norfolk with half of his crew on liberty. The Navy promised to send the missing men when they returned to base, and the errant sailors did come aboard a few at a time. Miller dodged unseen Soviet submarines by patrolling the south side of the Dominican Republic on a shelf where the water was only sixty to ninety feet deep—too shallow for subs.[79]

Over the weekend, the White House began recalling congressional leaders to Washington. Rep. Hale Boggs, a Louisiana Democrat, was deep-sea fishing in the Gulf of Mexico when he saw a U.S. Air Force plane above him. As the aircraft circled, a crewman dropped a bottle into the water. When Boggs retrieved it, he found a message telling him to contact JFK.[80]

MONDAY, OCTOBER 22

The Joint Chiefs of Staff dispatched detailed instructions for operation of the blockade. Included were a checklist of banned items, rules of engagement with foreign ships, directions on the conduct of ship searches, and a master plan for defense of the 45-square-mile Guantanamo base. Military leaders agreed that if a U-2 was shot down, the United States would continue one or two flights a day until another plane was lost. At that point, plans for continuing surveillance would be based on "whether the projected attrition rate was acceptable."[81]

At Guantanamo, the Navy evacuated 2,432 women and children. For the military dependents, the departure came with little warning. One then-8-year-old girl recalled, "As we were driving home [from school], there were suitcases on everybody's lawn. . . . My mother said, 'We're leaving in about five minutes. Go up to your room and take anything you can carry.'"[82] Women at the base had standing orders to keep a suitcase packed, but the suddenness of this departure forced many to leave in the middle of chores and without speaking to their spouses. With both an air and sea escort, four ships delivered the military dependents to the Atlantic Fleet's home base in Norfolk. During three days at sea, sailors helped mothers by rocking babies and making formula.[83] Teen-aged boys handled KP duties, while their female counterparts helped to clean areas of the ships.[84] At Guantanamo, reinforcements began arriving to support the 4,000 sailors and marines based there. Construction battalions created new frontline positions, bunkers, access roads, command posts, and other facilities. At the start of the crisis, Guantanamo had only twelve artillery weapons; Cuban forces nearby had more weaponry and much greater opportunity to re-position guns to serve their needs.[85]

By this time, more than 150 naval vessels were forming an arc around Cuba. Thirty Soviet ships were underway to Cuba. One, the *Aleksandrovsk*, carried nuclear warheads, and four were transporting intermediate-range missiles. The *Aleksandrovsk*, which was close to the island, received orders to proceed to the nearest Cuban port rather than remaining at sea until it reached its assigned destination. Soviet leaders still hoped the ships carrying missiles would reach Cuba without interference, but they had already decided that other ships carrying offensive weapons should return to the Soviet Union rather than create a direct military contest with the United States.[86]

On this morning, Kennedy placed calls to former presidents Herbert Hoover, Harry Truman, and Eisenhower. He called Hoover and Truman just to make them aware of the crisis. Eisenhower had been briefed by McCone, so JFK's conversation with him held greater substance. When Kennedy expressed concerns that the Soviet Union might move against Berlin in reaction to his speech, Eisenhower expressed skepticism. "The damn Soviets will do whatever they want, what they figure is good for them," the former president said. "And I don't believe they relate one situation to another."[87] (Events later proved Eisenhower's judgment to be correct, but Kennedy apparently did not give Eisenhower's assertion much weight: In his meeting with congressional leaders later in the day, he said, "We should keep our eye on the main site, which would be Berlin.")[88] In a recording of the conversation with Eisenhower, Kennedy discusses the likelihood of nuclear war in a tone of voice that sounds surprisingly— and almost eerily—casual. "General, what if Khrushchev announced tomorrow which I think he will, that if we attack Cuba, it's going to be nuclear war? What's your judgment as to the chances they'll fire these things off if we invade Cuba?" he asked. Eisenhower's reply was simple: "Oh, I don't believe they will."[89]

In an 11:30 a.m. meeting of the National Security Council, Kennedy predicted Khrushchev's response: accelerate construction of missile bases in Cuba, announce that Soviet missiles would be used if the United States attacked Cuba, and possibly seize control of West Berlin.[90] Kennedy's expectations of Khrushchev reflected a belief that the Soviet leader would act recklessly. In the real world, Khrushchev wholeheartedly embraced caution to avoid war.

On this busy day, congressional liaison Lawrence F. O'Brien invited members of Congress to meet with Kennedy shortly before his televised speech. To return to Washington, some traveled by commercial airliner, but others were transported by the Air Force. Presidential Press Secretary Pierre Salinger announced Kennedy's 7 p.m. address at noon. To preserve secrecy about the speech's topic, State Department staffers with responsibilities that did not include the Soviet Union or Cuba were asked to visit the White House in conspicuous limousines.

In Moscow, Khrushchev received news of Kennedy's address with a sense of foreboding. It was already evening in Moscow, and although Salinger's announcement did not reveal Kennedy's topic, Khrushchev was sure that the United States had discovered the missiles in Cuba. He called a nightime meeting of the Presidium. During that meeting, General Semyon Ivanov told the Presidium that some of the medium-range missiles were operational and that all of their warheads were in Cuba; however, he added that the intermediate-range missiles and their warheads had not yet reached the island. "The point is we didn't want to unleash a war," Khrushchev told the group. "All we wanted to do was to threaten them, to restrain them with regard to Cuba."[91] He spent the evening anxiously awaiting Kennedy's speech. "The tragedy is," he said, "that they can attack, and we shall respond. This may end in a big war."[92] Facing that prospect, Khrushchev ordered that Pliyev's conventional forces, but not the nuclear weapons, be placed on alert. There was some debate about giving Pliyev complete control over the Lunas, but the proposal was rejected. The general was required to receive approval from Moscow before using the Lunas. Khrushchev stayed in his office through the night and advised colleagues to sleep in the Kremlin. The new U.S. Ambassador Foy Kohler was under orders to deliver a copy of the address to the Kremlin one hour before Kennedy delivered it; however, because the delivery time was after midnight in Moscow, he was unable to make arrangements to meet with a senior official.

In Washington, Dobrynin was called to meet with Rusk at 6 p.m., and Rusk gave him the text of Kennedy's speech. Previously unaware of what was happening in Cuba, Dobrynin was jolted by the seriousness of the situation and the dark tone of Kennedy's message. There were reports, which were denied many years later, that secret documents were destroyed that night as the Soviet embassy in Washington prepared for the possibility of war. KGB officers within the embassy had both an emergency generator and a private oxygen supply available in case of war.[93]

When they arrived at Evreux Air Force Base near Paris around 1:30 a.m., Acheson and Kent were rushed to the home of Cecil Lyon, U.S. chargé d'affaires. Riding in small French cars with curtains drawn, the two men traveled like spies because their hosts feared that Acheson, well known for his service in Truman's Cabinet, would be recognized. Kent provided information on the crisis to the American mission to the North Atlantic Council, dignitaries in the American embassy, and the U.S. military attaché. In the afternoon, under a shroud of secrecy, drivers whisked both men to Elysée, where they met De Gaulle. In this period of high intrigue, Kent was reminded of *The Three Musketeers*. At one point, he turned to Acheson and asked, "D'Artagnan, is that saber loose in the scabbard?" Acheson responded by saying, "Aye, Porthos."[94]

At the State Department, officials checked to be sure that all appropriate governments had received messages explaining U.S. plans. Two Department of State officers were to be on duty around the clock through the coming week in the National Military Command Center at the Pentagon.[95] To block a flood of diplomatic cables, Rusk promised to send regular updates and urged American diplomats to maintain "cable silence" unless they had urgent messages.[96]

At the White House, the full Cabinet met. Although the exact nature of the crisis had not been announced, hundreds of protesters carried signs outside of the executive mansion. Among them were: "Don't chicken this time, Jack," "Cuba can be negotiated," and "Peace, Mr. President."[97] Though U.S. reconnaissance flights continued to spot additional missile sites in Cuba, Kennedy was not ready to assume that U.S. intelligence had located all of them. During the hours before Kennedy's speech, Newton Minow, chairman of the Federal Communications Commission, and Salinger called the managers of eleven radio stations with strong broadcast signals and asked them to beam Kennedy's speech to Cuba in Spanish. All agreed.

The president had a stormy meeting with congressional leaders, many of whom thought instituting a blockade was an inadequate response to Khrushchev's actions. Richard Russell, a Democrat from Georgia and chairman of the Senate Armed Forces Committee, argued forcefully that invasion was the only viable option.[98] At the same time, Ball and Hilsman briefed ambassadors from forty-six allied nations.

In the hour leading up to Kennedy's speech, there was great excitement and curiosity among the press. Reporting for NBC, Abel told his audience: "In just a few minutes now, the suspense will have ended. At this moment, Soviet Ambassador Dobrynin has just been to the State Department, where he was told just what the president has decided. The diplomatic entrance to the department has seldom—if ever before—been so choked with ambassadors coming and going."[99]

When he faced the cameras, a somber Kennedy told Americans that nuclear missiles in Cuba were pointed at them. In response to this threat, he drew a line in the sand—or, more literally, in the sea around Cuba.

> This secret, swift and extraordinary buildup of Communist missiles—in an area well known to have a special and historical relationship to the United States and the nations of the Western hemisphere, in violation of Soviet assurances, and in defiance of American and hemispheric policy—is a deliberately provocative and unjustified change in the status quo which cannot be accepted by this country, if our courage and our commitments are ever again to be trusted by either friend or foe.

He said that construction of the missile sites must end and that all missiles must be removed. JFK described the blockade using a less inflammatory term, "quarantine," and he requested supportive action from the Organization of American States and the United Nations. "We no longer live in a world where only the actual firing of weapons represents a sufficient challenge to a nation's security to constitute maximum peril," he said. "Nuclear weapons are so destructive and ballistic missiles are so swift, that any substantially increased possibility of their use or any sudden change in their deployment may well be regarded as a definite threat to peace." He concluded by telling Americans:

> Our goal is not the victory of might, but the vindication of right— not peace at the expense of freedom, but both peace and freedom, here in this hemisphere, and, we hope, around the world. God willing, that goal will be achieved.[100]

More than 100 million Americans viewed the speech. On the streets of Los Angeles, up to seventy-five people lined up outside the Southern California Music Company to watch the address on a row of TVs in the window.[101] Anticipating some kind of public reaction, New York City police stationed extra officers around the United Nations as well as at City Hall, Gracie Mansion (the mayor's home), and broadcast stations.[102] Instant polls by the *Atlanta Constitution*,[103] *Kansas City Times*,[104] *Baltimore Sun*,[105] and *The (Columbia, South Carolina) State* showed the cities' residents strongly supported Kennedy.[106] In Detroit, the speech cast a dispiriting mood over the annual auto show.[107] As the evening passed, Richard C. Hottelet reported on CBS News that "a Latin American diplomat had told him, 'We are now in the most dangerous situation since World War II. The next forty-eight hours will be decisive.'"[108] American TV networks interrupted regular programming repeatedly during this evening, as they would throughout the crisis, to provide updates.

As Kennedy spoke, the Joint Chiefs raised the nation's military readiness status to Defense Condition 3, on a scale in which DefCon 5 indicated total peace and DefCon 1 represented a state of war. *Polaris* subs sailed to their assigned launch points. Strategic Air Command B–52s and other bombers assumed alert status. This move placed five times as many B–52s in the air as usual, but to achieve that feat, the military reportedly ignored several safety regulations. Some planes flew with nuclear weapons whose circuitry had not been confirmed to be safe. SAC also readied more than 100 ICBMs for firing, and some men trying to bring the missiles to alert status violated precautionary regulations.[109] As many as 200 planes flew to dispersal fields with nuclear weapons aboard. (Dispersing the planes would prevent attacking Soviets from easily wiping out the nation's nuclear weapons.) General John Gerhart, head of the North American Defense Command, ordered technicians to install nuclear weapons in fighter–interceptor jets. Because these planes carried only a pilot, the installations violated accepted Air Force policy requiring at least two officers to be responsible for each nuclear weapon.[110] On its first day carrying a nuclear weapon, an F–106 overran the runway at Hulman Field in Terre Haute, Indiana, and crashed into a webbed barrier. The plane was damaged, but the warhead remained intact.[111] In this way, readiness procedures opened the door to accidental war. While the military assumed alert status, key civilian officials in the federal government received orders to keep a packed bag ready in case of evacuation to government bunkers.

In Cuba, Castro announced a nationwide mobilization before Kennedy spoke. By calling up the reserves, he could triple the size of the Cuban armed forces to about 270,000.[112] He later reported that he had spies among civilians working at Guantanamo who had leaked information about American military actions.[113] Cuban reaction was dominated by grim determination. Many expected a future of guerilla warfare against American invaders. "Soft intelligence" gathered by the CIA reported that fire sirens in Matanzas, Cuba, sounded to call out the militia after Kennedy's speech. Some militia members reportedly failed to report.[114] This scene does not appear in Castro's spoken memories of the crisis. "After the crisis became public on the night of the 22nd," he said decades later,

> from that moment on, measures for our defense occupied almost all of our time. We worked feverishly, night and day, on . . . the mobilization of our forces, support for the surface-to-surface missiles—for the medium-range missiles. We gave the Soviet installations practically all our antiaircraft batteries.[115]

The top headline on the next day's edition of *Revolución* read: "Preparations for Yankee Aggression." Below the headline, an article, possibly dictated by Castro himself, stated that Cuba was on "a war footing."[116] In Havana, university students chanted, "Cuba si, yanqui no." As Cubans prepared for war, they did not fully understand the likely results of an American attack because the Soviets had left Castro almost completely unaware of the missiles' time-consuming launch procedures, their vulnerabilities, and the likelihood of their destruction in an American attack.[117]

Following JFK's speech, the United States called for a special meeting of the Organization of American States. Meanwhile, Rusk briefed ambassadors in Washington who represented neutral nations. At the United Nations, Stevenson requested a meeting of the Security Council and began working on his speech with the help of White House aide Arthur M. Schlesinger Jr., two CIA officers, and two photo-interpretation experts.[118] On the other side of the Atlantic, Acheson explained American actions to the NATO Council.

Across the United States, civilians became aware that neighboring military bases and civilian airports were buzzing with activity as U.S. military planes were dispersed around the country. Meanwhile, both men and equipment shipped out to the American southeast to form a potential invasion force. The 1st Marine Division's ready battalion was mobilized within two hours at Camp Pendleton in California, and the 1,910 officers and men were airborne aboard troop transports to Guantanamo within twenty-four hours.[119] Among the men called back to duty were would-be bridegrooms, such as Radioman Second Class Ronald Dale Taylor, who was destined to miss his own wedding. He departed Lubbock, Texas, with a hope that he would return by Christmas. His bride had mailed 150 invitations to their November 1 wedding.[120]

At a Pentagon briefing later in the evening, reporters learned that the U.S. Navy planned to "hail, stop, and search vessels proceeding toward Cuba. . . . In the event that vessels refuse search we will use force if necessary to halt them." Reporters received assurance that air surveillance of Cuba would continue while defense of the East Coast would be strengthened.[121]

By coincidence, a leading U.S. spy within the Soviet Union was arrested on this day. Realizing that he was in danger, Colonel Oleg Penkovsky, an officer in Soviet military intelligence's GRU, called his American handlers, but instead of leaving the agreed-upon message to signify that he was in danger of apprehension, he delivered the pre-arranged coded signal to report that the USSR was preparing to launch a nuclear attack on the United States. Those receiving his message fortunately did not take it seriously. Information provided by Penkovsky had made it easier for those analyzing the U-2 film to identify Soviet missiles.[122]

CHAPTER 4

A World on Edge

COUNTING DOWN TO WAR

After John F. Kennedy's October 22 speech, what Americans call "the Cuban Missile Crisis" rattled the nerves of ordinary people like few international confrontations before it. It was less than a war, but in a way it was much more. The threat of fast and devastating destruction was much bigger than in any previous crisis. While nervous citizens proceeded with their daily lives, leaders of the United States and the Soviet Union looked for a way out of a dilemma that had been built upon a bedrock of aggressive rhetoric and brinkmanship.

Most of Kennedy's constituents embraced his belief that the Soviet Union held full responsibility for the confrontation: In their eyes, Nikita Khrushchev had threatened world peace by secretly installing nuclear weapons in Cuba. Soviet leaders, on the other hand, blamed Kennedy for creating what they came to know as "the Caribbean Crisis." They thought that the American president dangerously overreacted to the placement of missiles on the soil of a Soviet ally. To Fidel Castro and his backers, "the October Crisis" was an outgrowth of the Bay of Pigs fiasco and the Kennedy administration's arrogant belief that it could and should decide what type of government ruled Cuba. Leaders in all three countries agreed on one thing: The ominous standoff threatened to erupt into war. As the clash evolved, all three nations contributed to the dangers of an international dispute in the Nuclear Age.

In public, Kennedy, Khrushchev, and Castro all acted provocatively to solidify their images as strong leaders. Kennedy openly prepared for a large U.S. military operation to oust the missiles; Khrushchev immediately threatened that Soviet ships would push through the American blockade and swore that he would not eliminate the missiles in Cuba; and Fidel

Castro's combative comments about Cuban readiness for war—even if that meant nuclear war—did nothing to ease international tensions. Each man engaged in "tough talk." For Kennedy and Khrushchev, this behavior represented a genuine belief that only a strong response could maintain the balance of power, but that reaction also represented an important step in appeasing hardliners in their own countries and allied leaders abroad.

In private, both Kennedy and Khrushchev displayed prudent decision-making, wise leadership, and a willingness to compromise in the interest of peace. They made no room for brinkmanship in the halls of power; that was a performance best limited to the court of public opinion. Both men feared that, once activated, the machinery of war might spin beyond their control. Castro could promise blood on the beaches if Americans invaded, but in the private interchanges between nuclear powers he was a pawn, not a king.

One small indicator of the week's grim nature can be found in the list of assignments given to JFK's Deputy Counsel Myer Feldman: Find out whatever he could about the White House bomb shelter; locate copies of all American declarations of war; determine who would run the government if the president, vice president, and Cabinet were killed in a single attack; and ascertain how the White House would be evacuated if nuclear war began.[1] Soviet and Cuban leaders pondered similar questions, but the United States' actions to prepare for nuclear war far exceeded theirs. Planning for every conceivable contingency and loading more and more planes on the ground and in the air with nuclear bombs was an extension of American industry's efficiency-conscious culture. These preparations, which were not mirrored in the Soviet Union, increased the odds of haphazardly tumbling into war.

TUESDAY, OCTOBER 23

In the aftermath of Kennedy's speech, a wary world awaited a Soviet military response, but none came. The Soviet Union seemed eager to join a verbal skirmish and unwilling to take hostile action. Historian Michael Beschloss has called Kennedy's speech "probably the most alarming ever delivered by an American president."[2] Certainly, its shock value affected Soviet leaders.

JFK's words so angered Khrushchev that he rashly considered challenging the blockade by telling Soviet ships to storm the quarantine line. He also ordered round-the-clock work on the missile sites in Cuba.[3] *The Huntley-Brinkley Report* on NBC described Moscow's response to the speech as "a combination of anguish and toughness." The unsettling nature of Kennedy's speech was clear: *Pravda*, the state-run newspaper, uncharacteristically rolled off the presses late.[4] TASS, the state news agency, reported that

> the Soviet government has repeatedly drawn attention to the governments of all countries and world opinion to the serious danger to the cause of peace created by the policy followed by the United States with regard to the Republic of Cuba.

It also accused the United States of imperialist efforts to take control of a sovereign state, and said Kennedy's speech showed that the United States is "prepared to push the world into the abyss of war catastrophe." TASS equated the quarantine with piracy and warned: "If the aggressors touch off a war, the Soviet Union will strike a very powerful retaliatory blow."[5] *Pravda* reported that "Washington is hatching another adventure." Soviet radio listeners heard that Kennedy was justifying a quarantine of Cuba by referring to a "mythical concentration of Communist rockets."[6] And, as far as Soviet listeners knew, the missiles were a product of the American imagination.

Despite the Soviet media's harsh words, Khrushchev consistently steered clear of an overt military response. He sought victory through diplomacy. In answer to American disapproval of Soviet weapons in Cuba, he started to push for the United States to withdraw its troops and equipment from bases in other nations.[7] Soviet officials gave Ambassador Kohler a 2,500-word response to Kennedy's speech. In it, Khrushchev began making use of his most valuable bargaining chip—the missiles already in Cuba. He did not want nuclear war, but he hoped to avoid losing the advantage provided by those weapons. While avoiding provocative actions such as massive troop movements or shuffling of military resources, he placed the Soviet military on alert, with all leaves and discharges canceled. Top Soviet and Warsaw Pact commanders were called to Moscow for a meeting. The military switched missiles in the Soviet Union to alert mode but avoided more provocative moves. The missiles in Cuba were not placed on alert. An apparently jovial Khrushchev attended the opera on this evening.[8]

Instead of waiting to reach its destination—Mariel—the *Aleksandrovsk*, which was carrying nuclear warheads, hurried into the nearest Cuban port, Isabel, before the blockade began. Workers unloaded warheads for cruise missiles, but the rest were left aboard the ship. They were intended for intermediate-range missiles that remained at sea. These warheads would remain in the ship's air-conditioned space.[9]

Meanwhile, U.S. intelligence struggled to discover what was happening among Soviet ships in the Atlantic. The National Security Council received a cable reporting that the Soviet Union had deployed several long-range torpedo attack submarines in the North Atlantic.[10] Some members of the Presidium wanted to move the subs closer to Cuba, but Mikoyan won the day when he argued that they should remain several hundred miles from the island, at least in part because shallow waters around Cuba were inhospitable to submarines.[11] A U.S. count of Soviet ships headed to Cuba on this day totaled twenty-two, including the *Aleksandrovsk*.[12] The Soviet Union had chartered fourteen ships to transport the larger intermediate-range missiles, associated troops, and related equipment. Only one of these ships had reached Cuba. Two more were only hours away, but all of the missiles were aboard vessels in the middle of the Atlantic.[13]

After going to bed fearful that Khrushchev might launch a nuclear attack as America slept, Rusk awoke at 6 a.m. and thought, "Well, I'm still here. This is very interesting."[14] Three hours later, he spoke before representatives of the Organization of American States (OAS), promoting a resolution that demanded the immediate dismantling and removal of all offensive weapons in Cuba. The resolution's goal was

> to ensure the government of Cuba cannot continue to receive from the Sino-Soviet powers[15] military material and related supplies which may threaten peace and security of the continent and to prevent missiles in Cuba with offensive capability from ever becoming an active threat to the peace and security of the continent.[16]

To win OAS authorization, the United States needed the support of two-thirds of the organization's members. The OAS endorsed the quarantine without a single vote cast in opposition.

The Ex Comm had its first two official meetings today, and Kennedy announced the existence of the panel to the public. The eight permanent members were JFK, LBJ, McNamara, Rusk, Dillon, Robert Kennedy, Taylor, and McCone. The announcement also stated that members of Kennedy's staff would attend some meetings. (These staffers included McGeorge Bundy and Sorensen, both of whom played significant roles, and O'Donnell, who did not.)[17]

Kennedy expressed frustration at the now-apparent inevitability of a clash. "There's no way we can stop this happening now. We could have stopped it four months ago, but the SAM sites and all the rest, mobile missiles, without an invasion some months ago you couldn't have stopped it."[18] On this day the Ex Comm addressed how to handle continued construction of the missile sites and how to respond if a U-2 was shot down by a surface-to-air missile. Planning for a massive invasion continued, and McNamara announced that the next big step was to charter more than 100 merchant ships to assist in transporting men and materiel. U.S. photo interpreters had now identified locations that might be storage facilities for warheads in Cuba; however, they had no way of knowing whether the structures were empty or filled to capacity. Meanwhile, Soviet forces moved warheads into caves until a bunker could be completed.

President Kennedy talked to Gilpatric about making sure that U.S. boarding parties could approach Soviet ships without provoking violence. Kennedy said, "It's very possible the Russians will fire at them as they board and we'll have to fire back and have quite a slaughter." Gilpatric assured him that contact with Soviet ships would be as peaceful as possible, beginning with a shot across their bows.[19]

At a 6 p.m. meeting of the Ex Comm, the president expressed concern about civil defense. Assistant Secretary of Defense for Civil Defense Steuart Pittman told him that while 92 million people lived within range of the medium-range missiles, shelter space existed for less than half of that number, and existing shelters had not been stocked with food, water, and other supplies.[20] Many also were unmarked, so desperate citizens would have no way of finding them. Pittman suggested one way to shelter a wider swath of the population: Lower standards for public shelters. Rather than requiring that shelters cut the level of radiation 100 times, the government could accept buildings that reduced radiation only forty times. This would offer space for more people but would provide less protection against the effects of radioactive fallout, probably leading to more widespread and more virulent radiation sickness. The Ex Comm also discussed emergency civil defense steps that could be taken before an invasion of Cuba—positioning food stocks around the country, as well as identifying and marking more shelters.

The civil defense issue rattled through the American consciousness as news events heightened anxieties. Civil defense offices in many cities were overrun by requests for information. In Duluth, there was good news: The city would be low on the Soviet Union's list of targets. New Orleans was not so lucky. That city's mayor admitted, "New Orleans is in as dangerous a position as any city in this area on the coast of the United States. We are in a dangerous area." New Orleans' terrain also did not lend itself to houses with basements, so few residents had the option of taking shelter at home. In Arizona, only one county had stocked shelters; in Indiana, only one shelter had been marked. Tests of air raid sirens in Little Rock revealed that several in the downtown area were inoperable.

Public reactions to the threat of nuclear war

The Cuban Missile Crisis generated fears of nuclear war among leaders in the U.S. and Soviet governments, and not surprisingly some ordinary Americans took action to protect themselves should war begin. We know this because competitive news media were prowling American towns and cities noting how people responded to the threat of a conflagration. Often, unusual behavior was isolated to individuals, but in other cases more widespread fears were clear.

The majority of Americans probably continued their routines, taking little if any unusual action in response to the crisis, but little record is kept of a failure to act. As a result, we know far more about those who made an effort to improve their chances of survival. These Americans did not represent a paranoid minority: They were typical Americans unwilling to accept a feeling of powerlessness in the shadow of nuclear war. It has been estimated that perhaps as many as 10 million Americans left urban areas during this week to seek refuge in rural areas far from likely military targets.[21] Mothers in many locations took on the mission of finding havens for children. About a dozen women reportedly left husbands in Washington and Baltimore and gathered in Cumberland, Maryland,[22] and entire families from places as far away as Chicago were reported to have taken refuge in Wisconsin.[23] In South Florida, word spread about one frantic woman's attempt to leave the area where the American military was congregating. When she was stopped by a military policeman, the woman told him, "I've got to get out of here. My husband's in the Navy and his ship has gone to sea, and he wants me to take the kids home to my mother." After looking in her car, the officer asked, "What kids?" and the red-faced woman gasped, "My God, I forgot them!"[24]

Residents of Jacksonville, Florida, a city ringed by three naval air stations, knew that their homes stood on a high-priority Soviet target. Not surprisingly, there was talk about evacuating the city—or at the very least taking children elsewhere. The Jacksonville-Duval County Civil Defense Council reported hundreds of inquiries about evacuation routes.[25]

Police patrolling the dark Memphis streets one night were surprised at 2 a.m. to find a car stopped in the middle of the street with its headlights glowing. In front of the car stood a man holding a pick above a manhole. "I'm not drunk," he told the startled officers by way of introduction. Then, he explained that he feared nuclear war and was attempting to determine whether his family could live in the city's sewer system.[26]

Shoppers in some American cities flooded stores seeking whatever they thought would be needed if a nuclear war began. Los Angeles residents swarmed into supermarkets on two consecutive days. One woman told a reporter: "I know a woman who bought forty jars of instant coffee. I asked her, 'If there really is an H-bomb attack, what are you going to use for water?' She'd never thought of that." The Los Angeles Times reported that "even in the early days of World War II, when it was believed that the Japanese were attacking the West Coast, people generally did not feel the deep, shapeless fear inspired by the thought of nuclear war." This phenomenon is particularly interesting because Los Angeles was just inside the zone that would have been vulnerable to the intermediate-range missiles that never reached Cuba. The city faced no danger whatsoever from medium-range missiles. Anchorage shoppers, who lived outside the range of missiles in Cuba, rushed to buy survival items, such as canned and dehydrated foods, portable stoves, flashlights, batteries, and water cans.[27]

In the Miami area, Dade County Manager Irving McNayr came under fire for urging residents to stockpile survival supplies and set up home shelters. He encouraged Miamians to store a two-week supply of food and water, first aid supplies, and a battery-powered radio. McNayr's speech received nationwide attention. Rumors spread that military personnel had taken over the city and that some foods were scarce.[28] A further rush on stores ensued, with some stores reporting as much as a 20 percent jump in grocery sales.[29] One housewife spent $102—$671 in 2008 dollars—on canned goods. She denied that she was stockpiling, telling a reporter that she and her husband had just finished a strict diet, and "we're a little hungry."[30]

Gun sales skyrocketed in Bakersfield, California. One dealer said it was "the biggest outbreak of panic buying since Japan bombed Pearl Harbor."[31] Residents of gun-friendly Dallas, too, joined in a firearm-buying spree.[32]

Fearful reactions were not restricted to the United States. Panic shopping was reported in some other countries. Among them was a Soviet ally, Czechoslovakia, where news of the U.S. quarantine helped to clear the shelves of items such as cooking oil.[33]

The absence of a free press and competitive media in the Soviet Union and Cuba makes it difficult to recapture civilian responses. We know that details of the crisis did not repeatedly invade daily life through television and radio broadcasts, as it did in the United States.[34] Journalist Stanislav Kondrashov went so far as to say: "The Soviet press treated the episode with socialist surrealism. The word 'missiles' never appeared in the newspapers."[35] Dobrynin wrote that Soviet citizens were most stunned by Khrushchev's October 28 announcement that he would remove the missiles because they had heard nothing about Soviet nuclear weapons in Cuba until that day.[36] In Cuba, Castro alerted militia members to be on alert and recommended primitive civil defense measures to the general population, but we have little indication of how individuals responded to the crisis and what they knew about the threat of war.

Scattered across the American landscape were signs of a nation preparing for war. In Cincinnati, the Western Union office processed a flood of telegrams to Washington, while Philadelphia military recruiters saw a mix of young men and veterans considering enlistment. The City of Brotherly Love canceled all vacations for police, fire, health, and public property workers. The mood in Miami was apparently calm, although bars and restaurants reportedly became silent and "dead still" when the news aired.[37] As the military reallocated resources and moved troops, families often said their goodbyes without knowing where soldiers were headed. Calls jammed the switchboard at the American Red Cross in South Florida as servicemen's families sought information on their whereabouts. Several churches in Miami scheduled special prayer services.

The Daily Californian at the University of California at Berkeley reported that given the international crisis, exams and classes seemed unimportant. More than 1,500 people gathered at the corner of Telegraph Avenue and Bancroft Way, where pro-blockade forces overwhelmed a peace protest by the Young Socialist Alliance. The debate, which began at noon, was still under way at midnight.[38] Nationally, the Student Peace Union condemned the quarantine. "Last night President Kennedy announced an action which may be the beginning of the nuclear holocaust all of the arms of both sides are supposedly preventing," the organization declared. Student protesters popped up around the country, often prompting "counter marches." At Indiana University in Bloomington, fistfights broke out between students supporting and opposing the quarantine. At the University of Florida, the managing editor of the school newspaper reported that students were "nearly panicked," and some were taking refuge off campus. Students at the University of Chicago were described as "scared stiff." Most university newspapers endorsed Kennedy's actions, with the Cornell Daily Sun standing out as an exception.[39] At a Cornell peace rally, hecklers loudly advocated military action. At one point, a speaker asked the hecklers, "Are you ready for nuclear war?" They replied with a thunderous roar: "YES!"[40]

All in all, it was not an easy day to be Robert McNamara. At a news conference, the secretary of defense learned that the British government had released aerial photos of the missile sites—images that the U.S. military had wanted to keep secret. Even worse, McNamara apparently spent part of his evening in a shouting match with the chief of naval operations. According to McNamara's recollection of that night, he sought specifics about blockade procedures, and Anderson resisted because he did not think a civilian should involve himself in operational details. Anderson told McNamara that U.S. ships would hail Soviet ships seeking to cross the blockade line, and when McNamara asked whether they would be hailed in English or Russian, Anderson replied, "How the hell do I know?" If there was a language barrier, Anderson told McNamara, the Navy would use flags. Then, American ships would shoot across their bow, and if that did not work, they would fire into the ships' rudders. Greatly alarmed by the thought of individual ship captains deciding to fire, McNamara insisted that no one should use weapons against Soviet ships without his permission.

Anderson replied by waving a 1955 manual on the laws of naval warfare in McNamara's face. The admiral showed McNamara that blockade procedures were codified right down to the point of destroying a ship that tried to cross the blockade line without being cleared. McNamara stood firm, and Anderson's anger erupted. "This is none of your goddamn business!" he told the civilian head of the military. McNamara replied by repeating that no shots would be fired on ships without his permission.[41] (Anderson remembered the discussion somewhat differently: He claimed that he and McNamara had a mild misunderstanding, which was resolved, and then, partly in jest, Anderson told McNamara that he could return to his office and let the military take care of the quarantine. McNamara's version has been predominant over the years, and Anderson later admitted that this incident was cited as one reason that he was not re-nominated to be Navy chief of staff a year later.)[42]

In Cuba, not long after midnight, Soviet troops had begun digging trenches around missile installations. Pliyev pressured his men to accelerate work on the missile sites and on assembly of the forty-two crated Il-28s.[43] Khrushchev did not want nuclear war, but he wanted to be ready. Pliyev was carrying out orders received the previous day from Soviet Defense Minister Rodion Malinovsky:

> In connection with possible landing on Cuba of Americans participating in maneuvers in the Caribbean Sea, undertake urgent measures to increase combat readiness and to repel the enemy by joint efforts of the Cuban army and all Soviet troop units, excluding Statsenko's weapons [the medium-range missiles] and all of Beloborodov's cargo [the nuclear warheads, including those for tactical battlefield weapons, such as the Lunas].[44]

As Pliyev struggled to fulfill his orders, Che Guevara was spending his second night at Sierra del Rosario, where he and 200 other fighters had brought a convoy of jeeps and trucks to form the core of an elite force challenging an American invasion.[45] While Guevara prepared to fight, Castro delivered a ninety-minute address about "Yankee aggression." He denied having offensive weapons but refused to allow inspections to verify that assertion. The CIA reported that none of its operatives had seen any signs of Cubans being trained to operate missiles and concluded that Soviet troops were controlling the weapons.

At the United Nations, American, Soviet, and Cuban ambassadors spoke. U.S. Ambassador Adlai Stevenson told the Security Council that

this is a solemn, I believe, and significant day for the life of the
United Nations and the hope of the world community. Let it be
remembered not as the day when the world came to the edge of
nuclear war, but as the day when men resolved to let nothing
thereafter stop them in their quest for peace.

Soviet representative Valerian Zorin labeled U.S. missile photos as a
CIA fabrication. He asserted that the United States considered itself to be
a "world policeman" and maintained bases in thirty-five nations.[46] Soviet
representatives promised that any U.S. aggression, such as stopping a Soviet
ship, would be considered an act of war.[47] Cuba's Mario Garcia-
Inchaustegui condemned the blockade, saying that the United States
seemed to feel that it could identify "when a base is good and when a
base is naughty."[48] In a conversation with a mid-level member of the Soviet
delegation, a neutral delegate heard that the USSR would arm its ships
to challenge the quarantine. He also suggested that the Soviet Union might
blockade an American ally, such as
Turkey.[49] The Security Council
adjourned without taking any
action.

American troops and equipment were on the move, especially
in Florida. Crowds gathered to
watch Air Force B-47 bombers
and antisubmarine planes arrive at
Palm Beach International Airport.
Runways all over Florida were
jammed with arrivals of military
aircraft. At Key West Naval Base,
thirteen submarines and a division
of destroyers left port. The city
was suddenly home to so many
soldiers that it was difficult to find

> As a NATO ally of the United States,
> Turkey had received Jupiter nuclear
> missiles under a 1959 treaty with the
> United States. Although these weapons
> were outdated by 1962, Soviet leaders
> saw them as a threat at their back door.
> Officially, the United States refused to
> acknowledge similarities between the
> Soviet missiles in Cuba and the U.S.
> missiles in Turkey, saying that there was
> nothing secret about the missiles in
> Turkey and that Turkey enjoyed the
> freedom to reject the missiles.

places where they could sleep. The Army requested permission to let troops
camp in a local baseball stadium. In scenes reminiscent of World War II,
troop trains rolled into the Sunshine State, carrying men, tanks, amphibious
tractors, ammunition, supplies, and food rations.[50] As the military presence
grew in South Florida, the civilian population dwindled, particularly in
Key West. Tourists fled as soldiers arrived. All civilians checked out of
the Key Wester Motel, and military men replaced them.[51] On this day,
one Key West bank executive reported that withdrawals outnumbered
deposits by a ratio of seven to one.[52]

At 7:06 p.m. Eastern Daylight Time, JFK signed the document establishing the naval blockade. He cited that day's meeting of the Organization of American States and the Rio Pact as authorization for the quarantine.[53] The declaration listed equipment to be intercepted: Surface-to-surface missiles, bomber aircraft, bombs, air-to-surface rockets and guided missiles, warheads for any of those weapons, and mechanical or electronic equipment to support or operate them.[54]

In a CBS News Special Report, Walter Cronkite reported that the blockade would begin the following day. In his words, "The world was given at least a fifteen-hour moratorium tonight." On the same broadcast, Robert Eiseman noted that Key West "has been virtually taken over by Navy, Marine, Army and Air Force contingents." A reporter asked Senate Majority Leader Mike Mansfield, "Could this mean war, senator?" And he replied, "It could."[55]

After the day's second Ex Comm meeting, the Kennedy brothers had a private chat. Jack and Bobby Kennedy agreed that JFK had no choice about taking an aggressive stand against Soviet missiles. If he had done less, they believed, he would have faced impeachment.[56] At 9:30 p.m., the younger brother met with Anatoly Dobrynin at the Soviet Embassy. He began by condemning the ambassador for previous assurances that the Soviet Union would not put missiles in Cuba. Dobrynin said as far as he knew, that was still true. Kennedy had been angry with Dobrynin for lying but became convinced that Khrushchev had not confided in his ambassador to the United States. Dobrynin asked why the president had not mentioned the missiles when Gromyko visited the White House days earlier, and the attorney general said JFK could have told Gromyko nothing that he did not already know.[57] Kennedy warned Dobrynin that Khrushchev's actions had ruptured whatever trust existed between JFK and the Soviet leader.[58] As he left around 10:15, Robert Kennedy asked whether Soviet ships headed for Cuba planned to stop, and Dobrynin said Soviet ships had orders to challenge the quarantine.[59] This was the first of several secret meetings between Dobrynin and the attorney general during the crisis.

When Robert Kennedy returned to the White House, he found the president meeting with his old friend, Ambassador David Ormsby-Gore of Great Britain. Ormsby-Gore expressed concerns about the quarantine line's location. The Navy planned to set the line 800 miles from Cuba because that would place ships beyond the range of MIG fighters based on the island. The ambassador thought this was a mistake. He noted that the first ships would reach the quarantined area within a few hours and that would give Soviet leaders little time to consider their options. JFK agreed and asked McNamara to situate the blockade line just 500 miles from Cuba.[60]

WEDNESDAY, OCTOBER 24

Castro awoke in his underground command post not far from the Havana Zoo. The bunker comprised a tunnel dug 200 yards into a hillside, with six rooms on each side of the tunnel. The entrance, with reinforced steel doors, had been chiseled into the side of a cliff high above the Almendares River.[61]

The Ex Comm began its morning meeting at 10, the moment when the blockade began. At the same time, the Strategic Air Command raised its alert status to the highest level ever—Defcon 2. Without consulting the president or McNamara, SAC chose not to make the Defcon change covertly; instead, the move was done "in the clear," allowing Soviets to monitor it. This change reportedly intensified anxiety among Soviet officials, who thought the United States might be preparing for a first strike in a nuclear war. While U.S. surveillance indicated continued construction on the missile sites, there was no indication of any effort "to achieve a higher degree of action readiness among Soviet and bloc forces . . . on a crash basis," a national security report noted. Furthermore, that analysis stated that the Soviet Union "continues to avoid any hint of specific counteractions to the announcement of the quarantine."[62]

The first few minutes on the quarantine line were the most harrowing. Two Soviet ships, the *Gagarin* and the *Komiles*, were within a few miles of the line, and there were reports that a Soviet submarine was submerged between them. Consequently, Navy commanders chose a hulking aircraft carrier, the *USS Essex*, to intercept them. However, both Soviet ships halted before reaching the *Essex*. Meanwhile, a Soviet submarine was reported to be within the quarantine line.[64]

> Within twenty-four hours of the change in Defcon status, SAC raised the ready force of bombers from 912 to 1,436, ready ICBMs from 134 to 145, and ready tankers from 402 to 916.[63]

As he participated in the Ex Comm meeting, McCone received a written message. "Mr. President," he said, "I have a note just handed to me. It says that we've just received information through ONI [the Office of Naval Intelligence] that all six Soviet ships that are currently in Cuban waters—and I don't know what that means—have either stopped or reversed course."[65] After some time, it became clear the message indicated that all freighters approaching the quarantine line were at a standstill or reversing course. The Atlantic fleet commander was immediately ordered to allow the ships to retreat without interference. It was after reception of this news that Rusk famously said, "We're eyeball to eyeball, and the other fellow just blinked."[66] Nevertheless, challenges lay ahead. McNamara briefed the Ex Comm on plans to use antisubmarine helicopters to harass Soviet submarines in the area.[67] As the Ex Comm prepared for each possible escalation of tensions, it was as if the crisis had taken on a life of its own: When one obstacle fell away, the Kennedy administration moved ahead to the next potential problem or escalation.

At the United Nations, Acting Secretary General U Thant proposed that the Soviet Union delay all weapons shipments to Cuba for several weeks and that the U.S. blockade be halted for the same period. He urged both sides to use that moratorium to negotiate an agreement. Khrushchev welcomed this suggestion. In his reply to U Thant, he endorsed the possibility of a summit meeting with Kennedy; however, JFK rejected the proposal because it would not affect the arms already in Cuba. Pressure was growing among neutral nations in the United Nations General Assembly for action forcing Soviet and American negotiators to meet.

British pacifist Bertrand Russell wrote letters to both Kennedy and Khrushchev urging that they abandon combative rhetoric and show more prudence. Khrushchev again responded positively. In a cable to Russell he said,

> I wish to assure you that the Soviet government will not make any rash decisions; will not let itself be provoked by the unjustified action on the part of the United States; and will do nothing in order to escalate the situation. . . . We will do everything in our power to prevent the launching of a war. We are fully aware of the fact that should such a war be launched, it will be from its first hour a thermonuclear world war.[68]

Kennedy's sardonic response to Russell suggested that the peace advocate's attention "might well be directed to the burglar rather than to those who caught the burglar."[69] This represented an example of Kennedy's renowned wit and offered insight into his feeling that the missile installations represented a violation of American sovereignty.

In Moscow, Khrushchev spent three hours meeting with an American businessman, William Knox, then president of Westinghouse International. He told Knox that he would direct Soviet submarines to sink any U.S. vessels that attempted to stop or search a Soviet ship, but he emphasized his support for a summit. Admitting for the first time that Soviet nuclear missiles were in Cuba, Khrushchev told Knox a story about a man who lived with a goat. The man did not like the smell of the goat, but he became accustomed to it. The Soviet Union had been living with a goat, he said, as the United States armed European allies. Khrushchev said his

The Cuban Missile Crisis and the Press

John F. Kennedy had an unusual rapport with members of the Washington press corps, counting a few reporters among his personal friends. He also was a voracious reader of newspapers and magazines. Kennedy even worked for a short while as a freelance journalist between his World War II service in the U.S. Navy and his election to the House of Representatives in 1946.

An accident of time and natural skill enabled JFK to become the first "television president." Beginning with his televised 1960 debates with Richard Nixon and continuing through his news conferences that were televised live, Kennedy demonstrated a flair for exploiting the new medium. As a result, some of Kennedy's detractors considered him a "darling" of the media. Nevertheless, like any president, Kennedy had complaints about coverage of his administration. At one point, he banned the *New York Herald Tribune* from the White House because he was upset about something the newspaper had published.[70]

The Cuban Missile Crisis created unusual dynamics between the media and the White House. Initially, there was a long period of secrecy within the U.S. government while policymakers decided how to respond to the missile implantations. In his crisis memoirs, Robert Kennedy wrote that the veil of secrecy "was essential" in enabling the Ex Comm to work its way from favoring a vengeful air strike to embracing a cautiously prepared quarantine line.[71]

Before JFK's speech to the nation, he had asked the *Washington Post* and the *New York Times* not to publish details of the crisis until he had addressed his constituents. Both complied, and they were just the first to feel pressure to bow to the White House's wishes.

Once the threat of nuclear war had been revealed, journalists faced a delicate task. "Here we had to keep the American people advised of what seemed to be an imminent exchange of nuclear weapons," said CBS' Walter Cronkite.

> And, you know, the horror of that was clearly evident. . . . Boy, that was a seven-day crisis. And in reporting that. . . . We couldn't report it to the American people to the depths it really went. If we had, I don't know what would have happened. . . . Nobody was saying: And therefore, we're going to burn—or their cities are going to be destroyed. Or with the nuclear rays, we're all going to die. We didn't do that kind of thing. The lessons were there.[72]

In addition, JFK ordered unprecedented restrictions on the media, raising concerns about how freedom of the press would fare in the Nuclear Age. The Kennedy administration announced that it would stop releasing information on many facets of the conflict. The administration asked newspaper and magazine editors as well as radio and television news directors not to report on these topics even if they acquired information from other sources. Many journalists equated this directive with a demand for self-censorship. Distress over these guidelines worsened when Arthur Sylvester, a Pentagon spokesman, indicated that he believed an administration facing the threat of nuclear war had a right to lie. He went further, stating that handling of the news was

> one of the power factors in our quiver. This precise handling of the release of news can influence developments in the kind of situation in which military, political, and psychological factors are so closely related.[73]

In mid-November 1962, the American Society of Newspaper Editors, the American Newspaper Publishers Association, and the National Editorial Association issued a joint statement about the administration's restrictions. In it, they argued that uniform censorship was preferable to media self-censorship in times of crisis. Furthermore, they contended that the best way to preserve American security is through thorough reporting of all information that is not harmful to the military.[74] In a December editorial, the St. Louis Post-Dispatch condemned the Kennedy administration's policy, saying, "It is precisely because a free society is incompatible with the concentration of power that the concentration of control over information in government must be resisted."[75]

A news media controversy of a different type emerged in December 1962. Two of President Kennedy's closest friends, Charles Bartlett and Stewart Alsop, authored an article in the Saturday Evening Post that cast Adlai Stevenson as a weak-kneed appeaser willing to compromise American security to avoid war. Because Stevenson had proposed removing U.S. weapons from allied nations in Europe, one White House official was quoted as saying, "Adlai wanted a Munich."[76] Kennedy made no secret of his aversion to Stevenson's intellectualism and his mannerisms, and some have argued that JFK actually read this article and approved it before it was published. The obvious irony is that Kennedy followed Stevenson's advice, which was so widely criticized in the article: He did promise Khrushchev that he would remove nuclear missiles from Turkey and Italy.

nation did not like it, but had learned to accept it. Similarly, he said, when the United States thinks about the missiles in Cuba, "You are not happy about it and you won't like it, but you'll learn to live with it."[77]

The New Yorker's "The Talk of the Town" column gave this description of the blockade's first day:

> For a whole day, we waited for something to happen . . . minute by minute, in something like pain, our ignorance of what the next minute would bring, and feeling the dead weight of the conviction that no one on earth—not the president, not the Russians—knew what it would bring.[78]

In the evening, Kennedy received a letter from Khrushchev. In it, he argued that Kennedy was inappropriately involving himself in Cuban affairs. "Our ties with the Republic of Cuba," he wrote, "like our relations with other states, regardless of what kind of states they may be, concern only the two countries between which these relations exist."[79]

In some American cities, civil defense directors began urging citizens to stock basements with food, water, and first-aid supplies rather than placing hopes in public shelters that were unmarked and unstocked. Tulsa officials inspected 180 buildings, but found that only forty-seven met the requirements to be shelters. The city promised to have those sites stocked with necessities by December 15.[80] To Oklahomans who feared war might begin at any moment, the promise of action in December was cold comfort.

The Joint Chiefs had a full plate today. JFK remained unsure about whether the Cuban crisis carried consequences for Berlin. Consequently, he ordered that a battalion-sized force be prepared to take the autobahn to West Berlin with two hours' notice. The enlistments of all active-duty naval and marine personnel were extended indefinitely, and the Strategic Air Command announced that all leaves had been canceled. At the crisis's start, all U.S. missile-detecting radar installations had been pointed north, along the route bombers would take from the Soviet Union. On this day, for the first time, the United States directed a radar in Moorestown, New Jersey, southward to monitor possible launches from Cuba.[81] The Herald Tribune Service reported that the Office of Emergency Planning was considering imposition of martial law if a limited nuclear war occurred.[82]

Addressing the need for military secrecy, the Kennedy administration unveiled a twelve-point plan to control the flow of information. The "Memorandum to Editors and Radio and Television News Directors" detailed twelve types of information that were considered vital to national security, and while the Pentagon planned to keep this information under wraps journalists were advised that if they obtained details from other sources they should understand that releasing it would not be in the public interest. Among forbidden topics were deployment of forces, estimates of U.S. capabilities, information concerning U.S. targets, evaluations of enemy plans, preparations for weapons deployment, numbers of U.S. troops, notifications of U.S. military alert status, placement of aircraft, and details of military capabilities and vulnerabilities.[83] Some journalists responded angrily, accusing the administration of "news management."

By the end of a day that had generated much trepidation, a certain degree of relief swept the United States as reports confirmed that Soviet freighters en route to Cuba had halted or had begun a return to the Soviet Union. Only tankers, which could not carry offensive weapons, appeared to be maintaining course. JFK, nevertheless, warned the Ex Comm against celebration. "We still have twenty chances out of a hundred to be at war with Russia," he told Bundy.[84] The day was not without tragedy for the United States: Seven airmen died when their jet crashed at Guantanamo.

THURSDAY, OCTOBER 25

The Joint Chiefs began the day with orders for ships on the blockade line to identify a ship to stop, specifically a freighter not registered in the Soviet Union or a Soviet bloc nation.[85] *The Bucharest*, a Soviet petroleum tanker, cooperated with the blockade by identifying its cargo and was allowed to pass with a warship trailing it. As of this day, there were only two Soviet freighters still headed for Cuba and four tankers, in addition to the *Bucharest*. One of the freighters was believed to be carrying helicopters. It was in the North Atlantic, while the other freighter was a few days west of the Panama Canal.[86] Reconnaissance over Cuba remained heavy, and the military estimated that if a U-2 was shot down, military forces could launch a reprisal strike on a single SAM site or an attack on all SAM sites within two hours. It would take twelve hours to implement a full air strike on missiles, bombers, and SAM sites. Staging an invasion would require a week to prepare.[87]

In a letter to Kennedy, Khrushchev declared that "the Soviet government considers that violation of the freedom of the use of international waters and international air space is an act of aggression which brings mankind toward the abyss of a world missile-nuclear war."[88] At the State Department, Hilsman wrote a memo arguing that the Soviet Union was forcing the United States to take the initiative. His analysis was that Soviet leaders were playing for time to see whether the United States was open to a trade for the missiles in Cuba or whether American forces would take more aggressive action.[89]

In his daily syndicated newspaper column, Walter Lippmann urged the withdrawal of U.S. missiles in Turkey in exchange for removal of Soviet missiles in Cuba. This idea was gaining popularity in the halls of the United Nations. Another favored option among UN delegates was designation of Latin America as a denuclearized zone.

Walt Rostow, chairman of the Policy Planning Council at the State Department, delivered a document to the Ex Comm on the likely effects of expanding the quarantine to include petroleum. Rostow estimated that the existing quarantine was harming Cuba's economy because the ships that had turned back probably carried more than weapons. Imported petroleum was essential to Cuban industry. Rostow believed that Cuba

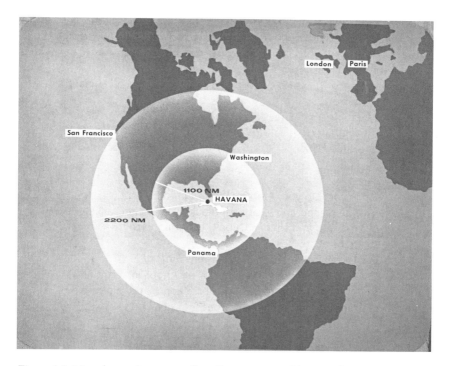

Figure 4.1 Map shows the range of medium-range and intermediate-range nuclear missiles based in Cuba. John F. Kennedy Library.

could stretch existing fuel stocks for six months at most, but a shortage would have "grave consequences for the economy and for public morale." The report anticipated opposition from American allies if the United States attempted to bring Cuba to its knees. For now, Rostow's panel recommended stopping shipments of missile fuel as a means of continually increasing pressure on Cuba.[90] Another document, also from Rostow's group, supported American agreement to a summit meeting if it was clear that removal of nuclear weapons from Cuba was a non-negotiable demand.[91] The same subcommittee suggested that the United States should begin talking to Turkish and Italian officials about replacing Jupiter missiles with Polaris submarines.[92]

This day's CIA report cited no signs of Soviet weapons transports approaching the quarantine line. However, it quoted Malinovsky as saying that Soviet armed forces remained at "highest battle readiness."[93] As the day progressed, new reconnaissance information showed that the missile sites were swiftly moving toward completion, and all twenty-four SAM sites apparently were operational. Soviet leaders had not yet assigned targets to the medium-range missiles, but they were expected to attack communications centers and industrial areas in American cities and towns.[94] On this afternoon and the following morning, the State Department provided regional briefings for members of Congress, most of whom were not in Washington.[95] And the White House canceled all social events for the crisis' duration.

A remarkable exchange occurred at the United Nations between Zorin and Stevenson. Speaking before the Security Council, Stevenson angrily responded to Zorin's repeated denials that Soviet missiles were in Cuba.

> *Stevenson:* Do you, Ambassador Zorin, deny that the U.S.S.R. has placed and is placing medium- and intermediate-range missiles and sites in Cuba? Yes or no. Don't wait for the translation. Yes or no.
>
> *Zorin:* I am not in an American courtroom, sir.
>
> *Stevenson:* You are in the court of world opinion right now.
>
> *Zorin:* I do not wish to answer a question that is put to me in the fashion that a prosecutor does. In due course, sir, you will have your reply.
>
> *Stevenson:* I am prepared to wait for my answer until Hell freezes over, if that's your decision.[96]

Television networks in the United States provided live coverage. On CBS, Cronkite called it "one of the most dramatic days in United Nations history."[97] A British delegate predicted that "the lights soon will be going out all over the world."[98]

In a letter to U Thant, JFK stressed that the United States could not resolve the crisis unless the Soviet Union removed the weapons already in Cuba. However, he told U Thant that Stevenson was prepared to discuss arrangements for preliminary talks. Kennedy did not address the secretary general's request that the quarantine be stopped while talks were under way.[99]

A U.S. report declared that public shelter space had been found for 60 million Americans in 112,000 locations. Although many shelter areas had not been marked, the Pentagon assured Americans that "local civil defense directors know where the space is."[100] These numbers were misleading. Some areas had virtually no shelters. In the sprawling city of Los Angeles, only 307 buildings had been designated as shelter space. Thus, in a metropolis with a population of more than two million, the shelter space would house less than 25 percent of the population, and survival supplies were available for only 40,000 Angelenos.[101] New Orleans had only forty-two approved shelters.[102] In Atlanta, a legislative subcommittee urged the state to accelerate civil defense planning or to abandon them and acknowledge that the government could not protect the civilian population.[103]

Civilian evacuees from Guantanamo reached Norfolk. There were yells from hundreds of people gathered at the dock to welcome the noncombatants and to celebrate their successful escape from Cuba. Awaiting the evacuees was a life of uncertainty spent in barracks equipped with Red Cross rations. They returned to the United States without knowing the fate of their husbands and fathers in Cuba.[104]

An internal CIA memo reported that the head of Operation MONGOOSE felt excluded from crisis discussions. Lansdale wanted to contribute to American strategy. Carter told McCone that the problem was a jurisdictional issue and that current intelligence-gathering in Cuba had to be done in coordination with the military and could not be accomplished through the cumbersome process required by Operation MONGOOSE, which was essentially run by a committee and often relied on operatives who were not professionals.[105]

A document prepared for an afternoon meeting of the Ex Comm called for taking a fresh look at the idea of an air strike against the missiles as a complement to the quarantine. This proposal urged that the blockade continue and be broadened to cover petroleum products.[106] President Kennedy and his advisers continued to consider and plan for all feasible military options.

Dobrynin reported to the Soviet Foreign Ministry that "noticeably fewer people could be seen on Washington's streets. Government offices are working until late at night. Preoccupation over the possibility of war is sensed in business circles, too." He mentioned that African embassies had notified students to be prepared to evacuate the United States, which was now viewed as a potential war zone. "In general," he wrote, "it is necessary to say that different sources in the journalist and diplomatic corps in Washington agree that currently the probability of a USA armed intervention against Cuba is great."[107] Also on this day, *Pravda* carried the full text of a statement from Communist China justifying its attack on India, and a *Pravda* editorial seemed to support China's action.[108]

The day's most important events occurred away from the public eye within the walls of the Kremlin. There, Khrushchev told colleagues that the time had come to make a deal that would preserve the peace and remove the missiles from Cuba. Speaking to the Presidium, he admitted his grave concerns following Kennedy's military response to discovery of the missiles: "The initiative is in our hands; there is no need to be afraid. We started out and then we got afraid." He argued Cuba's defense was not important enough to risk waging nuclear war. In exchange for removing the missiles, he wanted a commitment from Kennedy not to invade Cuba. The Presidium again voted unanimously to support his recommendation.[109]

CHAPTER 5

Into the Dark

FRIDAY, OCTOBER 26

Within Kennedy's Ex Comm, there was agreement on one important issue: The time had arrived for the quarantine line—150 ships, 250 aircraft, and about 30,000 men—to show some teeth by stopping and searching at least one vessel bound for Cuba.[1] Officials chose the *Marucla* precisely because it was unlikely to carry Soviet weapons. It was a Lebanese freighter with a Greek crew, and its port of departure was in Latvia, one of the Baltic nations absorbed by the Soviet Union. By stopping the *Marucla*, the United States could add meaning to the quarantine without risking direct contact with a Soviet ship. The *USS John R. Pierce* started pursuing the freighter on the previous night, but naval authorities chose a more symbolic vessel to stop and board the *Marucla*. They opted for the *USS Joseph P. Kennedy Jr.*, a destroyer named after the president's older brother who had been killed in World War II. The executive officer of the *Pierce* joined six officers and men from the *Kennedy* when they boarded the *Marucla*. Ironically, the Navy had authorized a $200 expenditure to provide items such as candy, magazines, and lighters to be given to the crews of each apprehended ship.[2] In return for those inexpensive gifts, the Greek crew offered the boarders hot coffee. The search was quick—and no missile parts were found. Later in the day, a Swedish freighter under a Soviet charter refused to stop at the quarantine line. The ship was carrying general cargo from Leningrad. The captain of the closest U.S. destroyer sent an urgent message to Washington asking for instructions. He was advised to let the ship pass.

The intelligence community still was struggling to estimate the dangers of having missiles in Cuba. A new American national security document asserted that the installation of all of the medium- and intermediate-range

weapons in Cuba would increase the number of missiles targeting the
United States by 40 percent. Moreover, it estimated that a first strike by
the Soviet Union could wipe out all soft bomber and missile sites as well
as moderately hardened Atlas missiles.[3] The United States remained
unaware that nuclear warheads had arrived in Cuba or that intermediate-
range missiles had not.[4]

In the Ex Comm, the split between hawks and doves was becoming
sharper. While the Joint Chiefs still favored attacking all offensive weapons
if the Soviet Union continued missile site construction, McNamara and
JFK supported a limited attack on the known missile sites and the Il-28
bombers as a next step.[5] Though everyone else was focused on which
military action to take, the visiting UN ambassador asked whether he could
offer to lift the blockade if the Soviets stopped work on the missile sites.
For a second time, Stevenson joined the Ex Comm and drew fire from
its members. McCone argued fiercely that invasion was the only way to
oust Castro, and the president interjected that the immediate goal was to
eliminate the missiles—not to overthrow Castro.[6]

Based on the latest estimates, an invasion would require 250,000 air,
sea, and ground personnel.[7] As a result, the largest gathering of U.S. forces

Figure 5.1 The Ex Comm meets October 29, 1962. White House photo by
Cecil Stoughton, John F. Kennedy Library.

since the Korean War was forming in the southeast.[8] Calling up reserve units to augment invasion forces was an important step not yet implemented.

The Ex Comm's job was not becoming any easier. Kennedy and his advisers decided not to broaden the quarantine line's list of banned cargo. If the United States expanded the quarantine to include missile fuel, that would inevitably lead to unnecessary and potentially unpleasant encounters between U.S. boarding parties and Soviet tankers that might be carrying fuel for civilian use. On another front, plans to drop leaflets on Cuba created concerns. The original plan had been to shower cities with flyers alerting Cubans to the dangers introduced by the presence of Soviet missiles on Cuban soil; however, JFK worried that this might create confusion later if the administration decided to launch an air strike and dropped leaflets warning civilians to take cover. For now, production of flyers would continue without specific plans to distribute them. The Ex Comm also worried about Pittman's desire to announce acceleration of civil defense preparations: Kennedy and his team feared that such action might cause panic. After the Ex Comm meeting in the afternoon, JFK turned to Salinger and said, "Do you think the people in that room realize that if we make a mistake, there may be 200 million dead?"[9]

Robert Kennedy continued his back-door diplomacy with Dobrynin. On this day, he warned the ambassador that the United States was preparing to escalate military action. If the Soviet Union did not agree to remove the missiles within forty-eight hours, he told Dobrynin, heightened military action was likely. Another form of informal diplomacy drew ABC News reporter John Scali into the heart of the crisis. Scali was approached by Aleksandr Fomin, who ostensibly served as a counselor at the Soviet embassy but actually was the KGB's Washington Station Chief Aleksandr Feklisov. He asked Scali to meet him for lunch.[10] At the restaurant, Feklisov reportedly said, "War seems about to break out. Something must be done to save the situation." Feklisov asked whether the United States would pledge not to invade Cuba so that Khrushchev could claim a victory while dismantling missile installations. After lunch, Scali reported the conversation to the State Department.[11]

In Cuba, a nervous Pliyev heard from Czech and Cuban sources that an American attack was imminent. He expected war within two days— and still his operable weapons were unarmed. Pliyev knew that it would take more than three hours to load each warhead onto a missile, so he issued a vague order for "a dispersal of technology," a clouded reference to moving warheads closer to the missiles.[12]

Castro, who also anticipated an invasion soon, told his General Staff that antiaircraft guns were free to fire on U.S. planes, starting on the following morning. U.S. planes were crisscrossing the island at tree level, and he believed this surveillance had one purpose: preparation for an invasion.[13] Castro wrote a letter to Khrushchev that generated new worries in an already-tense Kremlin. The Soviet premier believed that Castro's letter was meant to encourage the Soviet Union to launch a pre-emptive nuclear strike against the United States.[14]

Edward A. McDermott, head of the Office of Emergency Planning (OEP), met with Supreme Court Chief Justice Earl Warren to discuss evacuation of Supreme Court members to the Mount Weather underground bunker complex in Virginia, where the president and other key Executive Branch officials would take shelter from nuclear war. McDermott asked Warren to consider whether it would be necessary to have a fully functional Supreme Court in the bunker.[17] (Members of

In 1990, Castro released his text of the letter and clarified his meaning — that the Soviet Union should use nuclear weapons only if the United States invaded Cuba with the intention of taking over the island.[15] He later explained that he wanted to be sure that the Soviet troops would not hesitate to use the weapons if necessary.[16] It is doubtful that even this interpretation would have eliminated Khrushchev's concerns.

Congress would be housed in a secret bunker at the Greenbrier resort in West Virginia—and that facility was equipped with space for both the House and the Senate to conduct business.) McDermott gave Warren a pass for the Virginia bunker, but when Warren learned that his wife could not accompany him, he returned it.[18] In the upper tiers of government, the crisis raised new, and deeply personal, fears about leaving families behind if top officials moved into bunkers. Consequently, Kennedy's naval aide, Tazewell Shepard, issued a memo saying that dependents of White House officials could assemble in a fenced-in lot in northwest Washington, and from there, they would be led in a motorcade to a safer location— not inside a bunker, but somewhere safer than being above ground in the nation's capital.[19] The memo made no comment on the likelihood that it would be difficult to maintain a motorcade on highways jammed with people fleeing Washington. (Looking back on the crisis in 1964, Jacqueline Kennedy recalled begging her husband to let her stay in the White House, along with him and their two children. She remembered telling him that she would prefer to die on the White House lawn rather than being somewhere safe without him. "I just want to be with you," she recalled telling him, "And I want to die with you, and the children do too.")[20]

On this day, an OEP memo revealed details of rationing plans that would be put into effect after a nuclear attack. Retail inventories of food, petroleum, and other "essential consumer items" would be frozen following an assault. A rationing board would prohibit sales for five days and prepare rationing documents. Reproduction proofs for essential paperwork already had been made. In the initial stage, local boards would handle rationing, but that work would move to the national level as soon as possible.[21]

The White House announced to the American public that the latest reconnaissance findings indicated Soviet workers were rushing to complete missile installations. This continued activity created jitters around the country, and prompted extra security measures. Some naval bases banned civilians. Near San Francisco, government employees closed some access roads to piers on the Golden Gate bridge. At Rock Island, Illinois, authorities blocked gates to the Mississippi River locks. In Duluth, Minnesota, an airport guard spotted a dark figure climbing a fence and sounded sabotage alarms at all military bases in the upper Midwest. When the klaxon awoke pilots at Volk Field in Wisconsin, it was interpreted as an order for planes to take off—and an unspoken verification that war had begun. Just as planes equipped with nuclear weapons prepared to race down the runway, a second message canceled the alarm. Because Volk Field had no control tower, the only way to stop the planes was for a jeep to drive onto the runway and block it. Takeoffs were aborted just moments before the planes would have become airborne. In Duluth, officials later concluded that the intruder probably was a bear.[22]

The missile detection radar operators in Moorestown had a few nervous minutes after spotting a missile in flight. They knew that there would be only five minutes between a missile launch from Cuba and devastation on American soil. It took several minutes to realize that the missile was headed southeast instead of north. It was a previously scheduled Titan II ICBM test launch.[23] No one had thought to warn the radar operators.

At a meeting about Operation MONGOOSE, a Lansdale memo provided updates on specific operations against Cuba. Included were incursions by sabotage teams on small water craft, efforts to sink or sabotage the cargo on Cuban ships, attempts to hamper sugar production, an operation that would float balloons bearing propaganda into Cuba, and attempts to convince low-level officials to defect.[24] During the course of the meeting, protests were raised about new MONGOOSE incursions at a time of heightened security,[25] and Robert Kennedy ordered that all operations be placed on hold.[26]

That evening in Moscow, Khrushchev sent Kennedy a private letter suggesting terms to end the crisis. He offered to withdraw the missiles if the United States pledged not to invade Cuba. Khrushchev argued that Soviet citizens were "normal people." As a result, he asked, "how can we permit the incorrect actions that you ascribe to us? Only lunatics or suicides, who themselves want to perish and to destroy the whole world before they die, could do this."[27] Rusk later remembered that the letter's "distraught and emotional tone bothered us, because it seemed the old fellow might be losing his cool in the Kremlin."[28]

In Denver, a reporter investigated one fallout shelter officially listed as ready for use. He found that it contained about twenty-four chairs, twelve empty water cans, fifteen stretchers, first aid and radiation kits, several hundred boxes of survival crackers, and multiple boxes of civil defense pamphlets. There were no cots, only twelve filled water containers, and no food except survival crackers. This shelter was intended to house 2,630 people.[29] In Richmond, Virginia's governor admitted that the state's fallout system had inadequacies, but he did not attribute the problem to underfunding or poor planning. Instead, he blamed the citizens' fatalistic attitude toward nuclear war.[30] In New York, the police department asked all able-bodied men to join civil defense efforts.[31] The *Washington Star* published a list of 1,083 approved District of Columbia shelter sites, but only 100 had been licensed and could be stocked with supplies.[32]

American business executives read in *The Wall Street Journal* that mobilization during the crisis could bolster the nation's economy and delay a recession. Sales received a boost from military and civilian spending for the possibility of war. Economists also expected some inventory stockpiling. Even better, a Soviet retreat could increase optimism and buoy American business.[33]

While many Americans remained glued to transistor radios and television sets to keep up with the latest news, some found themselves strangely out of touch. After leaving Paris for New York on the *Queen Mary*, ocean liner passengers were largely cut off from the world. On this morning, they read in the ship's newspaper, the *Ocean Times*, North Atlantic Edition, about U.S. ships lying in wait for Cuban-bound Soviet freighters. Although a ship in the middle of the Atlantic Ocean would be an exceptionally safe location in nuclear war, much of the conversation aboard ship focused on the crisis.[34]

SATURDAY, OCTOBER 27

On this, the darkest day of the crisis, war seemed especially close. In both the 10 a.m. and the 4 p.m. Ex Comm meetings, American leaders struggled to grasp a peace that seemed to be slipping away. In Moscow similar scenes unfolded. While Kennedy attempted to find a way out of this morass without war, Khrushchev fretted about the possibility of losing control and watching helplessly as a conflagration began. The Soviet leader's fears were amplified by the feeling that Castro had become indifferent to the dangers of nuclear war. On his island, Castro directed the population to prepare for an invasion without realizing that his relationship with the Soviet Union had ceased to be a partnership as Khrushchev and Kennedy grappled toward a peaceful resolution.

This was the day when the crisis's first and only combat death occurred, raising difficult issues on all sides. Air Force Major Rudolf Anderson was killed when his U-2 was shot down over Cuba. Anderson, 29, departed from McCoy Air Force Base in Orlando at 8:10 a.m. on what was supposed to be a 3.5-hour reconnaissance mission over eastern Cuba. At 10 a.m., without any verbal communication or any sign of trouble, all indications of his flight terminated. More than four hours passed before the Joint Chiefs of Staff received notification that something was wrong. At 2 p.m., they knew only that Anderson's return was overdue.

Rudolf Anderson Jr. was one of two pilots who flew on the fateful October 14 U-2 mission that first captured evidence of ballistic missiles in Cuba. Born in 1927 in Spartanburg, South Carolina, Anderson graduated from Clemson Agricultural College. He worked briefly as a cost accountant before joining the Air Force. He served in the Tactical Reconnaissance Squadron in Korea from 1953 to 1955 and became a U-2 pilot in 1957.

Because Anderson had not indicated that he was under attack, Air Force officials initially thought he might have experienced a failure of his oxygen system; however, investigation revealed evidence that his U-2 had been hit by a missile fired from a base near Banes. The Ex Comm, which did not know about the plane's downing until early evening, had foreseen this possibility and had planned to order destruction of the SAM site used to strike the plane. Therefore, as soon as Air Force General Curtis LeMay received confirmation of the plane's loss, he ordered F-100 jet fighters to prepare for an air strike. The White House quickly notified him that no action should be taken. "He chickened out again," the general complained. "It will never come!"[35] Later, in a meeting of the Joint Chiefs, LeMay appeared to agree with the decision. He said that an air strike "would open ourselves to retaliation. We have little to gain and a lot to lose."[36] In the early evening, the Joint Chiefs received news of pilot debriefings for that day: All but two of the low-altitude planes had reported Cuban anti-aircraft weapons fired upon them. Having escaped the first shots, all of the pilots ascended to higher altitudes and avoided destruction. By evening, intercepted information revealed that Cubans had recovered wreckage of Anderson's plane and his body.[37]

Khrushchev, Kennedy, and Castro were equally ignorant about who was responsible for the U-2's downing. Initially, both Soviets and Americans suspected that overly aggressive Cubans had downed the U-2. In fact, Khrushchev accused Castro of attacking the plane, and Castro did not deny it.[38] However, that conclusion was implausible: Castro had given an order for his men to take action against low-level reconnaissance planes, but only a SAM, supposedly under the control of Soviet troops, could have reached the high-flying U-2. The fact that some Russian troops were wearing Cuban uniforms only added to confusion. With the prospect of nuclear war, Kennedy's team felt an unexpected hesitancy to retaliate. In the Soviet Union, the U-2's destruction baffled Khrushchev because he had ordered the Soviet military to avoid direct military conflict.

Once the U-2 had crashed, it is hard to say which side was more alarmed. Both American and Soviet leaders saw it as a potential trigger for war. Despite difficulty assigning blame, Malinovsky seemed sure that his own men were responsible. He sent a telegram to Soviet forces in Cuba asserting that they had made a grave mistake.[39] Decades later, it became clear that Soviet Generals Leonid Garbuz and Stepan Grechko had ordered the attack after unsuccessfully trying to locate Pliyev and get authorization from him.[40]

Four American airmen also died in an accident on this date. When they took off in an RB-47 low-level reconnaissance plane from a runway in Bermuda, the plane failed to gain sufficient altitude. As the pilot struggled for control, a wing struck a cliff, and the plane exploded. Maintenance men unfamiliar with this type of aircraft had serviced it with the wrong kind of water-alcohol injection fluid.[41] The opportunities for accidents were perhaps at an all-time high for the American armed forces: Dispersal of planes had sent many pilots to unfamiliar airports; the number of nuclear weapons on planes had reached an unprecedented high; and the elevated alert status meant that strict adherence to procedures sometimes was sacrificed to accelerate operations. More American bombers, missiles, and warheads were on alert on this day than on any other day in history. Approximately 12 percent of the B-52 heavy bomber force was in the air at all times.[42] In preparation for a possible invasion, there were about 850 military aircraft in Florida, and the number of military personnel in the state reached almost a million.[43]

There were dangers at sea as well. Going beyond Ex Comm guidelines, the United States military was pushing relentlessly to make Soviet submarines surface. As long as the subs remained submerged, they seemed especially ominous, like famished sharks waiting to strike without warning. The arrival of these subs so close to the United States created problems for both the American and the Soviet military. Their proximity to the

United States raised new fears of attack among American military leaders who saw them as a hidden yet vital threat to the nation.[44] At the same time, Soviet crews were miserable as they worked in warm temperatures on boats with no air conditioning or equipment to cool the batteries. The USSR's submarines typically remained in the Arctic Ocean close to their home bases, and logically, they were built to function in frigid conditions rather than warmer waters. Staying underwater too long could drain batteries and threaten the crews' survival. As nervous Americans sought to reduce the danger posed by unseen submarines, tempers became short among the subs' crews, who were subjected to annoying, repetitive assaults by U.S. anti-submarine weapons while sweltering in temperatures above 100 degrees. One Soviet captain, Valentin Savitsky, reportedly threatened to fire his nuclear torpedo rather than surrender to American harassment, but cooler heads prevailed.[45]

On the quarantine line, U.S. ships prepared to confront a Soviet tanker that had failed to stop before reaching the established boundary. Several destroyers loaded their big guns and prepared to attack the *Grozny* as they awaited clearance from superiors. The only order they received was to clear their guns—an event occurring sufficiently close to the *Grozny* that its captain reversed course, crossed outside the quarantined area, and lay dead in the water.[46]

In Cuba, five of the six medium-range missile sites had been completed. Despite the appearance of readiness in U-2 photos, only half of the thirty-six missiles were prepared for the eighteen-hour fueling process, and none had been programmed for flight or armed with warheads.[47] Pliyev notified Moscow that the Cubans expected an attack, possibly as early as today.[48] American reconnaissance flights confirmed that Soviet Lunas were in Cuba, but because the weapons could be armed with either conventional or nuclear charges, the American military could not be sure whether they represented a nuclear threat. The American equivalent—the Honest John—was expected to be used in a Cuban invasion, but McNamara refused to authorize use of nuclear warheads.[49]

Planning for an American air strike and invasion continued, with action expected within seventy-two hours. Planners had narrowed the list of potential targets to the Soviet missile sites, air bases, and antiaircraft installations. To bolster the operation, the Pentagon called up twenty-four trooper carrier reserve squadrons and supporting reserve units, totaling around 14,000 men. Privately, McNamara said he saw an invasion of Cuba as "almost inevitable" at that point.[50] The government had printed five million pamphlets warning Cuban civilians to take cover. At Rusk's request, Scali met with Feklisov again, and he stressed the White House's sense that reaching a resolution was urgent.[51]

Tensions ran high at the Kremlin. The previous day's letter from Castro weighed heavily on Khrushchev, who feared that the Cuban leader was advocating a reckless pre-emptive nuclear strike that could expand into full-scale nuclear war. A distraught Castro had visited the Soviet embassy in Havana on Friday night and remained there until 5 a.m. on this day. Castro worried Khrushchev. The troubled Soviet leader's anxiety may have been exacerbated by knowledge that, for the first time, U.S. Air Force Quick Response Alert planes in Europe were preparing to carry nuclear weapons.[52]

Eager to add momentum to the push for peace and to draw more chips onto his side of the bargaining table, Khrushchev released a public offer, but to the Ex Comm, this particular olive branch was unwelcome. In addition to seeking a U.S. promise not to invade Cuba, Khrushchev added a plea for the United States to remove missiles from Turkey. By winning an additional American concession, Soviet leaders hoped to strengthen their international standing.[53] And by releasing this letter to the press, Khrushchev probably expected that Kennedy would feel international pressure to make the missile swap. The missiles in Turkey were not strategically meaningful to U.S. or NATO defenses because the rapid development of missile technology had transformed the Jupiters into virtual antiques. Moreover, assigning Polaris submarines to those areas could offer greater protection. Nevertheless, the idea of removing missiles generated misgivings among American allies. Those missiles had value that was more symbolic than military. In a Cold War that often occurred more in psychological space than in the real world, symbolism was important. Years later, McNamara remembered JFK's feelings on this topic: "I recall him saying very well, 'I am not going to go to war over worthless missiles in Turkey.'"[54]

The different tones and demands of the two consecutive Khrushchev letters baffled the Ex Comm. Khrushchev's request for a Turkey–Cuba swap generated significant discussion among American leaders. Hilsman predicted that U.S. allies would be stunned by such a trade and might see it as an American move to distance the United States from its obligations to European allies. He anticipated a sense of abandonment in Turkey.[55] Anatoly Dobrynin later conjectured that Khrushchev wrote the first while in the throes of deep distress about an impending U.S. attack and did not want to muddy the waters by raising the Turkey issue; however, as the hours passed and as he felt growing pressure from hardliners to take a tougher stand, he decided to write the second message.[56] Among those most alarmed by the idea of making concessions to Khrushchev was Johnson. He warned against making a deal with the devil, as he saw it: "All I know is that when you were walking along a Texas road and a rattlesnake rose up ready to strike, there was only one thing to do—take a long stick and knock its head off."[57] However, Johnson argued that the United States would be doing Turkey a favor by swapping Polaris submarines for outdated Jupiter missiles.[58]

After brainstorming with the Ex Comm, Kennedy chose to answer the previous night's more conciliatory message from Khrushchev and to ignore the push for action in Turkey. Kennedy's response to Khrushchev began optimistically: "I have read your letter of October 26th with great care and welcomed the statement of your desire to seek a prompt solution to the problem. The first thing that needs to be done, however, is for work to cease on offensive missile bases in Cuba and for all weapons systems in Cuba capable of offensive use to be rendered inoperable, under effective United Nations arrangements." In his letter, Kennedy offered to end the quarantine and "to give assurances against an invasion of Cuba."[59]

As Americans debated strategy, Cuba's government prepared for full-scale war, with expectations of more than 100,000 casualties.[60] Hospitals rejected cases except true emergencies so that beds would be available for battle casualties. To prepare for American air strikes, officials advised civilians to amass buckets of sand to extinguish house fires. Cubans also were directed to avoid meeting in groups, to store food for only two to three days because hoarding would create unnecessary shortages, and to keep small pieces of wood handy to be placed between one's teeth during an air raid.[61]

Castro was totally uninvolved in the diplomatic back-and-forth between Kennedy and Khrushchev, and he had no chance to present his case to Khrushchev, who later described him as a "young and hotheaded man."[62] Castro never even knew exactly what Soviet weapons had been placed on his island.[63] Decades later, he remained angry about his exclusion from the decision-making process. "Judging by the letter Nikita sent me on the 23rd," Castro said, "I didn't see the slightest indication that he would solve the problem simply by caving in to American demands."[64]

As skittish Soviet radar operators watched the skies for signs of an American attack, they were surprised to see an American plane entering Soviet airspace. The plane, a U-2 taking air samples to measure radioactive fallout from Soviet weapons tests, had drifted off course and quickly became a target for Soviet fighters. The American pilot, realizing his error, radioed a distress call on an open channel and started toward Alaska. MiG fighters broke off their pursuit as the plane left Soviet air space. When the U.S. military realized what had happened, American fighter planes from Alaska were quickly mobilized to meet the U-2, piloted by Captain Charles Maultsby. An individual, outside the control of his commander-in-chief, had committed an error that could have become a catalyst for war.

Fidel Castro Biography

Fidel Castro, the illegitimate son of a wealthy sugar plantation owner and one of his maids, was officially accepted by his father when he was a teenager. That acknowledgment enabled him to share in the benefits of wealth. He attended a private Jesuit boarding school and received a college degree from El Colegio de Belén, where he pitched for the baseball team. He studied law at the University of Havana, beginning in 1945, and during that period he became involved in the Caribbean Legion, a regional political group that aimed to oust all political dictators from Latin America. He traveled to the Dominican Republic in 1947 and participated in a failed attempt to topple the right-wing dictator Rafael Trujillo. The following year, while visiting Colombia with fellow students, he took part in left-wing rioting.

Castro practiced law for a few years in Havana, but in 1953 he decided to take military action against Cuban President Fulgencio Batista, a right-wing leader backed by the United States. Batista had come into power in a 1952 coup, and during his tenure Havana served as an amusement park for rich Westerners, while many Cubans suffered in abject poverty. Castro led 165 rebels who made a failed attack on the Moncada Barracks on July 26, 1953. Facing defeat, Castro and others escaped and took refuge in the mountains. Some of their captured comrades were executed. Later, he and other escapees were arrested. Castro received a fifteen-year sentence; however, he served only nineteen months, including some time in solitary confinement.

When he was released in 1955 under an amnesty deal, Castro soon found himself in the midst of a government crackdown on opposition activity. His compatriots began guarding him against assassination attempts, and he eventually left Cuba. He and his brother Raul went to Mexico, where they met other displaced leftists, including Argentinian revolutionary and doctor Che Guevara.

Castro knew that if he wanted to return to Cuba and overthrow Batista, he would need money, so he toured the United States trying to attract donations from sympathetic Americans. In December 1956 he and eighty-one other revolutionaries secretly sailed to Cuba. After reaching the island, they set up camp in Cuba's Sierra Maestra mountain range and recruited other fighters. Batista eventually sent 10,000 soldiers into the mountains to find Castro and his 300-man army. Calling his organization the 26th of July Movement, Castro began an armed campaign against Batista's forces and successfully seized control of some of the island's regions. After years of battling the insurgents, Batista followed advice from the United States and fled the island. A triumphant Castro marched into Havana on January 9, 1959. Initially, he was military commander-in-chief, while Jose Miro Cardona was prime minister. After a few months, Cardona resigned, and Castro assumed the prime minister's duties.

He immediately confiscated property belonging to Batista and his allies. He nationalized the telephone company and redistributed land to the peasant caste. This included land owned by the Castro family and property held by Americans.

Then, he successfully enacted a new law that made foreign ownership of Cuban land illegal. He urged young people to go into the countryside and teach fellow citizens how to read. He also attempted to spread medical care throughout the nation and set up three new schools to educate doctors. In 1960, he seized U.S. assets worth more than $1 billion.

While the U.S. government was unhappy with Castro's decisions to nationalize property held by Americans, many people in the United States were initially unsure about whether Castro was a Communist or just a big-hearted revolutionary. Immediately after claiming power, he denied being a Communist, but in 1960 his friendship with the Soviet Union became public, triggering the Eisenhower administration's plans to overthrow Castro in what would later evolve into the Bay of Pigs fiasco. This operation, in turn, stimulated Cuban and Soviet fears about a U.S. invasion and contributed to Khrushchev's decision to place nuclear weapons in Cuba, sparking the Cuban Missile Crisis. At that episode's end, Castro was devastated by his exclusion from negotiations about removing the missiles from Cuba, but he continued to rule Cuba decades after the deaths of Kennedy and Khrushchev. The collapse of the Soviet Union in 1991 damaged Cuba's economy, especially because the United States steadfastly refused to lift its trade embargo against Cuba, but Castro's regime survived in a nation riddled with poverty. His health began to decline in the 1990s. At the age of 81, he gave up leadership in 2008 and was succeeded by his 76-year-old brother Raul.

Outside the White House, about 500 protesters marched. Some considered Kennedy's blockade reckless, while others condemned his failure to launch a massive military assault against Cuba. Police arrested three dissenters for disorderly conduct. About 2,000 people attended San Francisco rallies at opposite ends of Civic Center Plaza. Roughly 75 percent opposed the blockade; the rest sought more aggressive action against Communist forces.[65]

On this day, Robert Kennedy received an eight-page report from FBI Director J. Edgar Hoover on his agency's monitoring of the Communist Party, peace advocates, and Cuban troublemakers. In a document that remains partially classified fifty years later, he described an alleged plot by a Cuban to blow up a Philadelphia oil refinery with a pipe bomb. He also quoted a California Communist Party leader as saying that the government planned to establish concentration camps to imprison 250,000 people, many of them Communist Party members.[66]

Speaking before the National Civil Defense Readiness Commission of the National Governor's Conference, Pittman claimed the civil defense program was ready for war, although there were not enough shelters, and very few had been stocked with necessary supplies. "The reaction of the

American people to the current international tension shows that as a nation we are prepared to face up to and meet the recurring threats we live with," he proclaimed.[67] Pittman announced a temporary and significant lowering of the fallout protection level necessary for a building to qualify as a public shelter.

After the second Ex Comm meeting of the day, Kennedy met with a smaller group, including Rusk, Bundy, and Robert Kennedy. From a myriad of options on the crisis's first day, the list now appeared to be limited to two: negotiation or invasion. JFK decided to send his brother

The Future of Civil Defense

Planning for nuclear war continued after the crisis. The Office of Emergency Planning reported to Kennedy in late 1962 that an Office of Rationing should be established before any crisis that might lead to nuclear war. It was impossible, the memorandum reported, to jump into a rationing situation without a full accounting of non-perishable foods and petroleum.[68]

In a post-crisis civil defense report, Steuart Pittman claimed that he had identified shelter space for more than 100 million Americans, although most of that space was not adequately prepared to house people in a nuclear war. His report was optimistic about being able to shelter the American public, but illusory civil defense propaganda gradually faded from public view.[69] In Pittman's view Americans were not capable of ordering their thoughts

> to consider the importance to national recovery of the difference between over half of the population surviving and one-quarter surviving. . . . We have gone overboard in exaggerating the concept of total destruction in order to persuade ourselves and our adversaries and our allies that nuclear war is impossible.[70]

Many Americans did not want to be nuclear war survivors, and as a result interest in civil defense declined. An April 1963 survey in eight cities showed that 64 percent of respondents believed living in a fallout shelter for a long period of time would drive occupants insane.[71] A drop in civil defense interest is apparent in press coverage. In 1961 the New York Times published more than 350 news items on the topic. That number dropped dramatically to seventy in 1963, twenty in 1966, and only four in 1969. The Readers' Guide to Periodical Literature shows a similar decline in interest as evidenced by the number of magazine articles on civil defense over the course of the 1960s.[72] A July 1964 report on public opinion related to civil defense found that 58 percent of Americans believed that "nuclear war would mean the end of civilization as we know it."[73]

to offer Dobrynin a deal—part of which would be public, while the rest would remain secret for decades. Robert Kennedy told Dobrynin that JFK would make a public promise not to invade Cuba and offer his private assurances that he would remove missiles from Turkey and Italy within a few months if Khrushchev agreed to remove all Soviet offensive weapons from Cuba. Robert Kennedy's version of these events, published as *Thirteen Days* after his 1968 assassination, portrays the U.S. position as tough and uncompromising, and Sorensen, who edited the book after the second Kennedy assassination, deleted any mention of the secret agreement to remove U.S. missiles from Turkey and Italy to protect the Kennedy myth. This version of events is at odds with Dobrynin's recollections, which reflect high anxieties on both sides and a strong desire to reach an agreement that would be palatable to the American public and to military leaders in Moscow and Washington. In Dobrynin's memory, Robert Kennedy expressed serious concerns about Soviet retaliation in Europe if the United States aggressively attacked Cuba, and he told Dobrynin that the military brass in the United States was exerting considerable pressure on JFK for quick, decisive action. From the attorney general's mood, Dobrynin recalled feeling that JFK might face a military coup if he did not move swiftly.[74]

President Kennedy took one additional step to bring a quick end to the crisis. In case the Soviets rejected the deal offered to Dobrynin, Kennedy asked Rusk to contact Andrew Cordier, a Columbia University professor and deputy UN secretary general. Rusk urged Cordier to convince U Thant to take specific steps to resolve the crisis peacefully. What Kennedy wanted was a United Nations request that the United States withdraw its missiles from Turkey in exchange for the Soviet Union eliminating its nuclear force in Cuba. Kennedy would have encountered political opposition for publicly making such a swap, but this was his last-ditch effort to guarantee that war would be averted and that the missiles would be withdrawn.

As McNamara left the White House at the close of this grim day, his senses beheld a beautiful fall evening. Perhaps, he thought, "I might never live to see another Saturday night." Donald M. Wilson, deputy director of the United States Information Agency, recalled "on Friday and Saturday nights at home I literally wondered whether I'd come home the next night."[75] In the 1990s, after the Soviet Union had fallen, making it possible for surviving Missile Crisis leaders in all three nations to meet and compare experiences, McNamara received a greater understanding of the dangers stalking the world on that night and realized that "I was understating the danger, rather than exaggerating it."[76] American military leaders who were planning an invasion were not ready for the more than 40,000 Soviet troops in Cuba, their tactical nuclear weapons, and the evolving sense among Cubans and Soviets on the island that war had already begun.

SUNDAY, OCTOBER 28

In the Soviet Union, leaders awoke to the same sense of foreboding that shrouded American policymakers. According to erroneous reports in Moscow, Kennedy planned a public address today, and Kremlin leaders feared a declaration of war.[77] Just in case the United States attacked, the Presidium decided to give Pliyev the authority to use force to defend Cuba, an order that might have led to use of tactical nuclear weapons.[78] Then, news of Dobrynin's meeting with Robert Kennedy reached the Kremlin. It indicated general agreement on the terms for peace and great urgency in ending the crisis immediately—before it was too late. Khrushchev quickly finalized a letter to Kennedy. According to Vladimir Malin's Presidium notes, Khrushchev had made the decision to withdraw the missiles and had prepared a message announcing their removal before hearing that Kennedy would make a deal on the missiles in Turkey.[79]

Malinovsky ordered Pliyev to begin dismantling the missile sites early in the morning. Pliyev was told unequivocally to "obey no orders to launch and under no cir-cumstances install the warheads."[80] That order suggests that Khrush-chev feared that he no longer had firm control of the military. Soon, Khrushchev's conciliatory message traveled via radio around the world, lifting the darkness to reveal a hopeful day.[81]

His message to Kennedy accepted the American president's publicly stated terms for removal of the missiles:

Although this was the Space Age, Khrushchev's messages began their travels to other countries by riding in the satchel of a Western Union bicycle messenger. The cable was then typed and transmitted, and when it reached the United States translators had to convert it to English before the president could read it. This delivery method was slow and unreliable. That is why he chose to make a public announcement on October 28 rather than sending Kennedy a telegram and taking a chance that some action might occur while the letter was in transit.

> In order to eliminate as rapidly as possible the conflict which endangers the cause of peace, to give an assurance to all people who crave peace, and to reassure the American people, who, I am certain, also want peace, as do the people of the Soviet Union, the Soviet Government, in addition to earlier instructions

> on the discontinuation of further work on weapons construction
> sites, has given a new order to dismantle the arms which you
> described as offensive and to crate and return them to the
> Soviet Union.[82]

To the world, it appeared that Khrushchev had won only one concession in return for his capitulation, a U.S. promise not to invade Cuba. In reality, that concession was not as large as the Soviets believed because the Kennedy administration had no plans to make such an attack. Furthermore, Khrushchev had received a clandestine concession from Kennedy, a commitment to remove missiles from Turkey and Italy—a secret so well hidden that even some members of the Ex Comm were unaware of it.

Hilsman made an analysis of Khrushchev's message and noted "great Soviet concern over the danger of war."[83] Khrushchev was relieved to end the crisis but unhappy that his gamble in Cuba had not paid off as expected. Still, one of his originally stated motives for placing the missiles in Cuba had been to protect the island from American invasion, and he had achieved that without ordering that a single shot be fired. His apparent surrender weakened his standing in the Soviet Union and the world, and as a result his unwavering silence about Kennedy's covert commitment is all the more striking.

Once the news had arrived from Moscow, Kennedy swiftly replied. "I welcome this message and consider it an important contribution to peace," he declared in a message broadcast immediately. He also expressed regrets about Maultsby's inadvertent violation of Soviet airspace.[84] In a public statement, Kennedy called Khrushchev's decision "statesmanlike," and characterized his actions as an "important and constructive contribution to peace."[85]

Across the United States, public reactions to the apparent end of the crisis ranged from delight to skepticism. In Key West, congregations found their numbers inflated by servicemen. At the Holy Innocent Episcopal Church, congregants knelt on the church's lawn under bright sunshine to offer thanks. On this day, Rostow wrote that "we shall emerge from this crisis with American prestige and influence in the world at its highest point since the latter months of 1944."[86]

Rep. Howard W. Smith of Broad Run, Virginia, was less certain about the settlement. "We must remember that dealing with Khrushchev is like negotiating with a rattlesnake," he warned.[87] Democrat Hale Boggs, the House majority whip, argued that Kennedy "has shown courage and unflinching determination throughout this week of tension and crisis . . . . I would also think that charges relative to my party being soft on

Communism now have a very hollow ring indeed." Republicans sought to benefit from the glow of success that now bathed Kennedy's White House. "The Republicans, in my judgment, by their firm attitude of immediate action helped greatly in fixing the climate of readiness for action in Cuba," said GOP Senator Hugh Scott of Pennsylvania.[88]

Despite the exchange of promises between the United States and the Soviet Union, thousands of pacifists flooded New York's streets in the city's largest peace demonstration to date. While pleased with the crisis's apparent conclusion, peace advocates remained concerned about the circumstances that had caused it. They sought a greater dialogue between the United States and the Soviet Union—a dialogue marked by less posturing and more communication.

As part of ongoing war preparations begun earlier in the week, Bundy issued National Security Action Memorandum 200 on acceleration of civil defense preparations. It recommended special attention to the region within striking distance of medium-range missiles in Cuba. Under Kennedy's orders, action was limited to steps that could be taken without arousing public alarm. The order further authorized discreet contacts with state and local governments in areas that might be susceptible to attacks from Cuba using conventional weapons.[89]

Despite the welcome blanket of relief that enwrapped much of the world, both Soviet and American military forces remained at the ready in case the agreement collapsed. The American Joint Chiefs of Staff ordered ships to stay in place on the quarantine line but discouraged any contact with Soviet ships. The Air Force reservists still had to report for duty. Even after a tentative agreement had been reached, preparations for a possible invasion marched onward. By now, the plan called for something akin to the D-Day landings in World War II, with eight divisions, including 120,000 soldiers, storming a forty-mile stretch of beaches.[90] Military hospitals continued preparations to handle an influx of casualties from the shores of Cuba, while sailors made aircraft carriers ready to launch fighters as part of the invasion force. When the Joint Chiefs met with Kennedy that afternoon, they voiced skepticism about Khrushchev's promise and about Kennedy's wisdom in vowing not to invade Cuba. Anderson declared, "We have been had!" And LeMay asked, "Why don't we go in and make a strike on Monday anyway?"[91]

To at least one government on Earth, the peace agreement represented bad news. Khrushchev's unilateral decision to remove the missiles stunned Castro and his followers. Hours after the release of Khrushchev's letter, Castro received a coded message from Moscow. In it, Khrushchev urged Castro to "show patience, self-control, and still more self-control."[92] The Cubans had expected an American invasion and declared themselves ready for it. They had not anticipated that Khrushchev would relinquish the missiles to avoid war. Although Castro freely expressed his anger thirty years later, he initially responded by saying, "Cuba will not lose anything by the removal of the missiles, because she has already gained so much." He argued that international attention to Cuba had increased awareness of his nation's plight as a prime enemy of the United States.[93] The Cuban leadership produced its own list of demands: cessation of the economic blockade and all trade boycotts by the United States, American abandonment of its program of covert activities against Cuba, an end to "pirate attacks" by U.S. ships, an American pledge to end violations of Cuban waters and Cuban airspace, and removal of the U.S. base at Guantanamo.[94] None of these demands received serious consideration. An American intelligence report hypothesized that "Castro probably feels that he has been sold out."[95]

Even as peace was assured, the closeness of war still lingered in the air. On this morning, American radar operators in Moorestown, New Jersey, wrongly reported the launch of a missile from Cuba.[96] By the time the North American Air Defense Command in Colorado Springs received word of the anticipated missile impact near Tampa, the missile already would have detonated and caused massive devastation. Yet, the Bomb Alarm System, a nationwide system of sensors placed on telephone poles, indicated that Tampa had not suffered a nuclear explosion.[97] Later, officials discovered that a test tape had been running on the newly re-directed radar system in Moorestown.

The crisis's many "what ifs" and near-misses tainted daily life on the planet Earth. The panic and trepidation would fade, but something had been lost in the raw moments when nuclear war seemed so near. Untethered from the security of mundane life, people around the world had confronted the prospect of unimaginable loss.

CONCLUSION

The Cuban Missile Crisis was, in many ways, a wake-up call for modern man. Militarily, it opened the way to a path strewn with catastrophic possibilities just waiting to be manipulated by flawed human beings—either by accident or by over-zealous leadership. For Americans, it carried a particularly strong shock value. Many residents of the Soviet Union had clear memories of the World War II fight to regain control of their homeland and defeat Nazi Germany. However, for the United States, the prospect of war on native soil was startling and almost unthinkable. No war had been fought in the United States since the Civil War 100 years earlier. "America for the first time felt the breath of war at its door. War knocked at the door of every American," said Georgi Bolshakov.[98] Khrushchev himself later wrote:

> In our estimation, the Americans were trying to frighten us, but they were no less scared than we were of atomic war. We hadn't had time to deliver all our shipments to Cuba, but we had installed enough missiles already to destroy New York, Chicago, and the other huge industrial cities, not to mention a little village like Washington. I don't think America had ever faced such a real threat of destruction as at that moment.[99]

Recognizing its inability to control certain things, such as the missiles in Cuba, the Kennedy administration tried to plan for every foreseeable contingency within its grasp. While the United States had extra bombers in the air with Soviet targets already set, the Soviet Union took few steps to prepare for general war beyond placing troops and missiles on alert. Despite the CIA director's repeated reports on this topic to the Ex Comm, the Soviets' decision not to move troops and weaponry in anticipation of war had no apparent effect on American efforts to put the military just one step short of a war footing. Kennedy's crisis management has won accolades, especially in the years immediately following the crisis, and from fifty years' distance his administration's penchant for planning is both amazing and a bit scary. The United States seemed compelled to plan for every possibility and to make military preparations to carry out each option, even if those actions had the potential to alarm Soviet leaders. All of the United States' planning may have offered a slight sense of security, but it heightened the dangers of accidental war and made Soviet leaders more open to the idea that the United States was ready for war.

Within the United States, the crisis also opened the public's eyes to the false promises of the nation's civil defense program. There were not enough shelters, not enough supplies, and not enough protection from the horrors of nuclear war. Public interest had never been intense, and in fact some cities and towns learned during the crisis that civil defense directors had resigned months or years before the crisis and no one had noticed.[100] Like Santa Claus, civil defense was a nice idea but not an answer to the world's problems. After a flurry of activity during the crisis, civil defense quietly fell off the nation's agenda. A 1964 Hudson Institute study performed for the Office of Emergency Planning found that the American population "[endorses] the belief that war is not an inconceivable possibility, supports the idea of shelter or other civil defense programs as a form of protection, but is little inclined to do anything about it."[101]

The crisis had made it clear that there was nowhere to hide from nuclear war. Like flight attendants' warnings about what to do in the event of a plane crash, civil defense lectures were often ignored by people who wanted to avoid thinking about the underlying threat that came packaged with the helpful advice. If less thoughtful leaders had been in command, the results of Khrushchev's gamble and Kennedy's dare could have been catastrophic. Fortunately, both men recognized their power and knew that all of their planning and care could have been undone by a single stray plane or weapon fired without authorization. They showed courage in their willingness to make peace—not popularity—their highest priority.

CHAPTER 6

Moving Ahead, Looking Back

THE IMMEDIATE AFTERMATH

In the Cold War, superpower crises carried added significance because they threatened not just war, but national devastation. Confrontations between superpowers were no longer challenges to be resolved through the power of might: With advancements in the development of nuclear weapons, they became puzzles to be deciphered while enduring the sound of a loudly ticking clock. The Cuban Missile Crisis was the best example of that development. At its conclusion, virtually the whole world shared a sense of relief. Though the immediate credit went to John F. Kennedy, history has proven that Nikita Khrushchev owns a solid share of that victory because both men chose caution as a means of making the crisis gravitate toward peace instead of spiraling out of control and into war. Seeing that the crisis was becoming self-propelled and no longer thoroughly under their command, Khrushchev and Kennedy helped each other find a way to end it and regain control of the machinery of war.

In the words of historian Robert A. Pollard in 1982, "the experience was sufficiently sobering so that Soviet and American leaders have never since engaged in anything akin to nuclear brinkmanship."[1] Arthur G. Neal has written:

> A serious crisis of meaning surfaces when we can no longer make assumptions about the continuity of social life as it is known and understood. Such was the case with the trauma of the Cuban Missile Crisis. For a few days in October 1962 there was a disturbing possibility that human life on this planet would be extinguished within a matter of days. There had been no previous episode in the history of the world in which the stakes were so

high and the fate of the world in so few hands. . . . The crisis
intruded into everyday consciousness and temporarily brought
into focus unthinkable prospects. . . . The continuity of social life
from one generation to the next seemed doubtful. The desire for
peace and tranquility came to be temporarily juxtaposed against
the possibility of annihilation.[2]

More than a year after the crisis's resolution, as he prepared for his
first state of the union address, Lyndon Johnson spoke to his staff about
the crisis and said, "I want to tell you that one of the deepest things in
me is the memory of going to bed at night and not knowing whether
there was going to be a nuclear war or not."[3]

Thirty years later, Robert McNamara said on a broadcast anchored
by JFK's niece, Maria Shriver, that "the indefinite combination of human
fallibility and nuclear weapons carries with it the certainty of nuclear
exchange."[4] The often-blinding dogmas of anti-Communism on the
American side and anti-imperialism in the USSR lowered the odds of
avoiding a nuclear disaster. The familiar dogma created a comfortable
feeling of moral superiority that blurred recognition of commonalities
between the two nations and limited each side's capacity for empathy.

While many Americans—and many members of the Ex Comm—
never saw a parallel between U.S. missiles in Turkey and Soviet missiles
in Cuba, it is to Kennedy's credit that he could distance himself enough
from anti-Communist rhetoric to see that the differences between the two
situations were quite small. Khrushchev, too, refused to blindly accept
stereotypes that cast JFK as nothing more than a rabid, acquisitive
imperialist. Each saw his adversary as a human being and tried to imagine
the pressures guiding the other's decisions.

Although the rough outlines of a resolution had been determined on
October 28, 1962, weeks of negotiations followed before either side could
be sure that the world's future was out of danger. Many of these days
were rocky. On October 29, U.S. military sources believed that aerial
reconnaissance showed continued construction at the missile sites; however,
in the coming days, it became apparent that workers were dismantling
them.

Initially, the Soviet Union's leaders sought to solidify the privately
made U.S. offer to remove missiles from Turkey and Italy. A private letter
from Khrushchev to JFK cited the deal, but Robert Kennedy returned
the letter to Dobrynin, telling him that there could be no official *quid pro
quo*. Both Dobrynin and Khrushchev accepted Kennedy's need for secrecy
and neither man attempted to make that part of the agreement public.
Raymond Garthoff has asserted that according to reliable sources, the Soviet

Children and the Missile Crisis

For youngsters in 1962, nuclear war was not a distant concept. Schools across the country had been running nuclear war drills of various types for more than a decade. In 1950, target cities like Los Angeles, New York, Chicago, Detroit, and Milwaukee began duck-and-cover drills that required students to seek shelter under their desks.[5] Elsewhere around the country, practice for nuclear war took different forms: Some children took shelter in school basements or hallways; others raced home from school to see whether they could make it in the fifteen minutes of warning time expected if an attack came from the Soviet Union.

The prospect of nuclear war intruded in the lives of the nation's youngest citizens on a daily basis. TV and radio stations routinely tested the emergency broadcasting system during hours when young people would be in the audience. Moreover, science fiction TV programs and films of this period envisioned a post-apocalyptic world. Children not only were familiar with the possibility of nuclear war: They could not escape reminders of what science had wrought and its potential effects on their lives.

There are verbal snapshots of children's reactions to the ongoing international tensions during the crisis period. In Atlanta, a fifth-grade girl passed a note to a boy asking whether he was afraid. When he replied that he was not, she told him, "I am."[6] A girl in Massachusetts wrote to a friend and asked: "Can you imagine not seeing another Christmas, Thanksgiving, Easter, birthday, dance or even Halloween? . . . We're just too young to die."[7]

At one Los Angeles elementary school, a telephone line problem led school officials to believe that war was at hand. Two days after Khrushchev's agreement to withdraw the missiles but long before the fear of war had faded, tearful children were rousted from their classrooms at Miraleste Elementary School. Teachers escorted groups of youngsters on foot to their homes. In an era when many middle- and upper-class mothers spent their days working at home rather than in offices, stores, or factories, many school systems embraced the idea of sending children home in the event of nuclear war, presumably so that they might have the opportunity to die in their mothers' arms. Obviously, sending children home also reduced the weight of responsibility on schools and their employees. Many of the Miraleste students had reached their homes before word arrived that it had all been a false alarm. With that good news, the children returned to school. One boy, who did not live within walking distance of school, had been left with administrators and presumably would have died with them if a nuclear attack on Los Angeles had occurred.[8]

In a study done in late 1961 and early 1962, Milton Schwebel, a professor of education at New York University, found that among hundreds of junior high school students surveyed in three different regions of the country, almost half thought war was likely to break out in the near future.[9] Jiri Nehnevajsa and Morris I. Berkowitz conducted interviews with Pittsburgh-area high school and college students during the Cuban Missile Crisis. When asked to rate the level of international anxiety on a scale of one to ten, the typical student in that study rated global tension between nine and ten. Among the high school students questioned, most thought that war was the crisis's most likely outcome. The majority of participants characterized civil defense programs as weak or non-existent.[10] This generation of children would provide the core of the anti-war movement that rose in opposition to the Vietnam War in the late 1960s and early 1970s.

Union was even prepared to accept a U.S. invasion of Cuba rather than risk nuclear war.[11]

Apparently, the events of October 27 convinced both sides that the time for brinkmanship had ended. In that single day, a stray American U-2 mistakenly flew into Soviet air space, Soviet missiles shot down a U-2 over Cuba without proper authorization, and war jitters flourished in Havana and Washington. Both sides needed to resolve the crisis quickly. "The Chinese say I was scared." Khrushchev later commented:

> Of course I was scared. It would have been insane not to have been scared. I was frightened about what could happen to my country—or your country and all the other countries that would be devastated by a nuclear war. If being frightened meant that I helped avert such insanity, then I'm glad I was frightened.[12]

After the crisis, both superpowers carefully considered steps to prevent accidental war. The Soviet Union's alliance with an apparently trigger-happy Castro led to tightening control over its weapons. Later, when the USSR placed nuclear weapons in other Warsaw Pact nations, there was no debate about who could act to launch the weapons: That responsibility always resided in the Soviet Union. Its Eastern European allies could serve as bases for weapons and as storage spaces for warheads, but these nations had no ability to use weapons because they were strictly maintained under Soviet control.

In the crisis's wake, public and private attitudes realigned. CBS newsman David Shoenbrun reported,

> A once-favored theory that war was unthinkable in the thermonuclear age has just about been atomized, for a lot of people have been thinking about war in these past few weeks and been preparing for it. As the president has been saying, we came right up to the brink and looked down into the abyss. And

now this is a grim fact of sudden death that we must live with. This has given new impetus for another attempt at some real step toward disarmament and any other measures to keep the world well back from the brink of that abyss. This is perhaps the greatest moral single lesson of this crisis, according to Washington.[13]

Novelist Don DeLillo, whose *Libra* explores JFK's assassination, called the missile crisis "the purest existential moment in the history of mankind."[14]

As tensions between the Soviet Union and the United States began to ease, friction between the Soviet Union and Cuba became clear. Castro was irate about being uninvolved in the decision-making process. On the day after Khrushchev's announcement that he would remove the missiles from Cuba, Castro wrote to United Nations Secretary General U Thant categorizing the American promise not to invade Cuba as meaningless as long as the United States maintained economic restraints on his nation. The following day, U Thant visited Cuba, where he and eighteen advisers met with an agitated Castro as well as Russian diplomats and military leaders. The diplomatic mission failed, with Castro refusing to allow United Nations inspections to confirm that the missile sites had been eliminated. Therefore, resolution of the inspection issue required cooperation between the United States and the Soviet Union.[15]

Cuba was at a crossroads. In Khrushchev's words, "the Chinese were making a lot of noise publicly as well as in Castro's ear, 'Just remember, you can't trust the imperialists to keep any promises they make!'" Khrushchev wrote to Castro attempting to pacify him by pointing out that millions might have died if nuclear war had begun.[16] Then, he sent Mikoyan to meet with the Cuban leader on November 2. The talks did not go well. After hearing his envoy's report, the Soviet leader again wrote to Castro, arguing that he should be satisfied because "the main point of the Caribbean crisis is that it has guaranteed the existence of a Socialist Cuba."[17] Khrushchev saw his letter as closing the door to the crisis, but Castro, who lived and ruled for almost half a century, never relinquished his anger and carried his wrath into a new century. In 1984 he told reporter Tad Szulc, "I never considered the withdrawal solution. Perhaps in the revolutionary fervor, passion, fever of those days, we did not consider as conceivable the removal of the missiles once they were established here."[18] He felt both betrayed and abandoned, but he was dependent on trade with the Soviet bloc to guarantee his nation's survival. Khrushchev, who wholeheartedly believed that Castro had wanted to launch a nuclear war, felt justified in distancing himself from the young revolutionary.

On November 1 the president of the United States turned his mind away from Cuba long enough to send a message to the Inter-Parliamentary Union, an international umbrella organization established in 1889 for nations with parliamentary forms of government. In it he deplored "armed aggression by Communist China" against India. He also expressed hope that the organization would be successful in ending the border conflict.[19] Three days before, Kennedy had heard from McCone that American analysts were impressed by the Chinese division of 10,000 men that had staggered an Indian force twice its size.[20] On November 5, Khrushchev pointedly stopped support for the Chinese invasion and agreed to give India material assistance.[21]

In remarks for the broadcast media November 2, Kennedy reported the findings of U.S. reconnaissance flights over Cuba: clear evidence that dismantling of the missile sites had begun. In the early days of November, U.S. reconnaissance flights verified the movement of missiles from launch sites to roads and eventually to ports. The first ship carrying missiles to the Soviet Union left Mariel on November 5, and seven additional ships carrying offensive weapons set sail from Cuba within a week of that date. Despite Castro's decision to forbid United Nations inspections of the missile sites, American planes and ships were able to track the shipments through the quarantine zone and all of the way back to ports in the Soviet Union. Under Khrushchev's orders, ship captains pulled back tarpaulin covers that might conceal their military cargo so that the U.S. military could count the number of missiles aboard.

In the weeks following the Soviet pledge to withdraw the missiles, growing concern developed among U.S. military leaders about bombers still under construction in Cuba. The Joint Chiefs learned on November 7 that at least four bombers had been assembled, and reconnaissance photos showed work under way on others.[22] The original plan, according to General Anatoli Gribkov, was for a regiment of thirty-three planes without nuclear bombs, but sources later reported that like the missiles in Turkey, which Kennedy would have been happy to give up if there had been no diplomatic ramifications, the IL-28s apparently had been disowned by the leader who controlled them. Felix Kovaliev, director of the Department of Archival Administration, reported that Khrushchev had sought to withdraw the bombers even before the crisis's end. However, when Kennedy upped the ante by calling up reservists, the Soviet Union saw new value in the IL-28s' ability to protect Cuba from invasion. In negotiations with the Soviet Union, the United States listed the planes among weapons considered to be offensive and formally requested their removal on November 2. Soviet hardliners resisted, but after much debate Kennedy announced November 20 that the Soviets would remove the planes within thirty days, and the United States would be allowed to observe the departing crates. Within the Soviet leadership, there was still fear that American military leaders might precipitate war if Kennedy failed to resolve issues involving the IL-28s and inspections—and that trepidation apparently contributed to Soviet concessions.[23] In diplomacy, appearances are a powerful factor: As Sergei Khrushchev commented, his father liked to threaten the United States with missiles he did not have; and at the crisis's conclusion, it appears that JFK won considerable mileage by allowing Soviet leaders to believe that crazed military leaders might interfere with his policies.

After resolution of these issues, Kennedy ordered an end to the quarantine. Momentarily happy to see the crisis apparently resolved, the president learned hours later about new allegations that some warheads had not been returned to the Soviet Union. This rumor was true. Small tactical warheads for the Lunas remained in Cuba. An anxious Robert Kennedy questioned Dobrynin. Once again in the dark, Dobrynin was able to argue convincingly that all warheads had been removed, and his obvious sincerity convinced the Kennedys. Worried that the peace agreement might collapse, Soviet leaders quickly withdrew the warheads.[24] One day after the quarantine ended, the USSR ended the joint military alert of Soviet and allied troops.

In the United States, Kennedy's tenacious and apparently forceful handling of the crisis drew plaudits from both political parties. JFK's presidential approval ratings, which had never been low, stood just under 60 percent before the crisis. Afterwards, 76 percent of Americans supported his work as president.[25] And the Democrats made a better-than-expected showing in the mid-term elections; however, the results were far from dramatic and could not be clearly attributed to Kennedy's success in the crisis. Typically, the party controlling the White House loses seats in Congress during off-year elections. At least in part, this is true because no one sits at the top of the ticket to provide coattails for the party's candidates. Before the crisis, GOP leaders predicted a gain of ten to twenty seats in the House, and they bragged that they might win the forty-four seats necessary to get a majority in the House. When the votes were counted on November 6, the Democrats had lost only four seats in the House, while the Republicans had gained just two.[26] In the Senate, the Democrats unexpectedly picked up four seats. The Ex Comm tapes show surprisingly little consideration of potential political effects of the crisis, but comments made by participants after the crisis have made it clear that Kennedy felt he must take a tough stand to silence his critics. However, because Republicans almost unanimously stood firmly behind the president, it is difficult to draw strong connections between the vote and Kennedy's crisis performance. In a way, Kennedy's starring role in the showdown may have created coattails, which he clearly did not have in 1960 when he barely won the White House. Redistricting, too, affected the outcome.[27]

Despite widespread backing for Kennedy's crisis policies, opponents remained vocal. Keating claimed that Cubans were hiding missiles and other equipment in caves and elsewhere on the island.[28] (Keating would remain a doubter: A year later, the New York senator proclaimed that Castro's regime had "extended its subversive activities to every corner of the hemisphere.")[29]

In the crisis's aftermath, Hoover reported to Rusk about a pro-Castro espionage operation foiled by the FBI. The plot, reportedly led by a low-level official in the Cuban mission to the United Nations, aimed to detonate bombs in prominent American locations, including the Macy's department store in Manhattan. Hoover asserted that Castro's supporters in the United States had joined in planning the attacks and acquiring the bombs.[30]

> One dramatic 1962 race pitted Kennedy's 1960 opponent, Richard Nixon, against Democratic Governor Edmund G. "Pat" Brown in the California gubernatorial race. When he lost, Nixon famously declared that his political career was over, and in what he called his "last" press conference he told reporters, whom he saw as adversaries, that they would not have Richard Nixon "to kick around anymore." As it turned out, Nixon's declaration came almost twelve years before he truly left politics by resigning his presidency in 1974 under the weight of the Watergate scandal, parts of which had been uncovered by the news media.

The United States and the USSR gradually backed away from a war footing. The Air Force reservists called to active duty in the crisis's final days returned to civilian life November 21. On the same day, Khrushchev unveiled a new foreign policy to the Presidium. His strategy would end secret military assistance to the Communist front in Laos, the Pathet Lao. This aid had continued despite pledges by the United States and the Soviet Union to keep Laos neutral. In the words of Aleksandr Fursenko and Timothy Naftali, "Khrushchev began to identify his own political future with that of Kennedy."[31] At around this time, the *New Republic* argued that the United States would be more likely than the USSR to start a nuclear war because of its dominance in the nuclear arms race. The magazine urged the United States to pledge not to make a first strike. Administration officials replied that such a promise would give a free rein to Communist aggression.[32] McNamara spoke to President Kennedy about the importance of ruling out a first strike. He believed that he had convinced JFK, although Kennedy never publicly disavowed the possibility of a first strike.[33]

In mid-December, Khrushchev dispatched two confidential messages to Kennedy. In them, he minimized the possibility of renewed trouble in Berlin and offered a new proposal for a test ban treaty. In an interview broadcast by all three major American television networks, Kennedy described a war-weariness in the United States that almost seems strange for a nation blessed with peace at home for almost a century.

> I think our people get awfully impatient and, maybe fatigued and tired and saying, 'We're been carrying this burden [of western leadership] for seventeen years. Can we lay it down, and I don't see how we're going to lay it down in this century. . . . The responsibilities placed on the United States are greater than I imagined them to be, and there are greater limitations upon our ability to bring about a favorable result than I had imagined it to be.[34]

Kennedy also described an event that had been much on his mind— all-out nuclear war involving the United States and the Soviet Union. He predicted 150 million fatalities in the first eighteen hours of conflict.[35]

When he met with the Joint Chiefs in Palm Beach, where his family was celebrating Christmas 1962, Kennedy privately expressed his continued determination to somehow oust Castro. Nevertheless, he stood by his no-invasion pledge, and Operation MONGOOSE was suspended after the crisis's resolution. A CIA document recording its demise indicates that Robert Kennedy and McNamara had pushed the program primarily to "remove the political stain left on the president by the Bay of Pigs failure."[36] That stain faded a bit when Cuba released the last of the captured invaders in December 1962 following American payments to buy their freedom. Despite Kennedy's desire to avoid another faceoff with the Soviet Union, Castro remained an irritant to him, literally until his dying day.

In early January 1963, Stevenson and the Soviet Union's First Deputy Foreign Minister V.V. Kuznetsov notified U Thant that they no longer considered it necessary to have the missile crisis on the UN Security Council's agenda. In a letter, both sides asserted that

> the governments of the United States and the Soviet Union express hope that the measures taken to avert the threat of war in connection with this crisis will lead to the settlement of other differences between them and to a general lessening of tension.[37]

In a special briefing February 6, McNamara sought to convince the American public that more than 400 reconnaissance flights over Cuba since

Figure 6.1 President Kennedy receives the flag of the Bay of Pigs invasion brigade at a Florida celebration marking the release of the last prisoners in December 1962, two months after the missile crisis. White House photo by Cecil Stoughton, John F. Kennedy Library.

July 1 had not just revealed the construction of missile sites: They had confirmed the missiles' removal.[38] At around the same time, Khrushchev told the Kennedy administration that he planned to withdraw several thousand troops from Cuba by mid-March.

The Soviet Union was facing tough economic problems that forced Khrushchev to all but abandon efforts to raise the standard of living. He reportedly considered reducing government expenses by leaving the space race; however, in March he did an about-face because he believed the competition gave his people a much-needed reason to celebrate. Interestingly, Kennedy, who had set the U.S. goal of reaching the moon before the end of the decade, increasingly saw the space program as overly expensive, given possible uses for the money on Earth. His administration first raised the idea of a joint space venture as early as 1961, and on September 20, 1963 Kennedy departed from the idea of the space competition when he spoke before the United Nations and expressed openness to a U.S.–Soviet lunar mission. Audio-tapes released in 2011 show that in 1963 he discussed the prospect of abandoning the lunar project.[39]

By the end of April the United States had removed all missiles from Turkey and Italy. Polaris submarines were expected to be in place nearby within less than a year. The number of viable weapons protecting Italians and Turks would increase when solid-fueled Polaris weapons replaced the Jupiters' obsolescent liquid-fueled arms. Spring also brought a new Khrushchev proposal on a nuclear test ban: He would accept a ban on tests in the atmosphere, in space, and underwater, making only underground tests legitimate.

Given his growing stature as a world leader, Kennedy decided the time had come for a speech about peace. In a graduation address at American University on June 10, he argued that peace is the "necessary rational end of rational men." In opposition to the anti-Communist dogma that portrayed the Soviet Union as pure villainy, he contended that "no government or social system is so evil that its people must be considered as lacking in virtue." Acknowledging the stark contrasts between the United States and the Soviet Union, he said, "If we cannot end now all of our differences, at least we can help make the world safe for diversity."[40] Kennedy himself inserted one key clause into the speech: "Total war makes no sense."[41] This speech emerged, in part, because of an honest feeling that only "fools" could believe that a nuclear war would end in victory for either side.[42] Khrushchev praised the speech, saying that it was "notable for its sober appraisal of the international situation."[43]

A July 1963 report from the United States Information Agency showed that western Europeans held a higher opinion of the United States following the crisis. The same analysis revealed that unfavorable sentiments toward the USSR outnumbered positive ratings. By this time, Khrushchev's relations with the United States were more cordial than his interactions with Communist China. Facing the United States' overwhelming lead in the arms race and economic disaster at home, he had attempted to show the United States that he was willing to negotiate, compromise, and make concessions. Once a provocateur, he now excelled in avoiding confrontations, even abandoning the issue of Berlin's future. In June, he agreed to the establishment of a hotline between the White House and the Kremlin for quick communication in a crisis. The following month, he reached agreement on a test ban treaty with the United

Kingdom and the United States that outlawed all nuclear tests except those underground.

Both Kennedy and Khrushchev decided to cast aside brinkmanship as a Cold War strategy, and that made the world a safer place. "Even now that so many years have passed," Dobrynin wrote in 1995, "the political and diplomatic solution at which the two states jointly arrived may be regarded as a model of successfully controlling a crisis. It showed that a third world war can be avoided."[44] A few weeks after the crisis's end, Kennedy himself described it as "an important turning point, possibly in the history of the relations between East and West."[45] Political scientist Michael Mandelbaum also has contended that much of the crisis's fame rose from its passing, and from the fact that participants felt the closeness of war and the need to write and speak about it.[46] Literature relating to the crisis intensified feelings about its importance. Dobrynin classified the missile crisis not just as an important moment in the Cold War. He called it "the most dramatic event of the Cold War" and "a watershed in understanding how far they [the United States and the Soviet Union] could go and taught us a major lesson in what had to be done to prevent nuclear war."[47]

Indeed, this frightening confrontation had opened gates that had once been sealed and revealed options that had once been unthinkable. Both leaders could reach out now in search of a new world order free from inextricable links to the prospect of nuclear war. Stalin had viewed war with the West as inevitable, and with the rise of nuclear weapons many of his disciples saw a nuclear conflagration as equally unavoidable. Khrushchev broke the mold by imagining a future for the Soviet Union that did not involve war with the United States.

When Kennedy was assassinated in Dallas on November 22, 1963, Khrushchev believed that an American conspiracy was responsible. Although the captured gunman, Lee Harvey Oswald, had spent three years in the Soviet Union and was an outspoken proponent of Castro's Cuba, the KGB attempted to confirm that a right-wing conspiracy had spawned the assassination. Ultimately, the agency's investigation found no evidence to support its contention. American assassination conspiracy theorists often have characterized Cuban issues as the likely source of the assassination. Some have blamed pro-Castro forces, while others pointed the finger at anti-Castro arch-conservatives dissatisfied with the U.S. decision not to invade the island. At the time of his death, peaceful resolution of the missile crisis loomed as one of JFK's greatest accomplishments. One child wrote a note after Kennedy's death that linked sharply contrasting ideas. It said, "If Kennedy wasn't killed he might have become the greatest president ever. He also might have started an atomic war and destroyed the world."[48]

Driven by a variety of issues, forces within the Presidium began to plot Khrushchev's ouster just months after Kennedy's death. Among his opponents' grievances were apparent defeat in the missile crisis, grand promises to Cuba at the expense of the Soviet Union, and collapsing ties with Communist China. Dobrynin believed that Khrushchev's agreement to keep the Turkey missile deal secret had made him more vulnerable.[49] However, Fursenko and Naftali conclude that his increasing authoritarianism at home was the chief factor in his defeat. Driven by a fear of the intelligentsia, Khrushchev persistently opposed efforts to expand public education. In August 1964, he unilaterally decided to eliminate the eleventh grade in all schools.[50] This added fire to the opposition, which was led by a Ukrainian and one-time Khrushchev ally, Leonid Brezhnev. The United States was taken by surprise on October 15, 1964 when TASS revealed that Khrushchev had been deposed and that Brezhnev and Alexei Kosygin now led the USSR.

The Cuban crisis may not have been responsible for Kennedy's assassination or for Khrushchev's toppling. Nonetheless, it made both men more susceptible to attack. They had stepped outside the constrained line of dogmatic policymaking in their own nations to reach a compromise and protect the peace.

FIFTY YEARS OF CUBAN MISSILE CRISIS ANALYSIS

After Kennedy's assassination, the triumphal American view of the Cuban Missile Crisis received added impetus by veneration of his memory. This trend was fueled by memoirs from Kennedy loyalists such as Theodore Sorensen and Arthur M. Schlesinger Jr. However, in the 1970s new interpretations drew support. Revisionist historians characterized Kennedy's handling of the crisis as reckless. They condemned his failure to quietly pursue a negotiated agreement without raising the threat of nuclear war. These views predominated after the Vietnam War and the Watergate scandal led Americans to forsake hero worship and lose faith in their leaders. Nonetheless, over time, the emergence of new information cast doubt on the revisionists' perspective. Their arguments collapsed as increased dialogue in the 1980s and 1990s showed Kennedy had been far more cautious than his public statements in 1962 had suggested.

Fresh insights on the crisis came from multiple sources. Khrushchev's memoirs, published under the title *Khrushchev Remembers* in 1970, cast new light on the Soviet side of the confrontation. For the first time, the crisis could be seen through the eyes of a key player, but his words were edited

Crisis Management Captured on Tape

In reviewing most crises, historians must rely on public statements and scrawled notes to unravel the thinking that provided the underpinning for decisions. This is not the case in study of the American side of the Cuban Missile Crisis because President Kennedy, using equipment that had been secretly installed a few months earlier, took the unusual step of recording most crisis-related meetings.

To activate the system, JFK had to flip a switch. Then, microphones hidden in light fixtures in the Cabinet Room and in the president's Oval Office desk transmitted signals to a reel-to-reel tape recorder in the basement of the White House. Kennedy also had an Oval Office system that enabled him to record telephone calls on a Dictabelt after signaling his private secretary, Evelyn Lincoln, to activate the machine. He started recording meetings in late July 1962 and telephone calls in September. He continued both practices until his assassination in November 1963.

Recordings were made without the knowledge of most participants. JFK obviously knew that his words were being recorded, and it is possible that his brother, Robert, also was aware of the system. However, neither appeared to consciously alter what he said during missile crisis meetings. Ernest R. May and Philip D. Zelikow, who edited and published the crisis transcripts, have written, "If Robert Kennedy was aware of being recorded, the fact did not restrain his candor. On the tapes, both he and President Kennedy make many remarks that appear unguarded and that could have been damaging politically, if disclosed."[51]

In many cases, the recordings are difficult to decipher. Those who transcribed them had to isolate overlapping voices and parse regional intonations ranging from the Kennedys' clipped New England accents to the southern drawls of Dean Rusk and Lyndon Johnson. President Kennedy held a few crisis discussions without activating the system. He may have forgotten to flip the switch, or he may simply have wanted some conversations to occur outside of history's hearing range.

The existence of the tapes and the taping system remained secret until 1973. During investigation of the Watergate scandal, President Richard Nixon's White House taping system was revealed, and that prompted rumors about similar systems in previous administrations. Consequently, JFK's only surviving brother Senator Edward Kennedy and other keepers of the Kennedy flame reported the existence of the tapes and vowed to deliver them to the National Archives. In all, there were 248 hours of meeting tapes and twelve hours of telephone conversations.[52] The John F. Kennedy Library in Boston processed the tapes as time allowed, and the definitive study of the missile crisis tapes was published in 1997 by May and Zelikow. The library completed releasing transcriptions of all Kennedy administration tapes in January 2012.

to avoid causing embarrassment to the Soviet government. While the missile crisis is often cited as the event that precipitated Khrushchev's fall from power, he wrote that "it was a great victory for us, though, that we had been able to extract from Kennedy a promise that neither America nor any of her allies would invade Cuba." Khrushchev praised Kennedy for showing "real wisdom and statesmanship when he turned his back on right-wing forces in the United States who were trying to goad him into taking military action against Cuba."[53] Later, when the collapse of Soviet authoritarianism made it possible for Khrushchev to be quoted more openly, an addendum to his memoirs quoted him as saying, "The aim of the American aggressors was to destroy Cuba. Our aim was to preserve Cuba. Today, Cuba exists. So who won? It cost us nothing more than the round-trip expenses for transporting the rockets to Cuba and back."[54]

In the United States, White House tapes of Ex Comm discussions provided historians with an unprecedented opportunity to hear conversations that occurred in a great crisis. The tapes reveal a cascade of emotions as American leaders mentally fumble toward rational and coherent decisions. In their raw form, the recordings offer no heroes or villains—just human beings honestly attempting to find solutions. On the tapes, we hear them wrestling with ideas and struggling to grasp a potentially horrendous possibility that no other leaders have ever faced, the very real prospect of all-out nuclear war.

Even more extraordinary in expanding historical perspectives on the crisis was a series of "alumni" gatherings that altered the world's understanding of what happened on all sides during the crisis. Beginning with a meeting in Hawk's Cay, Florida, in March 1987 and going on to include sessions in Cambridge, Massachusetts later that year, in Moscow in January 1989, in Antigua in January 1991, and in Havana in January 1992, these gatherings brought together historians, actual participants, and family members and aides of those key players who were no longer alive. These exchanges clarified the astounding depth of misunderstanding between nations that existed in 1962. In addition, the release of new information, especially about Soviet troops and equipment in Cuba, made clear that the crisis was more dangerous than the most fearful observers had believed. On the other hand, revelations about steps taken by Kennedy and Khrushchev to avoid war demonstrated their painstaking caution in bringing the crisis to a peaceful end. While both men talked tough, they scrambled to find any excuse to save their nations and their citizens.

The emotions expressed at these meetings provided windows into national perceptions. In Cambridge, Georgi Shaknazarov, a key aide to then-General Secretary Mikhail S. Gorbachev, contended that American claims to superiority went far beyond a count of weapons:

> All of you believed yourselves in both a military and a moral
> position of superiority. You speak of deception, and so on. But,
> according to international law, we had no reason to inform you
> beforehand. You did not inform us of your intention to put
> missiles in Turkey.[55]

His words hit home, though few Americans would have acknowledged
their accuracy in 1962. The Spanish–American War probably represented
the coming-out party for America's self-image as the epitome of freedom
and as the world's policeman—an identity that was all too clear in the
Korean War, Vietnam War, Gulf War, and the War on Terrorism's two
fronts in Iraq and Afghanistan. This drive was submerged during periods
of American isolationism before both World Wars, but recaptured center
stage as soon as U.S. involvement had begun. Shakhnazarov later correctly
noted that without the Cuban Missile Crisis, the danger of nuclear war
would have been "incomparably greater" in the following years.[56]

In these interchanges, former officials outlined what their nations
believed about their adversaries but also what their nation's leaders learned
about themselves. Abram Chayes, who worked in Kennedy's State
Department, spoke about American leaders' new understanding of their
own feelings. They were not just appalled by the prospect of nuclear
devastation on a national scale but were unwilling to face the possibility
of even one American city being destroyed.[57] Despite the nation's vast
superiority in nuclear weaponry, Kennedy and his advisers hustled to avert
the possibility of a single weapon striking the United States. The level of
national shock that Ex Comm members expected seems to have been borne
out on September 11, 2001, when two hijacked airliners struck and
destroyed the World Trade Center, one smashed into the Pentagon, and
one crashed in western Pennsylvania. The death toll in this terrorist assault
was surely lower than it would have been if one nuclear missile had struck
the United States in 1962, and the physical destruction was much less
widespread. However, the nation was gripped by astonishment, largely
because of an unfamiliar and almost-crippling sense of vulnerability on
American soil. The Al Qaeda hijackers struck two symbolic targets on a
single day, but a nuclear weapon hitting New York City or Washington
in 1962 could have eliminated many more physical representations of
American identity.[58]

Each of these discussions about the missile crisis opened possibilities
for broader give-and-take and each new piece of information seemed
to rewrite common conceptions of the crisis. Details of the secret deal to
trade missiles in Turkey and Italy for missiles in Cuba demonstrated that
Kennedy had not been a thrill-seeker who blithely risked his country's

safety through a macho display of brinkmanship. Later, Rusk's statement that Kennedy had an additional fallback plan to avert war through the United Nations again changed the accepted image of Kennedy's work to resolve the crisis. Furthermore, Americans learned that Khrushchev's initial plans were far more dangerous than the Kennedy administration had guessed. U.S. intelligence's tremendous underestimate of the number of Soviet troops in Cuba and the presence of tactical nuclear weapons raised frightening possibilities. Expecting minimal opposition to a U.S. invasion force might have inadvertently launched a world war. Realization of this bigger threat made Kennedy's initially hidden peace initiatives seem smarter and more important.

Despite competing claims of moral superiority, the United States and the Soviet Union proved over the coming years that they were equally capable of stumbling into wars for the wrong reasons. This became apparent in the 1960s and 1970s when the United States cumulatively sent almost 3 million soldiers, sailors, Air Force personnel, and marines to Vietnam because fear of monolithic Communism made American leaders see a nation torn by civil war as a Cold War domino that must not be allowed to fall. The same image of America faltering on foreign soil re-emerged in the first decade of the twenty-first century when U.S. forces invaded Iraq to remove non-existent weapons of mass destruction and subsequently caused thousands of Iraqi civilian deaths. These wars, which took thousands of lives, can be seen as the wicked stepchildren of the missile crisis. In both cases, leaders drew the wrong lessons from the crisis and set into motion blueprints for disaster. At least to some extent, American involvement in each war sprang from the belief that once the most powerful nation in the world had expressed its will and drawn a line in the sand, nothing could stand in its way. As a result, tough talk replaced reasoned negotiation. The Soviets also became deeply entrenched in a meaningless and unsuccessful war in Afghanistan in 1979 and failed to withdraw until the late 1980s.

Like these misadventures, the missile crisis featured faulty judgments on both sides, at least partially because misperceptions were a dangerous by-product of Cold War secrecy and dogmatic ideology. Khrushchev thought he could secretly place missiles in Cuba, and Kennedy's advisers

> The Domino Theory contended that if one non-aligned nation was allowed to fall into Communist hands, its neighbors also would be overwhelmed by Communism, falling like a line of dominoes in a child's game.

believed that Khrushchev would never put nuclear weapons on the island. Khrushchev imagined that Kennedy would not respond aggressively to placement of missiles in Cuba, and Kennedy thought implantation of Soviet arms in Cuba must be tied to a planned Soviet move on Berlin. Soviet leaders planted the missiles at a time when they wrongly believed that the United States planned to invade Cuba in 1962, and Kennedy's Ex Comm never settled on a solid and reasonable understanding of Khrushchev's motives, even though Khrushchev spelled them out in his many letters to Kennedy. It would have been far easier for the Ex Comm if Khrushchev had clearly demonstrated a single motive, but, like Kennedy, Khrushchev was driven by complex forces. He made his decisions to achieve multiple goals that were not susceptible to the kind of simplistic analysis that reigned during the Cold War.

At gatherings where American and Soviet veterans of the missile crisis spoke, both sides acknowledged a failure to gauge how one nation's actions might be interpreted by the other. In many ways, this represented a failure of imagination as well as a lack of empathy. Both nations were so locked into their self-images and their views of the adversary that neither noticed obvious cues that misunderstandings were occurring. JFK identified this as a key problem in a televised interview in December 1962:

> I think, looking back on Cuba, what is of concern is the fact that both governments were so far out of contact, really. I don't think that we expected that he would put the missiles in Cuba, because it would have seemed such an imprudent action for him to take, as it was later proved. Now, he obviously must have thought that he could do it in secret and that the United States would accept it. So that he did not judge our intentions accurately.

He argued that "the Communists have a completely twisted view of the United States and that we don't comprehend them. That is what makes life in the Sixties hazardous."[59]

In the end, these gaps in comprehension did not block efforts by Khrushchev and Kennedy to reach a peaceful resolution. In its aftermath, the crisis's many surprises made each side more cautious and more eager to avoid future misunderstandings. As a result, both leaders demonstrated far more wisdom at the end of the crisis than they had displayed in the months leading up to it. Kennedy succeeded for several reasons: He did not allow his decisions to be rushed; he sought out the opinions of a divergent group of advisers; he refused to give military arguments more weight than other considerations; and he labored to offer Khrushchev a way out that did not require Soviet humiliation. Khrushchev did not draw on other opinions to a great extent, but he did embrace prudence.

Moreover, both men took significant steps to avoid accidental war. American political scientist Richard Neustadt said the crisis revealed that "the president's office is a lonely one, and the burden of responsibility is very personal. If we expect so much of the presidency," he argued, "we should also provide it with the advice it needs."[60]

Much has been written about the introduction of the terms "hawk" and "dove" within the Ex Comm discussions. James G. Blight and David A. Welch have asserted that the hawks' world was "relatively understandable, predictable, controllable, and safe," while the doves' world was "inexplicable, unpredictable, uncontrollable, and, above all, dangerous."[61] The doves, with JFK among their ranks, won the argument within the Ex Comm, and their world view seems to square with a rational analysis of life in the twenty-first century. Even Khrushchev was a dove in the end. He later wrote: "What good would it have done me in the last hour of my life to know that though our great nation and the United States were in complete ruins, the national honor of the Soviet Union was intact?"[62] Newspaper columnist Art Buchwald found humor in the new terminology. "We weren't a dove or a hawk," he wrote. "We were chicken. It had nothing to do with the issues. We just didn't want to die."[63] In a sermon delivered on Thanksgiving Day 1962, Martin Luther King Jr. took a more serious look at the crisis, saying,

> With war clouds hanging low; strife and bitterness in our own ranks; truth forever on the scaffold, wrong forever on the throne— we must know that, behind the scaffold, in the dark, dim, unknown, standest God in the shadow, keeping watch above His own.[64]

In the 1964 presidential campaign, Johnson was able to use Americans' fears of nuclear war as a campaign vehicle. By emphasizing the apparent willingness of his Republican opponent Senator Barry Goldwater to use nuclear weapons, Johnson made himself the candidate representing peace, moderation, and rationality. This campaign tactic was most clearly represented in a famous TV ad that began by showing a little blonde girl plucking petals from a daisy and ended with the explosion of a nuclear bomb. The so-called "Daisy Ad" was broadcast as a paid commercial only once, but its impact remains well known today. The Arizona senator lost in a landslide when many moderate and typically Republican voters cast their ballots for Johnson.

The drama of the crisis has provided fertile ground for cinematic imaginations. Alfred Hitchcock tried to emulate the real-life suspense story in the 1969 film *Topaz*, based on a novel by Leon Uris. In 1974's TV movie, "The Missiles of October," the closing scene takes a kernel from Sorensen's book, *Kennedy*, and the stage directions alone tell a story about the president and the Ex Comm:

> They have been in various positions, some standing, most sitting, all relaxing. Now, as they see the president, there is a moment of very deep feeling. It flows between them, and from them to JFK. The members of the Executive Committee all come to their feet. They stand, in place, for the president as a gesture of respect. And more than respect: gratitude in the sharing of the task. Love.[65]

Twenty-six years later, Kevin Costner's casting in 2000's *Thirteen Days*,[66] very loosely based on Robert Kennedy's memoir about the crisis, turned the Ex Comm saga upside down by making White House aide Kenneth O'Donnell, seldom heard on the White House tapes, a pivotal figure in the crisis.

Unfortunately, there will always be an important gap in our knowledge of the crisis because we lack John F. Kennedy's perspective. His assassination erased the possibility of revealing memoirs on the subject. Even Robert Kennedy's account was not published in a pure form because he was slain before its publication, and Sorensen, who was committed to protecting JFK's memory, chose to delete details about the missile swap. Granted, JFK's recollections might have been colored by prejudices and self-interest, but their absence forces historians to indulge in a significant amount of guesswork. There are snippets of Kennedy's thoughts filtered through the recollections of others. Journalist and friend Ben Bradlee remembers the president saying in November 1962, "The first advice I'm going to give my successor is to watch the generals and to avoid feeling that just because they were military men their opinions on military matters are worth a damn."[67] (He shared this conclusion with his Soviet adversary: Khrushchev said to his military advisers that the biggest tragedy "was not that our country might be devastated and everything lost, but that the Chinese or the Albanians would accuse us of appeasement or weakness.")[68] In a similar vein, Schlesinger reported that Kennedy believed the crisis demonstrated the importance of air and sea power, but he recalled that Kennedy said, "An invasion would have been a mistake—a wrong use of power. But the military are mad."[69]

A decade after the Cuban Missile Crisis, the Soviet Union and the United States reached the first agreement on arms control since the development of the atomic bomb in 1945. The Anti-Ballistic Missile Treaty limited development of defensive missiles to strike down an attacking

The Journey of Robert McNamara

Of the central figures on the American side of the missile crisis, Robert McNamara was one of the longest-lived and remained a prominent figure until his death at 93 in 2009. During the last fifteen years of his life, McNamara reclaimed a share of the nation's attention by voicing regrets about his role as an architect of U.S. policy regarding Vietnam. He persistently tried to derive lessons from his mistakes.

Before his service in the Kennedy administration, McNamara graduated with a degree in economics from the University of California at Berkeley and received a master's degree from Harvard's Business School. He worked for a while as a professor at Harvard before serving in the U.S. Army Air Corps in World War II. After the war, he was hired by Henry Ford II to work at Ford Motor Company in Detroit, and he rose to the company's presidency, becoming the company's first leader who was not a member of the Ford family.

In 1960, President-Elect Kennedy asked him to serve as secretary of defense. Kennedy wanted to fill that position with someone who could make the Pentagon run more efficiently. During the Cuban Missile Crisis, McNamara became an outspoken "dove," seeking to avoid war at all costs.

After Kennedy was assassinated in 1963, McNamara made a smooth transition to the Johnson administration, while some of his colleagues never could accept Johnson's leadership. Along with Rusk and McGeorge Bundy, he became a key participant in the Johnson administration's escalation of the Vietnam War, ultimately raising U.S. troop levels to more than 500,000 soldiers. This foursome met weekly to discuss the war, and many analysts have suggested that this concentration of power inexorably led to deeper and deeper involvement in Vietnam. Those who questioned U.S. policy, such as Vice President Hubert Humphrey, were excluded from the decision-making process. Questions of why the United States was involved in Vietnam became lost in the operational details of running a war. In 1967, as he began to develop doubts about the conflict, McNamara ordered a study analyzing U.S. conduct of the war. This report later was leaked to the press and became known as the Pentagon Papers. Toward the end of 1967, Johnson dismissed McNamara after he raised questions about Vietnam policy. LBJ made McNamara head of the World Bank, where he remained for thirteen years until his retirement. McNamara's replacement as secretary of defense, Clark Clifford, recognized the flaws in Vietnam policy within months of taking office, but peace remained elusive. By the end of U.S. military involvement in Vietnam in 1973, more than 58,000 Americans had died in Southeast Asia.

In the five gatherings of missile crisis participants during the 1980s and 1990s, McNamara returned to the national spotlight as an eager and thoughtful contributor. He often challenged his Soviet counterparts' analyses of what happened and provided great insight into American motives and U.S. military actions. He learned from these sessions that misconceptions had made the crisis much more dangerous than it appeared to be.

McNamara published a memoir in 1995 about the Vietnam War entitled *In Retrospect: The Tragedy and Lesson of Vietnam*. Some people responded to the controversial book with anger. Many of those who had fought in the rice paddies of South Vietnam or lost loved ones in the conflict voiced resentment toward McNamara because he seemed to want forgiveness for something too huge to be forgiven. In the back of the book, McNamara included an appendix on the Cuban Missile Crisis, and throughout the book's pages, he cites the crisis repeatedly as a problem handled deftly and Vietnam as a disaster that the Johnson administration carelessly brought upon itself. In the book, McNamara argued that JFK never would have become entrenched in Vietnam.[70]

In 2003, McNamara again offered a *mea culpa* in Erroll Morris's documentary, *The Fog of War*. In the film, Morris used McNamara as a focal point to show how details in conducting a war can obscure the important questions, such as: Why are we fighting? In the film, as in his book, McNamara focused on lessons that could be learned. In his mind, the missile crisis provided positive lessons to be followed, while Vietnam primarily showed how not to manage foreign policy. In particular, he felt that JFK made the most of many knowledgeable people and took every plausible step to avoid involving the United States in a war, while Johnson isolated himself from diplomats who truly understood Southeast Asia and engaged in a war under the belief that American power could crush Ho Chi Minh's North Vietnamese army as well as the rebellious Viet Cong in South Vietnam.

By living into the twenty-first century, McNamara had a rare opportunity to look back on these major events from a vantage point four decades later. He knew that Ho Chi Minh's ultimate victory in Vietnam had no calamitous effect on the United States and its allies. He also witnessed Castro's continuing rule of an impoverished island—a reign that lasted more than forty years beyond John F. Kennedy's death without harming the United States or its sphere of influence. In both cases, the dire effects feared during the Cold War never materialized. Because McNamara's apologies came after the fears of the Cold War had been extinguished by the Soviet Union's collapse, his arguments garnered less sympathy than they would have in the 1970s and 1980s. The Communist giant's demise made the Vietnam War seem even more meaningless.

nation's weapons. By cutting short development of this new generation of weapons, the treaty began the slow and as-yet-unfinished move toward disarmament. Unfortunately, the crisis did more than encourage arms negotiation: It fed Soviet ambition to close the missile gap. Kuznetsov told U.S. diplomat John McCloy soon after the crisis that "the Soviet Union would never again face a 4-to-1 missile inferiority." Soviet spending began to shift increasingly to military efforts, such as development of Polaris-like submarines. Soviet missile production skyrocketed after the crisis, with the number of ICBM launchers growing from a handful to about 200 just two years later. Khrushchev's successors, instead of embracing his growing belief that the Soviet Union could not afford an arms race, hastened production of nuclear weapons. McNamara believed that Soviet leaders interpreted the United States' nuclear arsenal not as a deterrent but as clear-cut evidence that the United States planned a crippling first strike in a nuclear war. "That was never our intention," he said in a 1992 interview, "It was not only not our intention, but we didn't believe we could possibly achieve such a capability." He argued that the United States never had great enough superiority to make a first strike worth the risk of a counterstrike by the Soviet Union.[71]

In *The Nuclear Revolution* Mandelbaum writes,

> Both sides subsequently assembled so much more nuclear firepower than they had in 1962 that it is unlikely either could achieve the same ratio of superiority that the United States then enjoyed. It is not at all clear that the Soviets had the capacity for the assured destruction of the United States.

"In the Cuban Missile Crisis," Mandelbaum asserts,

> since war of any kind might become nuclear war, war of any kind had to be avoided at all costs. And carried one step further, it has meant that the United States and the Soviet Union have scrupulously sought to avoid political conflicts that could raise the specter of war, which in turn could raise the specter of nuclear war.[72]

This crisis effectively silenced the small group of right-wing conservatives, such as General Curtis LeMay, some of whom had argued that it was possible to destroy the Soviet Union in a nuclear war. What the crisis made clear was that the USSR's destruction could not be achieved without significant—and unacceptable—havoc in the United States.

Thirty years after the crisis, as he met with American and Soviet officials who had been involved in it, Castro voiced admiration for Kennedy, who, despite his hostility to Castro's regime, never attacked Cuba with U.S. forces. Castro praised JFK's "new ideas," saying "some of them were brilliant or at least very intelligent." He included the Alliance for Progress on that list and speculated that with consolidated power in the aftermath of the crisis, Kennedy "might have been one of the presidents—or perhaps the president best able—to rectify American policy toward Cuba."[73]

Now, the Cuban Missile Crisis has receded into distant memory. In the words of Spencer R. Weart, "When the crisis ended most people turned their attention away as swiftly as a child lifts up a rock, sees something slimy underneath, and drops the rock back."[74] Nevertheless, it has not been forgotten: Perhaps more than any other event in human history, the Cuban Missile Crisis has been the subject of exhaustive studies intended to derive lessons from thirteen days in October 1962. In some cases, the lessons seem obvious. Many Americans undoubtedly wished that George W. Bush had made a study of the caution exhibited in 1962 before he plunged the United States into a war in Iraq based on the unfounded belief that Iraqi leader Saddam Hussein controlled weapons of mass destruction. However, it is dangerous to assume that understanding the missile crisis would provide a roadmap for future international conflicts. Just as both Kennedy and Khrushchev were perhaps too much driven by "lessons" from World War II, future leaders likely would falter if they tried to recreate the successful resolution in 1962.

Documents

DOCUMENT 1: PRESIDENT KENNEDY ADDRESSES THE NATION OCTOBER 22, 1962

In one of history's most dramatic presidential addresses, Kennedy orders a naval blockade in response to the Soviet Union's placement of nuclear missiles in Cuba.[1]

Good evening, my fellow citizens:

This Government, as promised, has maintained the closest surveillance of the Soviet military buildup on the island of Cuba. Within the past week, unmistakable evidence has established the fact that a series of offensive missile sites is now in preparation on that imprisoned island. The purpose of these bases can be none other than to provide a nuclear strike capability against the Western Hemisphere.

Upon receiving the first preliminary hard information of this nature last Tuesday morning at 9 a.m., I directed that our surveillance be stepped up. And having now confirmed and completed our evaluation of the evidence and our decision on a course of action, this Government feels obliged to report this new crisis to you in fullest detail.

The characteristics of these new missile sites indicate two distinct types of installations. Several of them include medium-range ballistic missiles, capable of carrying a nuclear warhead for a distance of more than 1,000 nautical miles. Each of these missiles, in short, is capable of striking Washington, D.C., the Panama Canal, Cape Canaveral, Mexico City, or any other city in the southeastern part of the United States, in Central America, or in the Caribbean area.

Additional sites not yet completed appear to be designed for intermediate-range ballistic missiles—capable of traveling more than twice as far—and thus capable of striking most of the major cities in the Western Hemisphere, ranging as far north as Hudson Bay, Canada, and as far south as Lima, Peru. In addition, jet bombers, capable of carrying nuclear weapons, are now being uncrated and assembled in Cuba, while the necessary air bases are being prepared.

This urgent transformation of Cuba into an important strategic base— by the presence of these large, long-range, and clearly offensive weapons of sudden mass destruction—constitutes an explicit threat to the peace and security of all the Americas, in flagrant and deliberate defiance of the *Rio Pact of 1947*, the traditions of this nation and hemisphere, the joint resolution of the 87th Congress, the Charter of the United Nations, and my own public warnings to the Soviets on September 4 and 13. This action also contradicts the repeated assurances of Soviet spokesmen, both publicly and privately delivered, that the arms buildup in Cuba would retain its original defensive character, and that the Soviet Union had no need or desire to station strategic missiles on the territory of any other nation.

The size of this undertaking makes clear that it has been planned for some months. Yet, only last month, after I had made clear the distinction between any introduction of ground-to-ground missiles and the existence of defensive antiaircraft missiles, the Soviet Government publicly stated on September 11 that, and I quote, "the armaments and military equipment sent to Cuba are designed exclusively for defensive purposes," that there is, and I quote the Soviet Government, "there is no need for the Soviet Government to shift its weapons for a retaliatory blow to any other country, for instance Cuba," and that, and I quote their government, "the Soviet Union has so powerful rockets to carry these nuclear warheads that there is no need to search for sites for them beyond the boundaries of the Soviet Union." That statement was false.

Only last Thursday, as evidence of this rapid offensive buildup was already in my hand, Soviet Foreign Minister Gromyko told me in my office that he was instructed to make it clear once again, as he said his government had already done, that Soviet assistance to Cuba, and I quote, "pursued solely the purpose of contributing to the defense capabilities of Cuba," that, and I quote him, "training by Soviet specialists of Cuban nationals in handling defensive armaments was by no means offensive, and if it were otherwise," Mr. Gromyko went on, "the Soviet Government would never become involved in rendering such assistance." That statement also was false.

Neither the United States of America nor the world community of nations can tolerate deliberate deception and offensive threats on the part of any nation, large or small. We no longer live in a world where only the actual firing of weapons represents a sufficient challenge to a nation's security to constitute maximum peril. Nuclear weapons are so destructive and ballistic missiles are so swift, that any substantially increased possibility of their use or any sudden change in their deployment may well be regarded as a definite threat to peace.

For many years, both the Soviet Union and the United States, recognizing this fact, have deployed strategic nuclear weapons with great care, never upsetting the precarious status quo which insured that these weapons would not be used in the absence of some vital challenge. Our own strategic missiles have never been transferred to the territory of any other nation under a cloak of secrecy and deception; and our history—unlike that of the Soviets since the end of World War II—demonstrates that we have no desire to dominate or conquer any other nation or impose our system upon its people. Nevertheless, American citizens have become adjusted to living daily on the bull's-eye of Soviet missiles located inside the U.S.S.R. or in submarines.

In that sense, missiles in Cuba add to an already clear and present danger—although it should be noted the nations of Latin America have never previously been subjected to a potential nuclear threat.

But this secret, swift, extraordinary buildup of Communist missiles in an area well known to have a special and historical relationship to the United States and the nations of the Western Hemisphere, in violation of Soviet assurances, and in defiance of American and hemispheric policy—this sudden, clandestine decision to station strategic weapons for the first time outside of Soviet soil—is a deliberately provocative and unjustified change in the status quo which cannot be accepted by this country, if our courage and our commitments are ever to be trusted again by either friend or foe.

The 1930s taught us a clear lesson: aggressive conduct, if allowed to go unchecked and unchallenged, ultimately leads to war. This nation is opposed to war. We are also true to our word. Our unswerving objective, therefore, must be to prevent the use of these missiles against this or any other country, and to secure their withdrawal or elimination from the Western Hemisphere.

Our policy has been one of patience and restraint, as befits a peaceful and powerful nation which leads a worldwide alliance. We have been determined not to be diverted from our central concerns by mere irritants and fanatics. But now further action is required, and it is under way; and these actions may only be the beginning. We will not prematurely or unnecessarily risk the costs of worldwide nuclear war in which even the fruits of victory would be ashes in our mouth; but neither will we shrink from that risk at any time it must be faced.

Acting, therefore, in the defense of our own security and of the entire Western Hemisphere, and under the authority entrusted to me by the Constitution as endorsed by the Resolution of the Congress, I have directed that the following initial steps be taken immediately:

First: To halt this offensive buildup a strict quarantine on all offensive military equipment under shipment to Cuba is being initiated. All ships of any kind bound for Cuba from whatever nation or port will, if found to contain cargoes of offensive weapons, be turned back. This quarantine will be extended, if needed, to other types of cargo and carriers. We are not at this time, however, denying the necessities of life as the Soviets attempted to do in their Berlin blockade of 1948.

Second: I have directed the continued and increased close surveillance of Cuba and its military buildup. The foreign ministers of the OAS [Organization of American States], in their communiqué of October 6, rejected secrecy on such matters in this hemisphere. Should these offensive military preparations continue, thus increasing the threat to the hemisphere, further action will be justified. I have directed the Armed Forces to prepare for any eventualities; and I trust that in the interest of both the Cuban people and the Soviet technicians at the sites, the hazards to all concerned of continuing this threat will be recognized.

Third: It shall be the policy of this nation to regard any nuclear missile launched from Cuba against any nation in the Western Hemisphere as an attack by the Soviet Union on the United States, requiring a full retaliatory response upon the Soviet Union.

Fourth: As a necessary military precaution, I have reinforced our base at Guantanamo, evacuated today the dependents of our personnel there, and ordered additional military units to be on a standby alert basis.

Fifth: We are calling tonight for an immediate meeting of the Organ of Consultation under the Organization of American States, to consider this threat to hemispheric security and to invoke articles 6 and 8 of the Rio Treaty in support of all necessary action. The United Nations Charter allows for regional security arrangements, and the nations of this hemisphere decided long ago against the military presence of outside powers. Our other allies around the world have also been alerted.

Sixth: Under the Charter of the United Nations, we are asking tonight that an emergency meeting of the Security Council be convoked without delay to take action against this latest Soviet threat to world peace. Our resolution will call for the prompt dismantling and withdrawal of all offensive weapons in Cuba, under the supervision of U.N. observers, before the quarantine can be lifted.

Seventh and finally: I call upon Chairman Khrushchev to halt and eliminate this clandestine, reckless, and provocative threat to world peace and to stable relations between our two nations. I call upon him further to abandon this course of world domination, and to join in an historic effort to end the perilous arms race and to transform the history of man. He has an opportunity now to move the world back from the abyss of destruction by returning to his government's own words that it had no need to station missiles outside its own territory, and withdrawing these weapons from Cuba by refraining from any action which will widen or deepen the present crisis, and then by participating in a search for peaceful and permanent solutions.

This nation is prepared to present its case against the Soviet threat to peace, and our own proposals for a peaceful world, at any time and in any forum—in the OAS, in the United Nations, or in any other meeting that could be useful—without limiting our freedom of action. We have in the past made strenuous efforts to limit the spread of nuclear weapons. We have proposed the elimination of all arms and military bases in a fair and effective disarmament treaty. We are prepared to discuss new proposals for the removal of tensions on both sides, including the possibilities of a genuinely independent Cuba, free to determine its own destiny. We have no wish to war with the Soviet Union—for we are a peaceful people who desire to live in peace with all other peoples.

But it is difficult to settle or even discuss these problems in an atmosphere of intimidation. That is why this latest Soviet threat—or any other threat which is made either independently or in response to our actions this week—must and will be met with determination. Any hostile move anywhere in the world against the safety and freedom of peoples to whom we are committed, including in particular the brave people of West Berlin, will be met by whatever action is needed.

Finally, I want to say a few words to the captive people of Cuba, to whom this speech is being directly carried by special radio facilities. I speak to you as a friend, as one who knows of your deep attachment to your fatherland, as one who shares your aspirations for liberty and justice for all. And I have watched and the American people have watched with deep sorrow how your nationalist revolution was betrayed—and how your fatherland fell under foreign domination. Now your leaders are no longer Cuban leaders inspired by Cuban ideals. They are puppets and agents of an international conspiracy which has turned Cuba against your friends and neighbors in the Americas, and turned it into the first Latin American country to become a target for nuclear war—the first Latin American country to have these weapons on its soil.

These new weapons are not in your interest. They contribute nothing to your peace and well-being. They can only undermine it. But this country has no wish to cause you to suffer or to impose any system upon you. We know that your lives and land are being used as pawns by those who deny your freedom.

Many times in the past, the Cuban people have risen to throw out tyrants who destroyed their liberty. And I have no doubt that most Cubans today look forward to the time when they will be truly free— free from foreign domination, free to choose their own leaders, free to select their own system, free to own their own land, free to speak and write and worship without fear or degradation. And then shall Cuba be welcomed back to the society of free nations and to the associations of this hemisphere.

My fellow citizens, let no one doubt that this is a difficult and dangerous effort on which we have set out. No one can foresee precisely what course it will take or what costs or casualties will be incurred. Many months of sacrifice and self-discipline lie ahead—months in which both our patience and our will will be tested, months in which many threats and denunciations will keep us aware of our dangers. But the greatest danger of all would be to do nothing.

The path we have chosen for the present is full of hazards, as all paths are; but it is the one most consistent with our character and courage as a nation and our commitments around the world. The cost of freedom is always high, but Americans have always paid it. And one path we shall never choose, and that is the path of surrender or submission.

Our goal is not the victory of might, but the vindication of right; not peace at the expense of freedom, but both peace and freedom, here in this hemisphere, and, we hope, around the world. God willing, that goal will be achieved.

Thank you and good night.

DOCUMENT 2: KHRUSHCHEV RESPONDS TO KENNEDY'S SPEECH

In an October 23 letter, Khrushchev warns Kennedy about the dangers of the course he has chosen.[2]

Department of State
Division of Language Services

[TRANSLATION]

Moscow, October 23, 1962

Mr. President:

I have just received your letter, and have also acquainted myself with the text of your speech of October 22 regarding Cuba.

I must say frankly that the measures indicated in your statement constitute a serious threat to peace and to the security of nations. The United States has openly taken the path of grossly violating the United Nations Charter, the path of violating international norms of freedom of navigation on the high seas, the path of aggressive actions both against Cuba and against the Soviet Union.

The statement of the Government of the United States of America can only be regarded as undisguised interference in the affairs of the Republic of Cuba, the Soviet Union and other states. The United Nations Charter and international norms give no right to any state to institute in international waters the inspection of vessels bound for the shores of the Republic of Cuba.

And naturally, neither can we recognize the right of the United States to establish control over armaments which are necessary for the Republic of Cuba to strengthen its defense capability.

We reaffirm that the armaments which are in Cuba, regardless of classification to which they may belong, are intended solely for defensive purposes in order to secure the Republic of Cuba against the attack of an aggressor.

I hope that the United States Government will display wisdom and renounce the actions pursued by you, which may lead to catastrophic consequences for world peace.

The viewpoint of the Soviet Government with regard to your statement of October 22 is set forth in a Statement of the Soviet Government, which is being transmitted to you through your Ambassador at Moscow.

N. Khrushchev

DOCUMENT 3: KENNEDY URGES KHRUSHCHEV TO HALT SHIPS

JFK tells Khrushchev that he should order the return of Soviet ships taking offensive weapons to Cuba.[3]

October 23, 1962

Dear Mr. Chairman:

I have received your letter of October twenty-third. I think you will recognize that the steps which started the current chain of events was the action of your government in secretly furnishing offensive weapons to Cuba. We will be discussing this matter in the Security Council. In the meantime, I am concerned that we both show prudence and do nothing to allow events to make the situation more difficult to control than it already is.

I hope that you will issue immediately the necessary instructions to your ships to observe the terms of the quarantine, the basis of which was established by the vote of the Organization of American States this afternoon, and which will go into effect at 1400 hours Greenwich time October twenty-four.

Sincerely,

John F. Kennedy

DOCUMENT 4: WHITE HOUSE PROVIDES UPDATE ON MISSILES IN CUBA

In an October 26 news release, the Kennedy administration tells the American people that construction is continuing on the missile sites.[4]

Immediate Release

October 26, 1962

Office of the White House Press Secretary

The development of ballistic missile sites in Cuba continues at a rapid pace. Through the process of continued surveillance directed by the President, additional evidence has been acquired which clearly reflects that of Thursday, October 25, definite buildups in these offensive missile sites continued to be made. The activity at these sites apparently is directed at achieving a full operational capability as soon as possible.

There is evidence that as of yesterday, October 25, considerable construction activity was being engaged in at the Intermediate Range Ballistic Missile sites. Bulldozers and cranes were observed as late as Thursday actively clearing new areas within the sites and improving the approach roads to the launch pads.

Since Tuesday October 23 missile related activities have continued at the Medium Range Ballistic Missile sites resulting in progressive refinements at these facilities. For example, missiles were observed parked in the open on October 23. Surveillance on October 25 revealed that some of these same missiles have now been moved from their original parked positions. Cabling can be seen running from the missile-ready tents to power generators nearby.

In summary, there is no evidence to date indicating that there is any intention to dismantle or discontinue work on these missile sites. On the contrary the Soviets are rapidly continuing their construction of missile support and launch facilities, and serious attempts are under way to camouflage their efforts.

DOCUMENT 5: CASTRO LETTER APPEARS TO CALL FOR NUCLEAR WAR

In a letter to Khrushchev, Castro appears to endorse a nuclear first strike against the United States.[5]

October 26, 1962

Dear Comrade Khrushchev:

Given the analysis of the situation and the reports which have reached us, [I] consider an attack to be almost imminent—within the next 24 to 72 hours. There are two possible variants: the first and most probable one is an air attack against certain objectives with the limited aim of destroying them; the second, and though less probable, still possible, is a full invasion. This would require a large force and is the most repugnant form of aggression, which might restrain them.

You can be sure that we will resist with determination, whatever the case. The Cuban people's morale is extremely high and the people will confront aggression heroically.

I would like to briefly express my own personal opinion.

If the second variant takes place and the imperialists invade Cuba with the aim of occupying it, the dangers of their aggressive policy are so great that after such an invasion the Soviet Union must never allow circumstances in which the imperialists could carry out a nuclear first strike against it.

I tell you this because I believe that the imperialists' aggressiveness makes them extremely dangerous, and that if they manage to carry out an invasion of Cuba—a brutal act in violation of universal and moral law— then that would be the moment to eliminate this danger forever, in an act of the most legitimate self-defense. However harsh and terrible the solution, there would be no other.

This opinion is shaped by observing the development of their aggressive policy. The imperialists, without regard for world opinion and against laws and principles, have blockaded the seas, violated our air-space, and are preparing to invade, while at the same time blocking any possibility of negotiation, even though they understand the gravity of the problem.

You have been, and are, a tireless defender of peace, and I understand that these moments, when the results of your superhuman efforts are so seriously threatened, must be bitter for you. We will maintain our hopes for saving the peace until the last moment, and we are ready to contribute to this in any way we can. But, at the same time, we are serene and ready to confront a situation which we see as very real and imminent.

I convey to you the infinite gratitude and recognition of the Cuban people to the Soviet people, who have been so generous and fraternal, along with our profound gratitude and admiration to you personally. We wish you success with the enormous task and great responsibilities which are in your hands.

Fraternally,

Fidel Castro

DOCUMENT 6: STILL-CLASSIFIED DOCUMENT OFFERS LITTLE INFORMATION

In an October 27 document that remains classified fifty years after the Cuban Missile Crisis, FBI Director J. Edgar Hoover tells Robert Kennedy about Soviet spy activity in the United States during the crisis.[6]

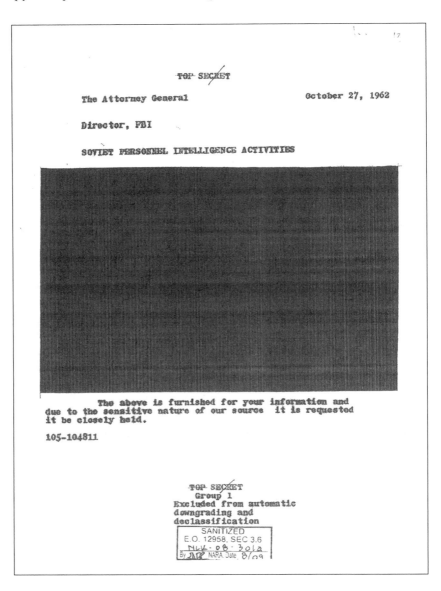

DOCUMENT 7: CIVIL DEFENSE READINESS REPORT ON OCTOBER 27, 1962

Assistant Secretary of Defense for Civil Defense Steuart Pittman delivers an optimistic report on the state of the United States' civil defense readiness. Though the nation has few marked and stocked shelters available, Pittman seeks to reassure civilians about their fate if nuclear war begins.[7]

PRESS RELEASE

A report on national civil defense readiness by Steuart L. Pittman, Assistant Secretary of Defense to the Committee on Civil Defense and Post Attack Recovery of the National Governors Conference, October 27, 1962

Following the meeting with the Governors' Committee, Steuart Pittman, Assistant Secretary of Defense for Civil Defense, made the following statement:

> "The reaction of the American people to the current international tension shows that as a nation we are prepared to face up and to meet the recurring threats we live with. According to our reports, people around the country are turning their attention to the sensible measures of self-protection which make up the rapidly developing civil defense programs of federal, state and local governments. We are in much better shape than we were a year ago. This sharpened public interest in civil defense gives us new opportunities to move ahead on the program we decided upon last year."

He went on to describe his report to the Governors:

> "We have asked the governors and mayors to join with the Federal Government in expediting the national civil defense effort. I laid before the Committee six steps being taken by the Office of Civil Defense to move the program as far as existing resources will permit in a three months' period. We can then take stock of what public funds are needed to meet the objectives of the President's program at about the time the new Congress convenes.

1   *Shelter Marking*—Procedures have been developed to accelerate the marking of shelter space and to nearly double the amount of available space by lowering the standards of shielding from radiation. Shelter

space qualifying under the higher standards would accommodate over 60 million people. By using areas in buildings which cut the radiation by 40 times or more, between 110 and 120 million people could be accommodated.

Studies of hypothetical attacks which might be possible over the next year indicate that shelter space meeting this lower standard would save lives in large areas of the country not exposed to the most intense radiation.

2 *Shelter Stocking*—Only the higher standard space is being stocked. Unstocked shelters can be used by people who have planned ahead to bring their own supplies.

3 *Rural Shelters*—Surveyed shelter space in existing buildings will provide for most of the urban population. The federal shelter program relies largely on home shelters for the rural population. In cooperation with the Department of Agriculture, the base has been laid for an intensified effort to provide technical civil defense help in the rural areas, particularly on the inexpensive home shelters.

4 *Training*—Short courses have been packaged for the wide-spread training of personnel to (a) monitor radiation, (b) give local, technical guidance on identifying and constructing shelters in smaller buildings not included in the national shelter survey program, and (c) provide leadership and direction to groups in community shelters.

5 *Matching Funds and Surplus Property for the States*—Requests for federal surplus property will receive priority treatment during the three months period; modified procedures will expedite matching funds applications; surveyed shelter space will be used for state and local emergency operating centers.

6 *Stand-By Military Reservists for Civil Defense Service*—The Department of Defense has authorized for the use of stand-by military reservists on a voluntary basis for civil defense service at the request of civil defense authorities. As an incentive, these reservists will be given retirement-point credit for such service."

DOCUMENT 8: KHRUSHCHEV ORDERS REMOVAL OF MISSILES FROM CUBA

Khrushchev's October 28 message announces his decision to order removal of missiles from Cuba in exchange for Kennedy's promise not to invade Cuba.[8]

Official English text of Khrushchev Message
Moscow Tass in English to Europe A611 28 Oct 62

Dear Mr. President:

I have received your message of October 27. I express my satisfaction and thank you for the sense of proportion you have displayed and for realization of the responsibility which now devolves on you for the preservation of the peace of the world.

I regard with great understanding your concern and the concern of the United States people in connection with the fact that the weapons you describe as offensive are formidable weapons indeed. Both you and we understand what kind of weapons these are.

In order to eliminate as rapidly as possible the conflict which endangers the cause of peace, to give an assurance to all people who crave peace, and to reassure the American people, who, I am certain, also want peace, as do the people of the Soviet Union, the Soviet Government, in addition to earlier instructions on the discontinuation of further work on weapons constructions sites, has given a new order to dismantle the arms which you described as offensive, and to crate and return them to the Soviet Union. . . .

Mr. President, I should like to repeat what I had already written to you in my earlier messages—that the Soviet Government has given economic assistance to the Republic of Cuba, as well as arms, because Cuba and the Cuban people were constantly under the continuous threat of invasion of Cuba.

A piratic vessel has shelled Havana. They say that this shelling was done by irresponsible Cuban émigrés. Perhaps so, however, the question is from where did they shoot. It is a fact that these Cubans have no territory, they are fugitives from their country, and they have no means to conduct the military operations.

This means that someone put into their hands these weapons for shelling Havana and for piracy in the Caribbean in Cuban territorial waters. It is impossible in our time not to notice a piratic ship, considering the concentration in the Caribbean of American ships from which everything can be seen and observed.

In these conditions, pirate ships freely roam around and shell Cuba and make piratic attacks on peaceful cargo ships. It is known that they even shelled a British cargo ship. In a word, Cuba was under the continuous threat of aggressive forces, which did not conceal their intention to invade its territory.

The Cuban people want to build their life in their own interests without external interference. This is their right, and they cannot be blamed for wanting to be masters of their own country and disposing of the fruits of their own labor.

The threat of invasion of Cuba and all other schemes for creating tension over Cuba are designed to strike the Cuban people with a sense of insecurity, intimidate them, and prevent them from peacefully building their new life.

Mr. President, I should like to say clearly once more that we could not remain indifferent to this. The Soviet Government decided to render assistance to Cuba with the means of defense against aggression—only with means for defense purposes. We have supplied the defense means which you describe as offensive means. We have supplied them to prevent an attack on Cuba—to prevent rash acts.

I regard with respect and trust the statement you made in your message of October 27, 1962, that there would be no attack, no invasion of Cuba, and not only on the part of the United States, but also on the part of other nations of the Western Hemisphere, as you said in your same message. Then the motives which induced us to render assistance of such a kind to Cuba disappear.

It is for this reason that we introduced our officers—these means as I had already informed you earlier are in the hands of the Soviet officers—to take appropriate measures to discontinue construction of the afore-mentioned facilities, to dismantle them, and to return them to the Soviet Union. As I had informed you in the letter of October 27th, we are prepared to reach agreement to enable United Nations Representatives to verify the dismantling of these means.

Thus in view of the assurances you have given and our instructions on dismantling, there is every condition for eliminating the present conflict.

I note with satisfaction that you have responded to the desire I expressed with regard to elimination of the aforementioned dangerous situation, as well as with regard to providing conditions for a more thoughtful appraisal of the international situation, fraught as it is with great dangers in our age of thermonuclear weapons, rocketry, spaceships, global rockets, and other deadly weapons. All people are interested in insuring peace.

Therefore, vested with trust and great responsibility, we must not allow the situation to become aggravated and must stamp out the centers where a dangerous situation fraught with grave consequences to the cause of peace has arisen. If we, together with you, and with the assistance of other people of good will, succeed in eliminating this tense atmosphere, we should also make certain that no other dangerous conflicts which could lead to a world nuclear catastrophe would arise.

In conclusion, I should like to say something about a détente between NATO and the Warsaw Treaty countries that you have mentioned. We have spoken about this long since and are prepared to continue to exchange views on this question with you and to find a reasonable solution.

We should like to continue the exchange of views on the prohibition of atomic and thermonuclear weapons, general disarmament, and other problems relating to the relaxation of international tensions.

Although I trust your statement, Mr. President, there are irresponsible people who would like to invade Cuba now and thus touch off a war. If we do take practical steps and proclaim the dismantling and evacuation of the means in question from Cuba, in so doing we, at the same time, want the Cuban people to be certain that we are with them and are not absolving ourselves of responsibility for rendering assistance to the Cuban people.

We are confident that the people of all countries, like you, Mr. President, will understand me correctly. We are not threatening. We want nothing but peace. Our country is now on the upsurge.

Our people are enjoying the fruits of their peaceful labor. They have achieved tremendous successes since the October Revolution, and created the greatest material, spiritual, and cultural values. Our people are enjoying these values; they want to continue developing their achievements and insure their further development on the way of peace and social progress by their persistent labor.

But during your term of office as President another violation of our border has occurred, by an American U-2 plane in the Sakhalin area. We wrote you about that violation on 30 August. At that time, you replied that that violation had occurred as a result of poor weather, and gave assurances that this would not be repeated. We trusted your assurance, because the weather was indeed poor in that area at that time.

But had not your planes been ordered to fly about our territory, even poor weather could not have brought an American plane into our airspace. Hence, the conclusion that this is being done with the knowledge of the Pentagon, which tramples on international norms and violates the borders of other states.

A still more dangerous case occurred on 28 October, when one of your reconnaisance planes intruded over Soviet borders in the Chukotka Peninsula area in the north and flew over our territory. The question is, Mr. President: How should we regard this. What is this: A provocation? One of your planes violates our frontier during this anxious time we are both experiencing, when everything has been put into combat readiness. Is it not a fact that an intruding American plane could be easily taken for a nuclear bomber, which might push us to a fateful step? And all the more so since the U.S. Government and Pentagon long ago declared that you are maintaining a continuous nuclear bomber patrol.

Therefore, you can imagine the responsibility you are assuming, especially now, when we are living through such anxious times.

I should like to express the following wish: it concerns the Cuban people. You do not have diplomatic relations. But through my officers in Cuba, I have reports that American planes are making flights over Cuba.

We are interested that there should be no war in the world, and that the Cuban people should live in peace. And besides, Mr. President, it is no secret that we have our people in Cuba. Under such a treaty with the Cuban Government we have sent there officers, instructors, mostly plain people: specialists, agronomists, zootechnicians, irrigators, land reclamation specialists, plain workers, tractor drives, and others. We are concerned about them.

I should like you to consider, Mr. President, that violation of Cuban airspace by American planes could also lead to dangerous consequences. And if you do not want this to happen, it would be better if no cause is given for a dangerous situation to arise.

We must be careful now and refrain from any steps which would not be useful to the defense of the states involved in the conflict which could only cause irritation and even serve as a provocation for a fateful step. Therefore, we must display sanity, reason, and refrain from such steps.

We value peace perhaps even more than other peoples because we went through a terrible war with Hitler. But our people will not falter in the face of any test. Our people trust their Government and we assure our people and world public opinion that the Soviet Government will not allow itself to be provoked. But if the provocateurs unleash a war, they will not evade responsibility and the grave consequences a war would bring upon them. But we are confident that reason will triumph, that war will not be unleashed and peace and the security of peoples will be insured.

In connection with the current negotiations between Acting Secretary General U Thant and representatives of the Soviet Union, the United States, and the Republic of Cuba, the Soviet Government has sent First Deputy Foreign Minister V.V. Kuznetsov to New York to help U Thant in his noble efforts aimed at eliminating the present dangerous situation.

Signed: Respectfully yours, N. Khrushchev
October 28, 1962

DOCUMENT 9: KENNEDY RESPONDS TO KHRUSHCHEV AGREEMENT

President Kennedy responds with relief to Khrushchev's message.[9]

Message in Reply to a Broadcast by Chairman Khrushchev on the Cuban Crisis. October 28, 1962

Dear Mr. Chairman:

I am replying at once to your broadcast message of October twenty-eight, even though the official text has not yet reached me, because of the great importance I attach to moving forward promptly to the settlement of the Cuban crisis. I think that you and I, with our heavy responsibilities for the maintenance of peace, were aware that developments were approaching a point where events could have become unmanageable. So I welcome this message and consider it an important contribution to peace.

The distinguished efforts of Acting Secretary General U Thant have greatly facilitated both our tasks. I consider my letter to you of October twenty-seventh and your reply of today as firm undertakings on the part of both our governments which should be taken through the United Nations, as your message says, so that the United States in turn will be able to remove the quarantine measures now in effect. I have already made arrangements to report all these matters to the Organization of American States, whose members share a deep interest in a genuine peace in the Caribbean area.

You referred in your letter to a violation of your frontier by an American aircraft in the area of the Chukotskiy Peninsula. I have learned that this plane, without arms or photographic equipment, was engaged in an air sampling mission in connection with your nuclear tests. Its course was direct from Eielson Air Force Base in Alaska to the North Pole and return. In turning south, the pilot made a serious navigational error which carried him over Soviet territory. He immediately made an emergency call on open radio for navigational assistance and was guided back to his home base by the most direct route. I regret this incident and will see to it that every precaution is taken to prevent recurrence.

Mr. Chairman, both of our countries have great unfinished tasks and I know that your people as well as those of the United States can ask nothing better than to pursue them free from the fear of war. Modern science and technology have given us the possibility of making labor fruitful beyond anything that could have been dreamed of a few decades ago.

I agree with you that we must devote urgent attention to the problems of disarmament, as it relates to the whole world and also to critical areas. Perhaps now, as we step back from danger, we can together make real progress in this vital field. I think we should also work hard to see if wider measures of disarmament can be agreed and put into operation at an early date. The United States Government will be prepared to discuss these questions urgently, and in a constructive spirit, at Geneva or elsewhere.

John F. Kennedy

Notes

Abbreviations

DDEL	Dwight D. Eisenhower Library in Abilene, Kansas
DNSA	Digital National Security Archive
JFKL	John F. Kennedy Library in Boston
JFK–NA	John F. Kennedy Assassination Records at National Archives II in College Park, Maryland
LBJL	Lyndon B. Johnson Library in Austin
LOC	Library of Congress
MLKL&A	Martin Luther King Jr. Library and Archives in Atlanta
NSA	National Security Archive
NY—RAC	Rockefeller Archive Center in Pocantico Hills
PC	Paley Center for Media in New York
RWWL	Robert W. Woodruff Library in Atlanta
SGMML	Seeley G. Mudd Manuscript Library in Princeton
WHS	Wisconsin Historical Society in Madison

1 The Chill of the Nuclear Age

1   Under the leadership of Tito, Yugoslavia adopted Communism but maintained greater independence than its Eastern European neighbors.

2   This term was introduced in an article published in 1947 in *Foreign Affairs*. The article, written under the pseudonym "X," was penned by professional diplomat George Kennan. Containment was not the only catch phrase born in the Cold War. Churchill became the first to refer to Stalin's isolation of Eastern Europe as an "Iron Curtain," sealing it away from the West.

3   Margaret Mead, *And Keep Your Powder Dry* (New York: William Morrow and Company, 1942), 234–5.

4   John F. Kennedy, "The Vigor We Need," *Sports Illustrated*, July 16, 1962, 12.

5   Reinhold Niebuhr, *The Children of Light and the Children of Darkness* (New York: Charles Scribner's Sons, 1959), ix.

6   Alton Frye, "VI.B." in *American Character and Foreign Policy*, ed. Michael P. Hamilton (Grand Rapids, Michigan: W.B. Eerdman's Publishing Company, 1986), 152.

7   John L. Gaddis, "II.A." in *American Character and Foreign Policy*, 29.

8   Anatoli I. Gribkov and William Y. Smith, with ed. Alfred Friendly, *Operation Anadyr: U.S. and Soviet Generals Recount the Cuban Missile Crisis* (Chicago: Edition Q, 1993), 80.

9   Louis Harris and Associates, "A Pilot Study of American Knowledge of and Attitudes Toward Communism in Russia and in the United States," Prepared for National Broadcasting Company, January 1962, 7, Theodore Sorensen Papers, Box 54, Folder 3, JFKL.

10   George H. Gallup, *The Gallup Poll: Public Opinion 1935–1971, Volume 3, 1959–71* (New York: Random House, 1972), 1753.

11   Aleksandr Fursenko and Timothy Naftali, *Khrushchev's Cold War* (New York: W. W. Norton & Co., 2006), 305.

12   Ibid., 328.

13   Gallup, 1758.

14   James G. Blight and David A. Welch, *On the Brink* (New York: Hill and Wang), 183.

15   Frank B. Ellis, "Basic Report of Civil Defense and Defense Mobilization," February 1961, 18, Presidential Office Files, Departments and Agencies, Office of Emergency Planning, Box 84a, Basic Report of Civil and Defense Mobilization Office Folder, JFKL.

16   Ernest R. May and Philip D. Zelikow, eds., "Introduction," *The Kennedy Tapes: Inside the White House During the Cuban Missile Crisis* (Cambridge: Belknap Press, 1997), 14.

17   Fursenko and Naftali, *Khrushchev's Cold War*, 430.

18   Lawrence Freedman, *Kennedy's Wars: Berlin, Cuba, Laos, and Vietnam* (Oxford: Oxford University Press, 2000), 47.

19   Stephen E. Ambrose, *Eisenhower, Volume 2: The President* (New York: Simon and Schuster, 1984), 494.

20   William R. Kintner, "The Communist Strategy of Protracted Conflict," Johns Hopkins University Operations Research Office, October 1956, 1, Rockefeller Brothers Fund Records, Special Studies, Box 14, Folder 157, Synopsis Folder, RAC.

21   Gallup, 1726.

22   Michael Mandelbaum, *The Nuclear Revolution: International Politics Before and After Hiroshima* (Cambridge: Cambridge University Press, 1981), 218.

23   Gallup, 1759.

24   "U.S. Nuclear Weapons Accidents (1950–1980) Acknowledged by the Pentagon," Operations—Atomic Weapons Accident Subject File, 6E-6F, United States Marine Corps Historical Center in Washington.

25   Caron Myers, "The Night the Sky Fell," *Our State*, June 2012, 52–5.

26   "U.S. Nuclear Weapons Accidents (1950–1980) Acknowledged by the Pentagon."

27   Dwight D. Eisenhower, Diary, January 11, 1956, Papers of the President of the United States (Ann Whitman File), DDE Diary Series, Box 12, January 56 Diary Folder, DDEL.

28   National Security Council, "A Federal Shelter Program for Civil Defense," March 29, 1957, 1, National Security Series, Policy Papers, Box 2, NSC 5709—Shelter Program for Civil Defense Folder, DDEL.

29   Curtis E. Harvey, "Civil Defense Abroad in Review," in *Survival and the Bomb* ed. Eugene Paul Wigner (Bloomington: Indiana University Press, 1969), 159–62.

30   "Discussion of the 318th Meeting of the National Security Council, Thursday, April 4, 1957," Papers of the President of the United States (Ann Whitman File), National Security Council Series, Box 8, 318th Meeting Folder, DDEL.

31   "Minutes of the Second Plenary of the Interim Assembly," Cabinet Series, Box 5, Special Cabinet Meeting of June 17, 1955 Folder, DDEL.

32   "The Human Effects of Nuclear Weapons Development," Papers of the President of the United States (Ann Whitman File), Nuclear Security Council Series, Briefing Notes, Box 9, Human Effects of Nuclear Weapons Development (2) Folder, DDEL.

33   David Oliver Relin, "The Era of Fear," *Scholastic Update*, September 7, 1990, 11.

34   Kenneth C. Rose, *One Nation Underground* (New York: New York University Press, 2001), 31.

35   Asher Byrnes and Garrett Underhill, "Civil Defense Muddle," *New Republic*, January 15, 1962, 8.

36   Alice L. George, *Awaiting Armageddon: How Americans Faced the Cuban Missile Crisis* (Chapel Hill: University of North Carolina Press, 2003), 59.

37   Gallup, 1741.

38   Ibid., 1732.

39   Ibid., 1745.

40   Rose, 188.

41   To examine the Eisenhower administration's stand on the prospect of creating a doomsday machine, see U.S. Information Agency, "Infoguide: *On the Beach*," December 4, 1959, 1–3, White House Office, Cabinet Secretariat: Records, 1953–60, Box 22, CP 64, DDEL. In 1961, analyst Herman Kahn testified before a U.S. House subcommittee that he expected development of a weapon that could eradicate human life by 1971. See "Civil Defense—1961," Hearing of the House of Representatives, Subcommittee on Military Operations, Committee on Government Operations, August 7, 1961, *Congressional Record*, 167.

42   The titles of U.S. civil defense operations changed often, possibly as a reflection of the programs' insubstantiality.

43   "Minutes of Cabinet Meeting," December 11, 1959, 2, Cabinet Series, Box 15, Cabinet Meeting of December 11, 1959 Folder, DDEL.

44   *On the Beach*, directed and produced by Stanley Kramer, screenplay by John Paxton, United Artists, 1959.

45   Eugene Burdick and Harvey Wheeler, *Fail-Safe* (New York: McGraw-Hill Book Company, 1962), 98.

46   Fletcher Knebel and Charles Bailey, *Seven Days in May* (New York: Harper & Row, 1962), 118.

47   C.L. Sulzberger, *Last of the Giants* (New York: MacMillan, 1970), 935.

48   See Theodore C. Sorensen, *Kennedy* (New York: Harper & Row, 1965), 606–7, and Richard Reeves, *President Kennedy: Profile in Power* (New York: Simon & Schuster, 1993), 305.

49   Interestingly, Robert Kennedy used a veiled suggestion of a military coup to convince Soviet leaders that they needed to make a deal with JFK quickly before things slipped beyond the president's control.

50   Rod Serling, "Time Enough to Last," *The Twilight Zone*, CBS, November 20, 1959, T82–0044, PC.

51   Serling, "The Shelter," *The Twilight Zone*, CBS, September 29, 1961, B:20062, PC.

52   James Aronson, *The Press and the Cold War* (Indianapolis: Bobbs-Merrill, 1970), 37.

53   Sidney Kraus, Reuben Mehling, and Elaine El-Assal, "Mass Media and the Fallout Controversy," *Public Opinion Quarterly* 27, no. 2 (Summer 1963): 198.

54   James G. Blight, Bruce J. Allyn, and David A. Welch, *Cuba on the Brink* (Lanham: Rowman and Littlefield Publishers Inc., 2002), 324.

55   These island territories were among the last remnants of Spain's once-massive empire.

56   Louis A. Pérez Jr., *Cuba In the American Imagination: Metaphor and Imperial Ethos* (Chapel Hill: University of North Carolina Press, 2008), 259.

57   Ibid., 252.

58   Ibid., 254.

59   Aleksandr Fursenko and Timothy Naftali, *"One Hell of a Gamble:" Khrushchev, Castro, and Kennedy, 1958–1964* (New York: W.W. Norton & Company, 1998), 40.

60   William J. vanden Heuvel, "Cuba: Its Refugees and its Liberation," September 6, 1962, National Security Files, Box 56, Cuba Subjects, Cuban Refugees, 8/61–3/63 Folder, JFKL.

61   "Soviet Control and Influence in Cuba," October 12, 1962, National Security Files, Box 415, Robert W. Komer, 10/10/62–10/25/62 Folder, JFKL. More than twenty-five years later, Cuba was virtually crippled when the Soviet Union and its allies collapsed.

62   Jim Rasenberger, *Brilliant Disaster: JFK, Castro and America's Doomed Invasion of Cuba's Bay of Pigs* (New York: Scribner, 2011), 55–6.

63   Fursenko and Naftali, *"One Hell of a Gamble,"* 39.

64   Fursenko and Naftali, *Khrushchev's Cold War*, 427–8.

65   Fursenko and Naftali, *"One Hell of a Gamble,"* 166.

66   Ibid., 61.

67   Rasenberger, 109.

68   Roger Hilsman, *To Move a Nation* (New York: Doubleday and Co., 1967), 32.

69   Roger Hilsman, "Soviet Public Statements with Respect to Cuban Security," September 14, 1962, Roger Hilsman Papers, Record Number 176–10030–10242, JFK-NA.

70   Fursenko and Naftali, *"One Hell of a Gamble,"* 85.

71   Rasenberger, 151.

72   Ibid., 164–5.

73   Arthur M. Schlesinger Jr., *A Thousand Days* (Boston: Houghton-Mifflin Company, 1965), 259.

74   Rasenberger, 1.

75   Sorensen, *Kennedy*, 308–9.

76   Mike Mansfield, Confidential Memorandum to John F. Kennedy, May 1, 1961, Vice Presidential Security File, Box 4, National Security Council (III) Folder, LBJL.

77   C.L. Sulzberger, "Foreign Affairs; And Nothing Fails Like Failure," *New York Times*, April 21, 1961, 24.

78   John F. Kennedy, "The President's News Conference of April 21, 1961," *Public Papers of the Presidents: John F. Kennedy 1961* (Washington: Government Printing Office, 1962), 313.

79   Arthur M. Schlesinger Jr., *Journals, 1952–2000* (New York: Penguin, 2007), 120–1.

80   James Reston, "Kennedy's First Defeat: How Will He React?" *New York Times*, April 23, 1961, 192.

81   Gribkov and Smith, 89.

82   Dr. Julio Amoedo, "Cuba's Situation Up to February 6th, 1962," Presidential Office Files, Box 114, Folder 29, http://www.jfklibrary.org/Asset-Viewer/ Archives/JFKPOF-114-029, last accessed May 29, 2012, JFKL.

83   National Security Council, "Strengthening Freedom in the Americas," April 26, 1961, Vice Presidential Security File, Box 4, National Security Council—1961 (1 of 2) Folder, LBJL.

84   Sorensen, *Kennedy*, 669–70.

85   Rasenberger, 357.

86   Central Intelligence Agency, "The Economic Situation in Cuba," April 25, 1962, Presidential Office Files, Box 115, Folder 4, http://www.jfklibrary.org/Asset-Viewer/Archives/JFKPOF-115–004, last accessed May 29, 2012, JFKL.

87   Blight, Allyn, and Welch, 163.

88   Ibid., 158.

89   William H. Craig, Report, January 24, 1962, 2, Rockefeller Commission Records, Box 3, Assassination Materials, Miscellaneous Rockefeller Commission and CIA Files Folder, Document number 178-10002-10414, JFK-NA.

90   Dobbs, 13.

91   Thomas A. Parrott, "Minutes of Meeting of the Special Group (Augmented) on Operation MONGOOSE," October 4, 1962, Rockefeller Commission Records, Box 3, Assassination Materials, Miscellaneous Rockefeller Commission and CIA Files (2) Folder, Document Number 157–10007–10289, JFK-NA.

92   John A. McCone, "Memorandum of Mongoose Meeting Held on Thursday, October 4, 1962," October 4, 1962, Rockefeller Commission Records, Box 4, Assassination Materials, Miscellaneous Rockefeller Commission and CIA Files (3) Folder, Record Number 178–10002–10405, JFK-NA.

93   "Introduction," May and Zelikow, 36.

94   Blight, Allyn, and Welch, 155.

95   Michael Dobbs, *One Minute to Midnight* (New York: Alfred A. Knopf, 2008), 10.

96   Select Committee to Study Governmental Operations, U.S. Senate, 94th Congress, "Alleged Assassination Plots Involving Foreign Leaders," November 20, 1975, 138–9, http://history-matters.com/archive/contents/church/contents_church_ reports_ir.htm, last accessed March 15, 2012.

2 Kennedy and Khrushchev

1   Fursenko and Naftali, *Khrushchev's Cold War*, 340.

2   It is not unthinkable that an unstable president could cause a nuclear war in an age when death could be delivered around the world within minutes. Colleagues

of both Lyndon Johnson and Richard Nixon have described them as mentally unstable at times during their presidencies—and either man had the power to launch a nuclear war, although those same colleagues might have averted such action.

3   The United States' allies in the North Atlantic Treaty Organization sometimes worried that if the Soviet Union moved against a European nation, the United States might hesitate to risk its own security by using nuclear weapons to stop the attack. This anxiety led to the placement of American missiles in Great Britain, Italy, and Turkey—weapons that did little to protect American interests and did not substantially increase the threat facing the Soviet Union.

4   Blight, Allyn, and Welch, 131.

5   Schlesinger, *A Thousand Days*, 374.

6   Robert Dallek, *An Unfinished Life* (Boston: Little Brown, 2003), 413.

7   Edwin O. Guthman and Jeffrey Shulman, eds., *Robert Kennedy In His Own Words* (New York: Bantam Books, 1988), 29.

8   The comment was later reported by Sergo Mikoyan, son of and assistant to Khrushchev's comrade, Anastas Mikoyan. See Blight and Welch, 289.

9   Fursenko and Naftali, *Khrushchev's Cold War*, 410.

10   Arnold L. Horelick, "The Cuban Missile Crisis: An Analysis of Soviet Calculations and Behavior," Rand Corporation, September 1963, 5.

11   Natural Resources Defense Council, "Table of USSR/Russian ICBM Forces: 1960–69," *Archive of Nuclear Data*, http://www.nrdc.org/nuclear/nudb/datab4.asp, last accessed June 2, 2012.

12   Natural Resources Defense Council, "Table of USSR/Russian Strategic Bomber Forces: 1960–69," *Archive of Nuclear Data*, http://www.nrdc.org/nuclear/nudb/datab8.asp, last accessed June 2, 2012.

13   Natural Resources Defense Council, "Table of US ICBM Forces: 1959–69," *Archive of Nuclear Data*, http://www.nrdc.org/nuclear/nudb/datab3.asp, last accessed June 2, 2012.

14   Natural Resources Defense Council, "Table of US Ballistic Missile Submarine Forces," *Archive of Nuclear Data*, http://www.nrdc.org/nuclear/nudb/datab5.asp, last accessed June 2, 2012.

15   "Table of US Strategic Bomber Forces: 1960–69," *Archive of Nuclear Data*, http://www.nrdc.org/nuclear/nudb/datab7.asp, last accessed June 2, 2012.

16   Natural Resources Defense Council, "Table of US Nuclear Warheads: 1945–1975," *Archive of Nuclear Data*, http://www.nrdc.org/nuclear/nudb/datab9.asp, last accessed June 2, 2012.

17   Natural Resources Defense Council, "Table of USSR/Russian Nuclear Warheads, 1949–75," *Archive of Nuclear Data*, http://www.nrdc.org/nuclear/nudb/datab10.asp, last accessed June 2, 2012.

18   Bruce J. Allyn, James G. Blight, and David A. Welch, eds., *Back to the Brink* (Lanham, MD: University Press of America, 1992), 23.

19   Nikita Khrushchev, *Khrushchev Remembers*, trans. and ed. Strobe Talbott, (Boston: Little, Brown and Company, 1970), 494.

20   Ibid., 494.

21   Sergei N. Khrushchev, *Nikita Khrushchev and the Creation of a Superpower* (University Park: Pennsylvania State University Press, 2000), 482.

22 Blema S. Steinberg, "Shame and Humiliation in the Cuban Missile Crisis: A Psychoanalytic Perspective," *Political Psychology* 12, no. 4 (December 1991), 662.

23 Allyn, Blight, and Welch, 38.

24 Gribkov and Smith, 11.

25 Stewart Alsop, "Kennedy's Grand Strategy," *Saturday Evening Post*, March 31, 1962, 14.

26 L.J. Legere, Memorandum, "Schröder–McNamara Meeting Tuesday, October 16," President's Office Files," Germany, Box 117, German Security, 1962 Folder; Digital identifier, JFKPOF-117–009, http://www.jfklibrary.org/Asset-Viewer/Archives/JFKPOF-117-009.aspx, last accessed June 2, 2012, JFKL.

27 Sergei N. Khrushchev, 489.

28 Ibid., 492.

29 Fursenko and Naftali, *Khrushchev's Cold War*, 437.

30 Sergei N. Khrushchev, 490.

31 Nikita Khrushchev, 492.

32 Gribkov and Smith, 28.

33 Ibid., 9.

34 Sergei N. Khrushchev, 494.

35 Anadyr is the name of both a river and a city in Siberia.

36 Fursenko and Naftali, *Khrushchev's Cold War*, 447.

37 Memcon between Udall and Khrushchev, September 6, 1962, in *Foreign Relations of the United States 1961–63*, Vol. 15, 308–10.

38 Gribkov and Smith, 15.

39 Ibid., 25.

40 Ibid., 27–8.

41 Dobbs, 27–8.

42 Gribkov and Smith, 30.

43 Preparedness Investigating Subcommittee of the Committee on Armed Services, U.S. Senate, *Investigations of the Preparedness Program: Interim Report* (Washington: Government Printing Office, 1963), 6.

44 Sergei N. Khrushchev, 512.

45 Gribkov and Smith, 46.

46 Ray S. Cline, Interview by William E. Ratliff and Roger W. Fontaine, Ray S. Cline Miscellaneous Papers, 1992–1993, Folder 94026–10.V, Hoover Institution.

47 Analyst Raymond Garthoff later concluded that among hundreds of reports from refugees about offensive weapons in Cuba, only two turned out to be correct. See Blight and Welch, 41.

48 Jay Mallin, "Mass Landings Confirmed," *Miami News*, August 16, 1962, 1.

49 "Castro Means Business," *Washington Daily News*, August 25, 1962, 12.

50 "Foreign Reds See Dividing Cuba 3 Ways," *Tampa Tribune*, September 19, 1962, 1.

51 McGeorge Bundy, "National Security Action Memorandum No. 181," August 23, 1962, National Security Files, Box 338, NSAM 181 Cuba (A) August 23, 1962 Folder, JFKL.

52 In the aftermath of Kennedy's murder, President Lyndon Johnson used sympathy for Kennedy and LBJ's own persuasive powers to push through much of Kennedy's legislative program, including the civil rights legislation.

53   Dino Brugioni, *Eyeball to Eyeball: The Inside Story of the Cuban Missile Crisis* (New York: Random House, 1990), 115.

54   John F. Kennedy, Secret Memo, September 4, 1962, Digital File, Cuba: General, 1962: 1 January-22 October, http://www.jfklibrary.org/Asset-Viewer/Archives/ JFKPOF-114-029.aspx, last accessed June 2, 2011, JFKL.

55   Christopher Andrew, *For the President's Eyes Only* (New York: Harper Perennial, 1996), 284.

56   John F. Kennedy, "The President's News Conference of September 13, 1962," *Public Papers of the Presidents: John F. Kennedy 1962* (Washington: Government Printing Office, 1963), 674.

57   Central Intelligence Agency, "Special National Intelligence Estimate 85–3-62: The Military Buildup in Cuba," Sept. 19, 1962 in *CIA Documents on the Cuban Missile Crisis,* ed. Mary S. McAuliffe (Washington: Central Intelligence Agency History Staff, 1962), 93.

58   Brugioni, 159.

59   Walter Lippmann, "On War over Cuba," as quoted by Senator Wayne Morse in *The Congressional Record*, October 9, 1962, 21648.

60   "Department of Defense Operations During the Cuban Crisis," Undated, 1, National Security Files, Box 55, Cuba Subjects, Cuba Testimony Defense and Military Responses Folder, JFKL.

61   Preparedness Investigating Subcommittee of the Committee on Armed Services, United States Senate, 8.

62   Preparedness Investigating Subcommittee of the Committee on Armed Services, United States Senate, 8.

3 The Ticking Clock

1   When Kennedy asked four months later why Bundy had not notified him the night before, Bundy replied in a memo that could be boiled down to one sentence: "What help would it be to you to give you this piece of news and then tell you nothing could be done till morning?" See Sorensen, *Kennedy*, 673.

2   Freedman, 169.

3   John Lewis Gaddis, *We Now Know: Rethinking Cold War History* (Oxford: Clarendon Press, 1997), 263.

4   Fursenko and Naftali, 39.

5   Dobbs, 45.

6   May and Zelikow, "Tuesday, October 16, 11:50 a.m., Cabinet Room," 65.

7   Dobbs, 3.

8   Former Soviet officials speaking at the various crisis conferences in the 1980s and 1990s unanimously agreed that the crisis in Cuba had no connection to Soviet claims on West Berlin. See Blight and Welch, 327.

9   Blight and Welch, 190.

10   In their book, *Essence of Decision*, Graham Allison and Philip Zelikow argue that Kennedy wholeheartedly endorsed logic in which Berlin's importance so outweighed Cuba's that the only way to explain Khrushchev's actions was through the perspective of Berlin's defender. See Allison and Zelikow, *Essence of Decision: Explaining the Cuban Missile Crisis*, 2nd edition (New York: Longman, 1999), 77–142.

11   "Tuesday, October 16, 11:50 a.m., Cabinet Room," 63.

12   Ibid., 59.

13   Ibid., 67.

14   Marshall S. Carter, Memorandum, "Operation MONGOOSE/Sabotage Proposals," October 16, 1962, Rockefeller Commission Records, Box 3A, Assassination Materials Miscellaneous Rockefeller Commission and CIA Files, Document Number 178–10002–10498, JFK-NA.

15   Richard Helms, Memorandum, "MONGOOSE Meeting with the Attorney General," October 16, 1962 in *The Secret Cuban Missile Crisis Documents*, 153.

16   Kennedy slightly misquoted a poem by Domingo Ortega.

17   Dobbs, 14.

18   "DOD, Transcripts, SECRET, Notes Taken from Transcripts of Meetings of the Joint Chiefs of Staff, October–November 1962," 4–5, *The Cuban Missile Crisis, 1962: The Documents,* http://www.gwu.edu/~nsarchiv/nsa/cuba_mis_cri/docs.htm, last accessed June 2, 2012, NSA.

19   Fletcher Knebel, "Washington Crisis: 154 Hours on the Brink of War," *Look,* December 18, 1962, 50.

20   Gribkov and Smith, 6.

21   Ibid., 4.

22   Fursenko and Naftali, *"One Hell of a Gamble,"* 242.

23   Blight, Allyn, and Welch, 354.

24   "Gallup Poll Being Released Sunday, October 14," National Security Files, Box 36, Cuba General 10/15/62–10/23/62 Folder, JFKL.

25   Robert F. Kennedy, *Thirteen Days* (New York: W.W. Norton & Company, 1971), 28.

26   Theodore Sorensen, "Summary of Agreed Facts and Premises, Possible Courses of Action and Unanswered Questions, October 17, 1962," eds. Laurence Chang and Peter Kornbluh, *The Cuban Missile Crisis, 1962: A National Security Archive Documents Reader* (New York: The New Press, 1992), 124.

27   *Cuban Missile Crisis of 1962—Studies in the Employment of Air Power, Volume 6* (Montgomery, Air University, 1988), 362–3.

28   "DOD, Transcripts, SECRET, Notes Taken from Transcripts of Meetings of the Joint Chiefs of Staff, October–November 1962," 7.

29   C.E. Bohlen, "Possible Soviet Reactions to the Following Alternatives," Presidential Office Files, Box 115, Cuba: Security, 1962 Folder 4, Digital Identifier, JFKPOF-115–004, http://www.jfklibrary.org/Asset-Viewer/Archives/JFKPOF-115–004.aspx, last accessed June 2, 2012, JFKL.

30   Gribkov and Smith, 51–2.

31   May and Zelikow, "Thursday, October 18, 11:00 a.m., Cabinet Room," 134.

32   Andrei Gromyko, *Memoirs,* trans. Harold Shukman (New York: Doubleday, 1989), 178.

33   Department of State, Memorandum, "Germany and Berlin; Possible Visit by Khrushchev," October 18, 1962, 11, Presidential Office Files, Box 115, Cuba: Security, 1962 Folder 4, Digital Identifier JFKPOF-115–004, http://www.jfklibrary.org/Asset-Viewer/Archives/JFKPOF-115–004.aspx, last accessed June 2, 2012, JFKL.

34   Elie Abel, *The Missile Crisis* (Philadelphia: J.B. Lippincott Co., 1966), 77.

35   "Thursday, October 18, 11 a.m., Cabinet Room," 121.

36   George W. Ball, "Excerpts from an interview with George W. Ball, May 1, 1987 in Princeton, NJ," 1, George Ball Papers, Box 69, Cuban Missile Crisis Folder, SGMML.

37   Brugioni, 290–1.

38   John M. McGuire, "The Day the Cold War Almost Ignited; Soldier Recalls Mystery of '62 Missile Crisis," *St. Louis Post-Dispatch*, October 27, 1997, 3E.

39   Gribkov and Smith, 209.

40   "DOD, Transcripts, SECRET, Notes Taken from Transcripts of Meetings of the Joint Chiefs of Staff, October-November 1962," 10–11.

41   Here, again, we see U.S. leaders struggling to understand the Cuban Missile Crisis by using World War II as a lens. See May and Zelikow, "Friday, October 19, 9:45 a.m., Cabinet Room," 178.

42   Introduction," May and Zelikow, 10.

43   Brugioni, 265.

44   Dobbs, 22.

45   George Ball, 2.

46   John Kenneth Galbraith, oral history interview by Vicki Daitch, September 12, 2003, 21, JFKL.

47   Dobbs, 18.

48   David Detzer, *The Brink: The Cuban Missile Crisis, 1962* (New York: Crowell, 1979), 162.

49   Brugioni, 306.

50   Fursenko and Naftali, *"One Hell of a Gamble,"* 233.

51   May and Zelikow, "Saturday, October 20, 2:30 p.m., Oval Room in Executive Mansion," 189.

52   Fursenko and Naftali, *"One Hell of a Gamble,"* 234.

53   Andrew, 291.

54   Sergei N. Khrushchev, 551.

55   McGeorge Bundy, Interview by Martin Agronsky, *Cuban White Paper*, NBC, Arthur M. Schlesinger Jr. Papers, Box W-6, McGeorge Bundy Interviewed Folder, JFKL.

56   "Draft Message to Cuban Government," October 20, 1962, National Security Files, Box 54, Cuba, NSC Meeting Papers, 10/20/62–10/21/62 Folder, JFKL.

57   "Cuba and Berlin—Some Hypothetical Questions," October 20, 1962, National Security Files, Box 36, Cuba, General, 10/15/62–10/23/62 Folder, JFKL.

58   Brugioni, 306.

59   Central Intelligence Agency, "SNIE 11–19–62: Major Consequences of Certain US Courses of Action on Cuba," http://www.gwu.edu/~nsarchiv/nsa/cuba_mis_cri/docs.htm, last accessed June 2, 2012, NSA.

60   Sergei N. Khrushchev, 489.

61   Paul Nitze, Steven L. Rearden, and Ann M. Smith, *From Hiroshima to Glasnost* (New York: Grove Press, 1989), 222.

62   William P. Bundy, "Possible Soviet Courses of Action against Overseas Bases and their Vulnerability to Such Actions," October 20, 1962, National Security Files, Box 36, Cuba, General, 10/15/62–10/23/62 Folder, JFKL.

63   General Horace M. Wade, U.S. Air Force oral history interview, October 10–12, 358–9, Albert F. Simpson Historical Research Center, Office of Air Force History.

64   May and Zelikow, "Saturday, October 20, 2:30 p.m.," 197.

65   Douglas R. Cornell, "Kennedy Ends 6-State Tour Due to Cold," *Sunday (Washington) Star*, October 21, 1962, A-1.

66   Galbraith, 18.

67   Robert S. McNamara, "Secretary of Defense Robert McNamara, Military Briefing: Notes on October 21 Meeting with the President," October 21, 1962, 1, *The Cuban Missile Crisis, 1962: The Documents*, http://www.gwu.edu/~nsarchiv/nsa/cuba_mis_cri/docs.htm, last accessed June 2, 2012, NSA.

68   McNamara, 2.

69   Dean Acheson, oral history interview by Lucius D. Battle, April 27, 1964, 24, JFKL.

70   Unsigned Memorandum for the Director, "Chronology of DCI's Position Re Cuba," October 21, 1962, Rockefeller Commission Records, Box 3A, Assassination Materials Miscellaneous Rockefeller Commission and CIA Files, Document Number 178–10002–10495. JFK-NA.

71   Brugioni, 336–7.

72   George, 92.

73   Theodore C. Sorensen, oral history interview by Carl Kaysen, March 26, 1964, 55, JFKL.

74   "DOD, Transcripts, SECRET, Notes Taken from Transcripts of Meetings of the Joint Chiefs of Staff, October-November 1962," 14.

75   "Department of Defense Operations During the Cuban Missile Crisis," 2.

76   Gribkov and Smith, 211–12.

77   Fursenko and Naftali, *"One Hell of a Gamble,"* 237.

78   Roger Hilsman, "Soviets Skirt Issue of Cuban Missile Buildup," October 21, 1962, Roger Hilsman Papers, Box 1, Cuba 1962 Folder, Document Number 176–10030–10242, JFK-NA.

79   Vice Admiral G.E. Miller, Oral history interview #3 by John T. Mason, March 22, 1976, 335–9, U.S. Naval Institute.

80   "The Air Force Response to the Cuban Crisis 14 October–24 November 1962," January 1963, Document CC02811, NSA.

81   "DOD, Transcripts, SECRET, Notes Taken from Transcripts of Meetings of the Joint Chiefs of Staff, October-November 1962," 16.

82   Liz Kovacs, oral history interview by Sheldon Stern, June 7, 1978, JFKL.

83   "Parisian Scurried From Cuba," *Paris (Texas) News*, October 29, 1962, 1.

84   James Daniel and John G. Hubbard, *Strike in the West* (New York: Holt, Rinehart and Winston, 1963), 80.

85   Major John M. Young, *When the Russians Blinked: The U.S. Maritime Response to the Cuban Missile Crisis* (Washington: History and Museums Division Headquarters, U.S. Marine Corps, 1990), 160–1.

86   Brugioni, 247.

87   Dwight D. Eisenhower and John F. Kennedy, "Telephone Recordings: Dictation Belt 30.2 Cuban Missile Crisis Update," October 22, 1962, http://ww.jfklibrary.org/Asset-Viewer/Archives/JFKPOF-TPH-30–2.aspx, last accessed June 2, 2012, JFKL.

88   May and Zelikow, "Monday, October 22, 5 p.m., Cabinet Room," 256.

89   Eisenhower and Kennedy.

90   May and Zelikow, "Monday, October 22, 11:30 a.m., Cabinet Room."

91   Fursenko and Naftali, *Khrushchev's Cold War,* 468–9.

92   Ibid., 468–70.

93   Brugioni, 249.

94   Ibid., 330.

95   Jeffrey C. Kitchen, Memorandum, "Department of State Duty Officers Assigned to the National Military Command Center, JCS," October 22, 1962, George Ball Papers, Box 147, George Ball Notebook, SGMML.

96   Anthony Akers, oral history interview by William Moss, July 17, 1971, 39, JFKL.

97   Special to the *New York Times,* "Cuban Crisis: A Step-by-Step Review," *New York Times,* November 3, 1962, 6.

98   "Memorandum of Meeting Between President Kennedy and the Congressional Leadership on October 22," *The Kennedys and Cuba: The Declassified Documentary History,* ed. Mark J. White (Chicago: Ivan R. Dee, 1999), 199.

99   Elie Abel, NBC-TV News, October 22, 1962, Elie Abel Papers, Box 3, Elie Abel Scripts, Sept.–Dec. 1962 Folder, Twentieth Century Archives, Boston University.

100   John F. Kennedy, "Radio and Television Report to the American People on the Soviet Arms Buildup in Cuba," October 22, 1962, *Public Papers of the Presidents: John F. Kennedy 1962,* 806–9.

101   Paul Weeks, "Crowd Gathers Silently on Street and Listens Intently to President," *Los Angeles Times,* October 23, 1962, A1.

102   "Police Here Act to Prevent Disturbances Over Cuba," *New York Times,* October 23, 1962, 18.

103   Marion Gaines and Dick Hebert, "Man-on-Phone Stands Solidly With Kennedy," *Atlanta Constitution,* October 23, 1962, 6.

104   "Reaction Here Favors the President on Cuba," *Kansas City Times,* October 23, 1962, 3.

105   "Man on the Street Gives his Views on New Crisis," *Baltimore Sun,* October 23, 1962, 40.

106   Staff and Bureau Correspondents, "'Man on the Street' Approves Cuba Stand," *The (Columbia) State,* October 23, 1962, 12A.

107   "Speech Spreads a Subdued Mood Over Auto Show," *Detroit Free Press,* October 23, 1962, 5C.

108   "CBS News Extra: U.S. Quarantines Cuba," Douglas Edwards, anchor, October 22, 1962, T77:0494, PC.

109   Gaddis, *We Now Know: Rethinking Cold War History,* 273.

110   Scott D. Sagan, *The Limits of Safety* (Princeton: Princeton University Press, 1993), 95.

111   Dobbs, 49.

112   Allyn, Blight, and Welch, 155.

113   Dobbs, 48.

114   Central Intelligence Agency, "Reaction in Cuba to Current Crisis," November 21–4, National Security Files, Box 52, Cuba Subjects, Intelligence7 DCS, 6/62–2/63 Folder, JFKL.

115   Blight, Allyn, and Welch, 211.

116   Dobbs, 53.

117   Blight, Allyn, and Welch, 20.

118   Knebel, 54.

119   "Battalion at Pendleton Mobilized in Two Hours," *Los Angeles Times*, October 23, 1962, Section 1, Page 17.

120   Charles Cullin, *Lubbock (Texas) Avalanche-Journal*, November 24, 1962, 1.

121   The Pentagon, "Background Briefing on Cuban Situation," K160–951–5, Albert F. Simpson Historical Research Center, Office of Air Force History.

122   Fursenko and Naftali, *Khrushchev's Cold War*, 465.

4 A World on Edge

1   Theodore C. Sorensen, *Counselor: A Life at the Edge of History* (New York: Harper, 2008), 288.

2   Ibid., 300.

3   Blight and Welch, 306.

4   United Press International, "*Pravda* Fails Its Deadline," *Wichita Eagle*, October 23, 1962, 1.

5   "Official Soviet Government Statement," TASS, October 23, 1962, 1–3, National Security Files, Box 64, Cuba, Subjects, USSR Miscellaneous Messages, 10/62 Folder, JFKL.

6   "Chronicle of Soviet Propaganda on the Cuban Crisis," October 30, 1962, National Security Files, Box 49, Cuba, Subjects, Foreign Reaction Reports, Foreign Information Service 10/23/62–11/3–62 Folder, JFKL.

7   Wolfgang Saxon, "Foy D. Kohler, Envoy to Moscow during Cuban Crisis, Is Dead at 82," *New York Times*, December 26, 1990, D-11.

8   *The Huntley-Brinkley Report*, October 23, 1962, National Broadcasting Company Records, Box 534, H.B. (N.Y. only) 1962 October 15–30 Folder, WHS.

9   Dobbs, 62.

10   "Soviet Submarine Deployment," National Security Files, Box 40, Cuba Cables 10/23/62 Folder, JFKL.

11   Dobbs, 56.

12   Memorandum, National Security Files, Box 46, Cuba, Subjects, CIA Memoranda, 10/23/62–10/25/62 Folder, JFKL.

13   Dobbs, 42–3.

14   Blight and Welch, 178.

15   There has never been any evidence that the Chinese government had anything to do with the influx of offensive weapons in Cuba. Still, the Western habit of assuming that all Communists functioned as a united front tended to obscure the reality of a sharp divide between the Soviet Union and China.

16   May and Zelikow, "Tuesday, October 23, 10 a.m., Cabinet Room," 300.

17   The 2000 film *Thirteen Days* cast O'Donnell in a starring role filled by Kevin Costner.

18   May and Zelikow, "Tuesday, October 23, 10 a.m., Cabinet Room," 297.

19   John F. Kennedy and Roswell Gilpatric, "Telephone recordings: Dictation Belt 32.3. Possible Naval Action, Blockade of Cuba," http://www.jfklibrary.org/Asset-Viewer/Archives/JFKPOF-TPH-32–3.aspx, last accessed June 6, 2012, JFKL.

20   John McCone, "Executive Committee Meeting on 23 October 1962 6 p.m. All members present plus Counsel for Defense Department," October 23, 1962 in *CIA Documents on the Cuban Missile Crisis*, 291–2.

21   The estimate that 10 million Americans fled their homes can be found in Roger Sullivan, "Memorandum to Distribution," January 10, 1978, Paul H. Nitze Papers, Box 65, Folder 5, LOC. Also see B. Wayne Blanchard, "American Civil Defense 1945–75: Evolution of Programs and Politics," Ph.D. diss., University of Virginia, 1980.

22   Eugene L. Meyer, "When the Bomb Falls, Head for Paw Paw," *Washington Post*, March 8, 1980, A1.

23   United Press International, Wire Dispatch, May 6, 1981.

24   Associated Press, "Ma Forgets Her Kids," *Philadelphia Inquirer*, October 29, 1962, 7.

25   United Press International, "Jacksonville Ready To Evacuate If –," *Charlotte Observer*, October 25, 1962, 3A.

26   Lydel Sims, "Crisis-Created Curiosity Offers Puzzle to Police," *Memphis Commercial Appeal*, October 26, 1962, 1.

27   Jack Smith, "City Feels Panic, Calm in Crisis," *Los Angeles Times*, October 28, 1962, 3.

28   "McNayr Criticized For Attack Alert," *Miami Herald*, October 26, 1962, 2.

29   "Query Editor," *Newsweek*, Undated, Newsweek MSS 629, Box 5, Item 3, RWWL.

30   "This 'Funny' Crisis," *Miami Herald*, October 27, 1962, 1A.

31   "Big Sale of Guns at Bakersfield," *Los Angeles Times*, October 28, 1962, 12.

32   "Crisis Builds Gun Demand," *Dallas Morning News*, October 28, 1962, Section 1, Page 15.

33   Special to the *New York Times*, "Czechs Halt Rush to Purchase Food," *New York Times*, October 27, 1962, 7.

34   In general, the Soviet Union has been heralded for having a better civil defense system than the United States.

35   Allyn, Blight, and Welch, 170.

36   Dobrynin, 90.

37   Juanita Greene, "Tense Talk of War—Without Panic," *Miami Herald*, October 24, 1962, 1C.

38   Bob Pimentel, "The Campus and Cuba," *Daily Californian*, October 24, 1962, 1.

39   Mary McGowan, "Nation's Students Scared By New Cuban Crisis," *Daily Californian*, October 24, 1962, 1.

40   Spencer R. Weart, *Nuclear Fear: A History of Images* (Cambridge: Harvard University Press, 1988), 259.

41   Dobbs, 71–2.

42   George Anderson, Interview by Joseph E. O'Connor, April 25, 1967, 18–19, JFKL.

43   Fursenko and Naftali, *"One Hell of a Gamble,"* 254.

44   See "Malinovsky's Order to Pliyev," October 22, 1962, in *On the Brink of the Nuclear Abyss,* ed. A.I. Gribkov, trans. Svetlana Savranskaya (Moscow: Gregory Page, 1998), 363, http://www.gwu.edu/~nsarchiv/nsa/cuba_mis_cri/621022%20Malinovsky's%20Order%20to%20Pliyev.pdf, last accessed June 6, 2012, NSA.

45   Dobbs, 80.

46   Adlai Stevenson, "To Secretary of State," October 23, 1962, Harlan Cleveland Papers, Box 76, 10/24/62 Folder, JFKL.

47   Central Intelligence Agency, "Reaction to President Kennedy's Televised Address Regarding the Cuban Problem on October 22," October 23, 1962, National Security Files, Box 40, Cuba Cables, 10/23/62 Part II Folder, JFKL.

48   Chet Huntley, *Chet Huntley Reporting*, National Broadcasting Company, October 23, 1962, 4, National Broadcasting Company Records, Box 306, CHR 1962, October 23 Folder, WHS.

49   Cable, "Soviet Threats of Retaliation," October 23, 1963, National Security Files, Box 40, Cuba Cables, 10/23/62 Folder, JFKL.

50   Norman H. Finkelstein, *Thirteen Days/Ninety Miles* (New York: Simon & Schuster,1994), 73.

51   Joseph W. Sullivan, "Cuban Crisis Upsets Tourist Industry in Florida and Caribbean," *Wall Street Journal*, October 25, 1962, 1.

52   Jack Heil, "Troops Reach Key West," *Washington Star*, October 25, 1962, A5.

53   The Rio Pact, otherwise known as the Inter-American Treaty of Reciprocal Assistance, stated in 1947 that an attack on any American republic would be treated as an attack against all of them.

54   John F. Kennedy, "Proclamation 3504: Interdiction of the Delivery of Offensive Weapons to Cuba," October 23, 1962, *Public Papers of the Presidents: John F. Kennedy 1962*, 810.

55   "CBS News Special Report," anchored by Walter Cronkite, October 23, 1962, T77:0495, PC.

56   This conclusion has been a topic of note for historians, many of whom believe that a more moderate course might have been unpopular among conservatives but probably would not have prompted impeachment.

57   Robert F. Kennedy, "Memorandum for the President from the Attorney General," October 24, 1962, Presidential Office Files, Box 115, Cuba: Security, 1962 Folder 4, http:www.jfklibrary.org/Asset-Viewer/Archives/JFKPOF-115–004.aspx, last accessed June 6, 2012, JFKL.

58   Anatoly Dobrynin, *In Confidence* (New York: Random House, 1995), 81.

59   Robert F. Kennedy, *Thirteen Days*, 65–6.

60   Ibid., 67.

61   Brugioni, 101.

62   Central Intelligence Agency, National Security Memorandum, "Summary Contents," October 24, 1962, 1–4, National Security Files, Cuba, Subjects, CIA Memoranda, 10/23/62–10/25/62 Folder, JFKL.

63   "The Air Force Response to the Cuban Crisis 14 October–24 November 1962," *Cuba Missile Crisis*, Document cc02811, 18, NSA.

64   Curtis A. Utz, *Cordon of Steel: The U.S. Navy and the Cuban Missile Crisis* (Washington: Naval Historical Center, 1993), 32.

65   May and Zelikow, "Wednesday, October 24, 10:00 a.m., Cabinet Room," 353.

66   Dobbs, 88.

67   May and Zelikow, "Wednesday, October 24, 10:00 a.m., Cabinet Room," 356.

68   Nikita Khrushchev, Cable to Bertrand Russell, October 24, 1962, National Security Files, Box 415, Robert W. Comer 10/10/62–10/25/62 Folder, JFKL.

69   Michael Beschloss, *The Crisis Years: Kennedy and Khrushchev 1960–1963* (New York: Edward Burlingame Books, 1991), 486.

70   Walter Cronkite, interview by Steven Fagan and Vicki Daitch, April 14, 2004, 12, JFKL.

71   Robert F. Kennedy, *Thirteen Days*, 111.

72   Cronkite, 17.

73   "How Much Censorship? How Much Distortion?" *Newsweek*, November 12, 1962, 29.

74   George, 106.

75   "Information is Power," *St. Louis Post-Dispatch*, December 9, 1962, 12.

76   Stewart Alsop and Charles Bartlett, "In Time of Crisis," *Saturday Evening Post*, December 8, 1962, 15–20.

77   William E. Knox, "Report on Mr. William E. Knox's Meeting during the Cuban Missile Crisis with Chairman Nikita S. Khrushchev in Moscow on October 24, 1962," September 20, 1977, 6, Oral history collection, JFKL.

78   "The Talk of the Town," *New Yorker*, November 3, 1962, 43.

79   Nikita Khrushchev, "Premier Khrushchev's Letter to President Kennedy," October 24, 1962, in *The Cuban Missile Crisis 1962*, ed. Laurence Chang and Peter Kornbluh (New York: The New Press, 1992), 173–4.

80   "CD to Stock 47 Buildings for Shelter," *Tulsa Daily World*, October 25, 1962, Section 2, Page 1.

81   Sagan, 124.

82   *Herald Tribune* Service, "Control Programs Are Under Study," *Cincinnati Enquirer*, October 25, 1962, 1.

83   "Memorandum to Editors and Radio and Television News Directors," Presidential Office Files, Box 114, Cuba: General, 1962: 24 October–31 December Folder, http://www.jfklibrary.org/Asset-Viewer/Archives/JFKPOF-114–031.aspx, last accessed June 6, 2012, JFKL.

84   Andrew, 297.

85   "DOD, Transcripts, SECRET, Notes Taken from Transcripts of Meetings of the Joint Chiefs of Staff, October–November 1962," 10.

86   Memorandum, October 26, 1962, National Security Files, Box 46, Cuba, Subjects, CIA Memoranda, 10/26/62–10/28/62 Folder, JFKL.

87   Gribkov and Smith, 217.

88   May and Zelikow, "Thursday, October 25, 10:00 a.m., Cabinet Room," 420.

89   Hilsman, Memorandum, "Soviets Continue to Seek Abandonment of Quarantine While Missiles Stay," October 25, 1962, National Security Files, Box 50, Cuba, Subjects, Intelligence—INR Material 10/15/62–12/31/62 (1 of 3) Folder, JFKL.

90   State Department Policy Planning Subcommittee, "The Possible Role of a Progressive Economic Blockade against Cuba," October 25, 1962, Presidential Office Files, Box 115, Cuba: Security, Missile Crisis Planning Subcommittee October 1962: 24–28 Folder, http://www.jfklibrary.org/Asset-Viewer/Archives/JFKPOF-115-011.aspx, last accessed July 23, 1011, JFKL.

91   State Department Policy Planning Subcommittee, "Summitry," October 25, 1962, Presidential Office Files, Box 115, Cuba: Security, Missile Crisis Planning Subcommittee October 1962: 24–28 Folder, http://www.jfklibrary.org/Asset-Viewer/Archives/JFKPOF-115-011.aspx, last accessed June 6, 2012, JFKL.

92   William Tyler, W.W. Rostow, and Phillip Talbot, "To the Secretary," October 25, 1962, Presidential Office Files, Box 115, Cuba: Security, Missile Crisis: Planning Subcommittee, October 1962: 24–28 Folder, http://www.jfklibrary.org/Asset-Viewer/Archives/JFKPOF-115-011.aspx, last accessed June 6, 2012, JFKL.

93   Central Intelligence Agency, "The Crisis USSR/Cuba," October 25, 1962, National Security Files, Cuba, Subjects, CIA Memoranda, Box 46, 10/26/62–10/28/62 Folder, JFKL.

94   At the Moscow conference about the missile crisis, Khruschev's son, Sergei, explained that Soviet missiles lacked the necessary targeting ability to zero in on military targets. See Allyn, Blight, and Welch, 161.

95   Dean Rusk and Robert McNamara, "Memorandum to Members of Congress," October 24, 1962, Vice Presidential Papers, Subject File 1962 Foreign Relations—Cuba, (3 of 4) Folder, LBJL.

96   Sorensen, *Kennedy*, 706–7.

97   "CBS News Special Report," October 25, 1962, anchored by Walter Cronkite, T77:0497, PC.

98   Ralph McGill, "Mood Piece from the U.N.," *Atlanta Constitution*, October 24, 1962, 1.

99   John F. Kennedy, "Message to the Acting Secretary General of the United Nations," October 25, 1962, *Public Papers of the Presidents: John F. Kennedy 1962*, 811.

100   Special to the *New York Times*, "Pentagon Issues Shelter Report," *New York Times*, October 26, 1962, 1.

101   "307 Buildings in L.A. Licensed as Shelters," *Los Angeles Times*, October 26, 1962, 18.

102   "N.O. Designates 42 CD Shelters," (New Orleans) *Times-Picayune*, October 25, 1962, 1.

103   Marion Gaines, "Speed Up Civil Defense or Drop It, State Urged," *Atlanta Constitution*, October 26, 1962, 1.

104   In the twenty-first century, when soldiers and their families are able to maintain face-to-face communication via the internet, it is difficult to imagine the uncertainty of an age when communications between troops and their families were inconsistent and unreliable.

105   Marshall S. Carter, "Memorandum to the Director," October 25, 1962, *The Secret Cuban Missile Crisis Documents*, 311.

106   "Scenario for Airstrike against Offensive Missile Bases and Bombers in Cuba," Harlan Cleveland Papers, Box 79, Cuba—Cuba Crisis—Top Secret Folder, JFKL.

107   Anatoly Dobrynin, Report to the Foreign Ministry, October 25, 1962, *Cold War International History Project Digital Archives*, Cuban Missile Crisis Collection, http://legacy.wilsoncenter.org/va2/index.cfm?topic_id=1409&fuseaction=home.document&identifier=5034F28C-96B6–175C-9D40F502A238FC9&sort=collection&item=Cuban Missile Crisis, last accessed June 6, 2012, NSA.

108   Moscow Embassy, "Attention Mr. Bundy," October 25, 1962, National Security Files, Box 179, USSR General, 10/9/62–10/31/62 Folder, JFKL.

109   Fursenko and Naftali, *Khrushchev's Cold War*, 484.

5 Into the Dark

1   Brugioni, 371.

2   Dobbs, 136.

3   "Annex 1: Cuba and the Strategic Threat," National Security Files, Box 36, Cuba: General, 1962 10/26/62–10/27/62 Folder, JFKL.

4   At the last meeting of Cuban Missile Crisis survivors in Havana in 1992, there was debate about the number of Soviet missiles that reached Cuba, with some discrepancies between Soviet and Cuban counts.

5   "DOD, Transcripts, SECRET, Notes Taken from Transcripts of Meetings of the Joint Chiefs of Staff, October-November 1962," 20.

6   Fursenko and Naftali, "*One Hell of a Gamble,*" 366–7.

7   May and Zelikow, "Monday, October 23, 5 p.m., Cabinet Room," 261.

8   May and Zelikow, "Friday, October 26, 10:00 a.m., Cabinet Room," 440.

9   Allyn, Blight, and Welch, 76.

10   Subsequent reports suggest that Feklisov was not acting on behalf of the Soviet government because a KGB agent would not typically have been used for this purpose. See Alexander Fursenko and Timothy Naftali, "Using KGB Documents: The Scali-Feklisov Channel in the Cuban Missile Crisis," *Cold War International History Project Bulletin*, Spring 1995, 60.

11   ABC News, *John Scali, ABC News*, April 13, 1964, Arthur M. Schlesinger Jr. Papers, Box W-5, ABC News Report Folder, JFKL.

12   Blight, Allyn, and Welch, 354.

13   Fursenko and Naftali, "*One Hell of a Gamble,*" 268.

14   See Nikita Khrushchev, *Khrushchev Remembers: The Glasnost Tapes*, trans. and ed. Jerrold L. Schecter and Vyacheslav V. Luchkov (Boston: Little, Brown and Company, 1990), 178.

15   George Gedda, "Letter Says Castro Opposed Pre-Emptive Strike Against the U.S. in '62," Associated Press, December 19, 1990.

16   Blight, Allyn, and Welch, 111.

17   Edward A. McDermott, Letter to Earl Warren, October 30, 1962, Office of Emergency Planning, Microfilm Roll #1, JFKL.

18   Jacob "Jack" Rosenthal, Interview by Vicki Daitch, December 8, 2004, 3–4, JFKL.

19   Tazewell Shepard Jr., "Relocation of Dependents of Personnel Involved in the White House Emergency Plan," Presidential Office Files, Box 114, Cuba: General, 1962: 24 October–31 December Folder, http://www.jfklibrary.org/Asset-Viewer/Archives/JFKPOF-114–031.aspx, last accessed June 6, 2012, JFKL.

20   Jacqueline Kennedy, *Jacqueline Kennedy: Historic Conversations on Life with John F. Kennedy* (New York: Hyperion, 2011), 263.

21   "Memorandum to the Director: The Rationing Situation," October 26, 1962, Office of Emergency Planning Records, Microfilm Roll #1, JFKL.

22   Dobbs, 133–4.

23   Sagan, 128.

24   "Operation MONGOOSE: Main Points to Consider," October 26, 1962, Rockefeller Commission Records, Box 3A, Record Number 178–10003–10010, JFK-NA.

25 John A. McCone, "Memorandum of MONGOOSE Meeting in the JCS Operations Room, October 26, 1962, at 2:30 p.m.," October 29, 1962, Rockefeller Commission Records, Box 3A, Record Number 178–10003–10008, JFK-NA.

26 Dobbs, 152.

27 May and Zelikow, "Friday, October 26 Afternoon and Evening, Oval Office," 487.

28 Andrew, 300.

29 Del W. Harding, "As a Fallout Shelter, This One's No Hotel!" *Rocky Mountain News*, October 26, 1962, 6.

30 "CD Setup of Virginia Is Assessed," *Richmond Post-Dispatch*, October 27, 1962, 1.

31 "WNBC News 7:25 a.m." NBC Records, Box 266, WNBC Television, October 26, 1962 Folder, WHS.

32 "1,083 Surveyed Shelter Sites in District List," *Evening [Washington] Star*, October 26, 1962, A10.

33 "Cuban Crisis Could Boost Economy, Delay a Recession, Economists Say," *Wall Street Journal*, October 26, 1962, 3.

34 John Handley, "Memories of the *Queen Mary*: Immensity, Beauty and Comfort," *Chicago Tribune*, January 19, 1986, Travel Section, 1.

35 Brugioni, 464.

36 "DOD, Transcripts, SECRET, Notes Taken from Transcripts of Meetings of the Joint Chiefs of Staff, October–November 1962," 23.

37 Ibid., 22.

38 See "Letter from Nikita Khrushchev to Fidel Castro," October 28, 1962, PBS, http://www.pbs.org/wgbh/americanexperience/features/primary-resources/jfk-ussrfirm and "Letter from Fidel Castro to Nikita Khrushchev," October 28, 1962, http://www.pbs.org/wgbh/americanexperience/features/primary-resources/jfk-airspace, both last accessed June 17, 2012.

39 Allyn, Blight, and Welch, 32.

40 Dobbs, 237.

41 Dobbs, 210.

42 Ibid., 276.

43 Gribkov and Smith, 142.

44 Dobbs, 92.

45 Sorensen, *Counselor*, 305.

46 Brugioni, 474.

47 Gribkov and Smith, 63.

48 Fursenko and Naftali, *"One Hell of a Gamble,"* 271.

49 Dobbs, 249.

50 Freedman, 219.

51 Roger Hilsman, Memorandum, "Implications of the Soviet Initiative on Cuba," October 27, 1962, Roger Hilsman Papers, Box 1, 10/27 Folder, Record Number 176–10030–10242, JFK-NA.

52 Sagan, 108.

53 Khrushchev's inspiration in making this plea may have been Walter Lippmann's column that suggested a Cuba/Turkey missile trade. See Fursenko and Naftali, *Khrushchev's Cold War*, 488.

54   Marc Trachtenberg, "The Influence of Nuclear Weapons in the Cuban Missile Crisis," *International Security* 10, no.1 (Summer 1985): 144.

55   Roger Hilsman, "Trading U.S. Missile Bases in Turkey for Soviet Bases in Cuba," October 27, 1962, Roger Hilsman Papers, Box 1, 10/27 Folder, Record Number 176–10030–10242, JFK-NA.

56   Dobrynin, 86.

57   Sorensen, *Counselor*, 304.

58   Contrary to claims by some Kennedy loyalists, Johnson demonstrated leadership on the Ex Comm, and according to Ernest R. May and Philip D. Zelikow, who edited the Ex Comm tapes, his strength was most evident when both Kennedys were out of the room. See May and Zelikow, "Introduction," 42.

59   John F. Kennedy, "Message to Chairman Khrushchev Calling for Removal of Soviet Missiles From Cuba," October 27, 1962, *Public Papers of the Presidents: John F. Kennedy 1962*, 813–14.

60   Allyn, Blight, and Welch, 156.

61   Dobbs, 240.

62   Nikita Khrushchev, *Khrushchev Remembers: The Glasnost Tapes*, 178.

63   Gribkov and Smith, 70.

64   Blight, Allyn, and Welch, 121.

65   George, 161.

66   J. Edgar Hoover, Report to the Attorney General: Cuban Crisis—1962, October 27, 1962, Presidential Office Files, Box 115, Cuban Security 1962 Folder, JFKL.

67   Steuart Pittman, "A Report on National Civil Defense Readiness," October 27, 1962, Office of Emergency Planning Records, Microfilm Roll #1, JFKL.

68   Edward McDermott, Memorandum to the President, November 7, 1962, Presidential Office Files, Departments and Agencies, Box 85, OEP 7/62–12/62 Folder, JFKL.

69   Steuart L. Pittman, "Report on the National Survey from the Assistant Secretary for Civil Defense, Steuart L. Pittman," February 20, 1963, Vice Presidential Papers, 1963 Subject Files, David Reardon Papers, Box 6, Civil Defense Shelters Folder, LBJL.

70   Steuart Pittman, "Government and Civil Defense," in *Who Speaks for Civil Defense?* ed. Eugene P. Wigner (New York: Scribner, 1968), 53–4.

71   *The Fallout Protection Booklet: A Report of Public Attitudes Toward and Information about Civil Defense*, Michigan State University, April 1963, Appendix A, 15.

72   Weart, 260.

73   *Civil Defense and Cold War Attitudes*, University of Pittsburgh, June 1964, 80.

74   Jim Hershberg, "Anatomy of a Controversy: Anatoly F. Dobrynin's Meeting with Robert F. Kennedy, Saturday, 27 October 1962," *Cold War International Historical Project Bulletin*, Spring 1995, http://www.gwu.edu/~nsarchiv/nsa/cuba_mis_cri/moment.htm, last accessed June 6, 2012.

75   Donald M. Wilson, oral history interview by James Greenfield, September 2, 1964, 30, JFKL.

76   Blight, Allyn, and Welch, 378.

77   Freedman, 217.

78   Fursenko and Naftali, "*One Hell of a Gamble*," 285.

79   Fursenko and Naftali, *Khrushchev's Cold War*, 480.

80 Sergei N. Khrushchev, 626.

81 Fursenko and Naftali, "*One Hell of a Gamble*," 287.

82 Nikita Khrushchev, "Official English Text of Khrushchev Message," TASS, October 28, 1962, National Security Files, Box 47, Cuba, Subjects, Kennedy, Khrushchev, U Thant, Castro Correspondence 10/28/62 Folder, JFKL.

83 Roger Hilsman, "Analysis of Khrushchev's Message," October 28, 1962, Roger Hilsman Papers, Box 1, 10/27 Folder, Record Number 176–10030–10242, JFK-NA.

84 John F. Kennedy, "Message in Reply to a Broadcast by Chairman Khrushchev on the Cuban Crisis," October 28, 1962, *Public Papers of the Presidents: John F. Kennedy 1962*, 814–15.

85 John F. Kennedy, "Statement by the President Following the Soviet Decision to Withdraw Missiles from Cuba," October 28, 1962, *Public Papers of the Presidents: John F. Kennedy 1962*, 815.

86 Walter W. Rostow, "To the Secretary," October 28, 1962, Box 115, Cuba: Security, Missile Crisis: Planning Subcommittee, October 1962: 24–8 Folder, http://www.jfklibrary.org/Asset-Viewer/Archives/JFKPOF-115-011.aspx, last accessed June 6, 2012, JFKL.

87 "Harrison, Congressmen Welcome Cuban Accord," *Richmond Post-Dispatch*, October 29, 1962, 1.

88 *CBS Washington Report*, October 28, 1962, PC.

89 McGeorge Bundy, "National Security Memorandum 200," October 28, 1962, National Security Files, http://www.jfklibrary.org/Asset-Viewer/tGfLmc1iKU2kf DuYbYwH4Q.aspx, last accessed February 18, 2012, JFKL.

90 Dobbs, 176.

91 Gribkov and Smith, 148.

92 Dobbs, 326.

93 Fursenko and Naftali, "*One Hell of a Gamble*," 288.

94 Blight, Allyn, and Welch, 214–15.

95 Central Intelligence Agency, "Implications of Khrushchev's Message of 28 October," October 28, 1962, 3, National Security Files, Box 46, Cuba, Subjects, CIA Memoranda 10/26/62–10/30/62 Folder, JFKL.

96 Blight, Allyn, and Welch, 406.

97 Dobbs, 336.

98 Allyn, Blight, and Welch, 137.

99 Nikita Khrushchev, *Khrushchev Remembers*, 496.

100 Dan Oberdorfer, "Survival of the Fewest," *Saturday Evening Post*, March 23, 1963, 17.

101 Rose, 201.

6 Moving Ahead, Looking Back

1 Robert A. Pollard, "The Cuban Missile Crisis: Legacy and Lessons," *Wilson Quarterly* 6, no. 4 (Autumn 1982): 158.

2 Arthur G. Neal, *National Trauma and Collective Memory*, 2nd edition (Armonk, NY: M.E. Sharpe, 2005), 30.

3 Walt Rostow, interview by Richard Neustadt, 1964, 71, JFKL.

4   Maria Shriver, *One Minute to Midnight: The Real Story of the Cuban Missile Crisis*, NBC, October 23, 1992.

5   Lisle A. Rose, *The Cold War Comes to Main Street* (Lawrence: University Press of Kansas, 1999), 311.

6   "Query Editor," Newsweek Atlanta Bureau, undated, Newsweek Atlanta Bureau Records, Box 5 (Cuba), 4 Folder, RWWL.

7   Beschloss, 487.

8   Lois Dickert, "They Thought the War Was On!" *McCall's*, April 1963, 96.

9   Milton Schwebel, "What Do They Think?" in *Children and the Threat of Nuclear War*, ed. Child Study Association (New York: Duell, Sloan and Pearce, 1964), 26–29.

10   Jiri Nehnevajsa and Morris I. Berkowitz, *The Cuban Crisis: Meaning and Impact* (Pittsburgh: University of Pittsburgh, 1962), 8–9.

11   Raymond Garthoff, *Reflections on the Cuban Missile Crisis* (Washington: Brookings Institution, 1987), 51.

12   Norman Cousins, *The Improbable Triumvirate* (New York: W.W. Norton, 1972), 46.

13   "CBS Special Report," November 1, 1962, PC.

14   Don DeLillo, *Libra* (New York: Penguin, 1991), 316.

15   Brugioni, 509–10.

16   See "Letter from Khrushchev to Castro," October 30, 1962, PBS, http://www.pbs.org/wgbh/americanexperience/features/primary-resources/jfk-defendcuba, last accessed June 17, 2012.

17   Nikita S. Khrushchev, *Khrushchev Remembers*, 504.

18   Blight, Allyn, and Welch, 22.

19   John F. Kennedy, "Message to the President of the Inter-Parliamentary Council," November 1, 1962, *Public Papers of the Presidents: John F. Kennedy 1962*, 820.

20   May and Zelikow, "Monday, October 29, 10:10 a.m., Cabinet Room and Oval Office," 638.

21   Fursenko and Naftali, *Khrushchev's Cold War*, 497.

22   "DOD, Transcripts, SECRET, Notes Taken from Transcripts of Meetings of the Joint Chiefs of Staff, October–November 1962," 27.

23   Fursenko and Naftali, *Khrushchev's Cold War*, 502.

24   Fursenko and Naftali, *"One Hell of a Gamble,"* 311–12.

25   Freedman, 249.

26   Democratic losses and Republican gains were not equal because the House of Representatives had 437 members in the 87th Congress and only 435 in the 88th. The new statehood of Alaska and Hawaii in 1959 temporarily raised the number of representatives in the House until reapportionment took effect in the 1962 election.

27   Thomas G. Paterson and William J. Brophy, "October Missiles and November Elections: The Cuban Missile Crisis and American Politics, 1962," *Journal of American History* 71, no. 1 (June 1986): 87–119.

28   Brugioni, 560.

29   Kenneth Keating, "Keating Reminds Senate of 1962 Cuba Resolution," September 20, 1963, 1, Kenneth B. Keating Papers, II:568:1, University of Rochester Rare Books Department.

30 Dean Rusk, Telegram to Adlai Stevenson, November 16, 1962, Harlan Cleveland Papers, Box 78, Cuba, Cuban Crisis—H.C.'s Book 1962 (Folder 1 of 2), JFKL.

31 Fursenko and Naftali, *"One Hell of a Gamble,"* 323.

32 "Defense in a Nuclear Age," *New Republic,* November 24, 1962, 3–4.

33 Robert S. McNamara, *In Retrospect: The Tragedy and Lessons of Vietnam* (New York: Random House, 1995), 345.

34 Transcript, *A Conversation with President Kennedy,* ABC, CBS, and NBC, December 17, 1962, 1, Eric Sevareid Papers, Box II 41, Folder 19, LOC.

35 Ibid., 22.

36 Central Intelligence Agency, Memorandum, November 5, 1962, Rockefeller Commission Records, Box 3A, Assassination Materials Miscellaneous Rockefeller Commission and CIA Files Folder, Digital Record Number 178–10003–10006, JFK/NA.

37 Gromyko, 180.

38 Robert S. McNamara, "Special Cuba Briefing," February 6, 1963, George McGovern Papers, Box 1293, Alliance for Progress Folder, SGMML.

39 Jay Lindsay, "JFK Moon Mission Tape Reveals Inner Doubts about Space Program," *The Huffington Post,* May 25, 2011, http://www.huffingtonpost.com/2011/05/25/jfk-moon-mission_n_866715.html; accessed June 13, 2012.

40 John F. Kennedy, "Commencement Address at American University in Washington," June 10, 1963, *Public Papers of the Presidents: John F. Kennedy 1963* (Washington: Government Printing Office, 1964), 460–2.

41 Mandelbaum, *The Nuclear Revolution,* 173.

42 Steinberg, 672.

43 Mandelbaum, *The Nuclear Question* (Cambridge: Cambridge University Press, 1979), 175.

44 Dobrynin, 93.

45 John F. Kennedy, "Toasts of the President and Chancellor Adenauer," November 14, 1962, *Public Papers of the Presidents: John F. Kennedy 1962,* 825.

46 Mandelbaum, *The Nuclear Question,* 133.

47 Dobrynin, 71.

48 John Compton, "John Kennedy," in *Children Write About John F. Kennedy,* ed. William G. Walsh (Brownsville, Texas: Springman-King Publishing Company, 1964), 119.

49 Dobrynin, 91.

50 Fursenko and Naftali, *Khrushchev's Cold War,* 533–4.

51 May and Zelikow, "Preface," x.

52 Sheldon M. Stern, *The Week the World Stood Still* (Stanford: Stanford University Press, 2005), 6.

53 Nikita S. Khrushchev, *Khrushchev Remembers,* 500.

54 Nikita S. Khrushchev, *Khrushchev Remembers: The Glasnost Tapes,* 180.

55 Blight and Welch, 247.

56 Allyn, Blight, and Welch, 67.

57 Blight and Welch, 26.

58 This nightmare of destruction seemed all too real to two Americans serving in the Peace Corps in Thailand during the crisis. At one point, the couple heard—and believed—that New York City, where their families lived, had been annihilated

by a Soviet nuclear attack. See James G. Blight, *The Shattered Crystal Ball* (Savage, MD: Rowman & Littlefield Publishers, 1990), 6.

59   John F. Kennedy, televised interview by George Herman, "Post Mortem on October Crisis," CBS, December 16, 1962, National Security Files, Box 61, Cuba Subjects Guidelines for Public Testimony, Presidential Comments Folder, 11/22/62–10/31/63 Folder, JFKL.

60   Blight and Welch, 108.

61   Ibid., 201.

62   Norman Cousins, "The Cuban Missile Crisis: An Anniversary," *Saturday Review*, October 15, 1977, 4.

63   Art Buchwald, "The Doves and the Hawks," *Herald Tribune* Syndicate, November 1962, Art Buchwald Papers, Box 4, Folder 1, WHS.

64   Martin Luther King Jr., "Thanksgiving Day Sermon at Ebenezer Baptist Church [in Atlanta]," November 22, 1962, Southern Christian Leadership Records, Box 58, Folder 18, MLKL&A.

65   Script, *The Missiles of October*, XII-180, George Ball Papers, Box 146, *The Missiles of October* Folder, SGMML.

66   Robert Kennedy's "thirteen days" referred to the period between the day JFK found out about the Soviet missiles until the day of Khrushchev's announcement that he would withdraw the missiles. Some people measure just the public phase of the crisis, October 22–28.

67   Benjamin C. Bradlee, *Conversations with Kennedy* (New York: W.W. Norton & Company, 1975), 122.

68   Cousins, 4.

69   Schlesinger, *A Thousand Days*, 831.

70   McNamara, 96.

71   Robert S. McNamara, interview by Robert Scheer, "How We Helped Push the Soviets into their Arms Buildup," *Washington Post*, August 1, 1982, B3.

72   Mandelbaum, *The Nuclear Question*, 143.

73   Blight, Allyn, and Welch, 193.

74   Weart, 259.

Documents

1   John F. Kennedy, "Radio and Television Report to the American People on the Soviet Arms Buildup in Cuba, October 22, 1962," *Public Papers of the Presidents: John F. Kennedy 1962*, 806–9.

2   Nikita Khrushchev, letter to John F. Kennedy, October 23, 1962, Presidential Office Files, Box 115, Cuba: Security, Missile Crisis: Khrushchev correspondence, 1962: 23 October–19 December Folder, http://www.jfklibrary.org/Asset-Viewer/Archives/JFKPOF-115–010.aspx, last accessed August 8, 2012, JFKL.

3   John F. Kennedy, "Draft Letter to Nikita Khrushchev," October 23, 1962, Presidential Office Files, Box 115, Cuba—Missile Crisis—Khrushchev Correspondence 10/23/62–12/19/62 Folder, http://www.jfklibrary.org/Asset-Viewer/Archives/JFKPOF-115–010.aspx, last accessed August 8, 2012, JFKL.

4   Office of the White House Press Secretary, Statement, October 26, 1962, Pierre Salinger Papers, Box 67, 9/2/62–11/27/62 Folder, JFKL.

5   Fidel Castro, Letter to Nikita Khrushchev, October 26, 1962, http://www.gwu.edu/~nsarchiv/nsa/cuba_mis_cri/621026%20Castro%20Letter%20to%20Khrushchev.pdf, last accessed August 9, 2012, NSA.

6   J. Edgar Hoover, "Soviet Personnel Intelligence Activities," Memorandum to the Attorney General, October 27, 1962, Presidential Office Files, Countries, Cuba, Box 115, Cuba: Security, 1962 Folder, http://www.jfklibrary.org/Asset-Viewer/Archives/JFKPOF-115–004.aspx, last accessed August 8, 2012, JFKL.

7   Steuart L. Pittman, "A Report on National Civil Defense Readiness," October 27, 1962, Office of Emergency Planning Records, Microfilm #1, JFKL.

8   Nikita Khrushchev, Letter to John F. Kennedy, October 28, 1962, *Digital History*, http://www.digitalhistory.uh.edu/disp_textbook.cfm?smtID=3&psid=3638, last accessed December 6, 2012.

9   John F. Kennedy, "Message in Reply to a Broadcast by Chairman Khrushchev on the Cuban Crisis," October 28, 1962, *Public Papers of the Presidents: John F. Kennedy 1962*, 814–15.

Selected Bibliography

Libraries, Archives

Archive of Nuclear Data of the Natural Resources Defense Council at http://www.nrdc.org/nuclear/nudb/datainx.asp

Cold War International History Project Digital Archive, http://www.wilsoncenter.org/digital-archive

Digital National Security Archive, http://nsarchive.chadwyck.com/marketing/index.jsp

Dwight D. Eisenhower Library in Abilene, Kansas

Hoover Institution in Palo Alto, California

Howard Gotlieb Archival Research Center in Boston

John F. Kennedy Assassination Records at National Archives II in College Park, Maryland

John F. Kennedy Library in Boston (JFKL)

Library of Congress in Washington, DC

Lyndon B. Johnson Library in Austin

Martin Luther King Jr. Library and Archives in Atlanta

National Security Archive in Washington

Paley Center for Media in New York

Robert W. Woodruff Library in Atlanta

Rockefeller Archive Center in Pocantico Hills, NY

Seeley G. Mudd Manuscript Library in Princeton

University of Rochester Rare Books Department

Wisconsin Historical Society in Madison

Individual sources

ABC News. *John Scali, ABC News*. April 13, 1964, Arthur M. Schlesinger Jr. Papers, Box W-5, ABC News Report Folder, JFKL.

Abel, Elie. *The Missile Crisis*. Philadelphia: J.B. Lippincott Co., 1966.

Allison, Graham, and Philip Zelikow. *Essence of Decision: Explaining the Cuban Missile Crisis,* 2nd edition. New York: Longman, 1999.

Allyn, Bruce J., James G. Blight, and David A. Welch. *Back to the Brink.* Lanham, MD: University Press of America, 1992.

Alsop, Stewart. "Kennedy's Grand Strategy." *Saturday Evening Post*, March 31, 1962, 11–15.

Alsop, Stewart and Charles Bartlett. "In Time of Crisis." *Saturday Evening Post*, December 8, 1962, 15–21.

Ambrose, Stephen E. *Eisenhower, Volume 2: The President.* New York: Simon and Schuster, 1984.

Andrew, Christopher. *For the President's Eyes Only.* New York: Harper Perennial, 1996.

Aronson, James. *The Press and the Cold War.* Indianapolis: Bobbs–Merrill, 1970.

Beschloss, Michael. *The Crisis Years: Kennedy and Khrushchev 1960–1963.* New York: Edward Burlingame Books, 1991.

Blight, James G. *The Shattered Crystal Ball.* Savage, MD: Rowman & Littlefield Publishers, 1990.

Blight, James G., Bruce J. Allyn, and David A. Welch. *Cuba on the Brink.* Lanham: Rowman and Littlefield Publishers Inc., 2002.

Blight, James G. and David A. Welch. *On the Brink.* New York: Hill and Wang, 1989.

Bradlee, Benjamin C. *Conversations with Kennedy.* New York: W.W. Norton & Company, 1975.

Brugioni, Dino. *Eyeball to Eyeball: The Inside Story of the Cuban Missile Crisis.* New York: Random House, 1990.

Burdick, Eugene and Harvey Wheeler. *Fail-Safe.* New York: McGraw-Hill Book Company, 1962.

Central Intelligence Agency, ed. *The Secret Cuban Missile Crisis Documents.* Washington: Brassey's Inc., 1994.

Chang, Laurence and Peter Kornbluh, eds. *The Cuban Missile Crisis 1962.* New York: The New Press, 1992.

Child Study Association, ed. *Children and the Threat of Nuclear War.* New York: Duell, Sloan and Pearce, 1964.

Cousins, Norman. "The Cuban Missile Crisis: An Anniversary." *Saturday Review*, October 15, 1977, 4.

——. *The Improbable Triumvirate.* New York: W. W. Norton, 1972.

Cuban Missile Crisis of 1962—Studies in the Employment of Air Power, Volume 6. Montgomery Air University, 1988.

Dallek, Robert. *An Unfinished Life.* Boston: Little, Brown and Company, 2003.

Daniel, James and John G. Hubbard. *Strike in the West.* New York: Holt, Rinehart and Winston, 1963.

"Defense in a Nuclear Age." *New Republic*, November 24, 1962.

DeLillo, Don. *Libra.* New York: Penguin, 1991.

Detzer, David. *The Brink: The Cuban Missile Crisis, 1962.* New York: Crowell, 1979.

Dickert, Lois. "They Thought the War Was On!" *McCall's*, April 1963, 96.

Dobbs, Michael. *One Minute to Midnight*. New York: Alfred A. Knopf, 2008.

Dobrynin, Anatoly. *In Confidence*. New York: Random House, 1995.

Eisenhower, Dwight D. Diary. Papers of the President of the United States (Ann Whitman File), Dwight D. Eisenhower Library.

The Fallout Protection Booklet: A Report of Public Attitudes Toward and Information about Civil Defense, East Lansing: Michigan State University, April 1963.

Finkelstein, Norman H. *Thirteen Days/Ninety Miles*. New York: Simon & Schuster, 1994.

Freedman, Lawrence. *Kennedy's Wars: Berlin, Cuba, Laos, and Vietnam*. Oxford: Oxford University Press, 2000.

Fursenko, Aleksandr and Timothy Naftali. *Khrushchev's Cold War*. New York: W. W. Norton & Co., 2006.

———. *"One Hell of a Gamble": Khrushchev, Castro, and Kennedy, 1958–1964*. New York: W.W. Norton & Company, 1998.

Gaddis, John Lewis. *We Now Know: Rethinking Cold War History*. Oxford: Clarendon Press, 1997.

Gallup, George H. *The Gallup Poll: Public Opinion 1935–1971, Volume 3, 1959–71*. New York: Random House, 1972.

Garthoff, Raymond. *Reflections on the Cuban Missile Crisis*. Washington: Brookings Institution, 1987.

George, Alice L. *Awaiting Armageddon: How Americans Faced the Cuban Missile Crisis*. Chapel Hill: University of North Carolina Press, 2003.

Gribkov, A.I., ed. *On the Brink of the Nuclear Abyss*. Translated by Svetlana Savranskaya. Moscow: Gregory Page, 1998.

Gribkov, A.I. and William Y. Smith, with ed. Alfred Friendly. *Operation Anadyr: U.S. and Soviet Generals Recount the Cuban Missile Crisis*. Chicago: Edition Q, 1993.

Gromyko, Andrei. *Memoirs*. Translated by Harold Shukman. New York: Doubleday, 1989.

Guthman, Edwin O. and Jeffrey Shulman, eds. *Robert Kennedy In His Own Words*. New York: Bantam Books, 1988.

Hamilton, Michael P., ed. *American Character and Foreign Policy*. Grand Rapids, Michigan: Wm. B. Eerdmans Publishing Company, 1986.

Harris, Louis and Associates. "A Pilot Study of American Knowledge of and Attitudes Toward Communism in Russia and in the United States." Prepared for National Broadcasting Company, January 1962, 7, Theodore Sorensen Papers, Box 54, Folder 3, JFKL.

Hershberg, Jim. "Anatomy of a Controversy: Anatoly F. Dobrynin's Meeting with Robert F. Kennedy, Saturday, 27 October 1962," *Cold War International Historical Project Bulletin*, Spring 1995, http://www.gwu.edu/~nsarchiv/nsa/cuba_mis_cri/moment.htm.

Hilsman, Roger. *To Move a Nation*. New York: Doubleday and Co., 1967.

Horelick, Arnold L. "The Cuban Missile Crisis: An Analysis of Soviet Calculations and Behavior." Rand Corporation, September 1963.

"How Much Censorship? How Much Distortion?" *Newsweek*, November 12, 1962.

Kennedy, Jacqueline. *Jacqueline Kennedy: Historic Conversations on Life with John F. Kennedy.* New York: Hyperion, 2011.

Kennedy, John F. *Public Papers of the Presidents: John F. Kennedy 1961.* Washington: Government Printing Office, 1962.

——. *Public Papers of the Presidents: John F. Kennedy 1962.* Washington: Government Printing Office, 1963.

——. *Public Papers of the Presidents: John F. Kennedy 1963.* Washington: Government Printing Office, 1964.

——. "The Vigor We Need." *Sports Illustrated*, July 16, 1962, 12–15.

Kennedy, Robert F. *Thirteen Days.* New York: W.W. Norton & Company, 1969.

Khrushchev, Nikita. *Khrushchev Remembers.* Translated and edited by Strobe Talbott. Boston: Little, Brown and Company, 1970.

——. *Khrushchev Remembers: The Glasnost Tapes.* Translated and edited by Jerrold L. Schecter and Vyacheslav V. Luchkov. Boston: Little, Brown and Company, 1990.

Khrushchev, Sergei N. *Nikita Khrushchev and the Creation of a Superpower.* University Park: Pennsylvania State University Press, 2000.

Knebel, Fletcher. "Washington Crisis: 154 Hours on the Brink of War." *Look*, December 18, 1962, 42–54.

Knebel, Fletcher and Charles Bailey. *Seven Days in May.* New York: Harper & Row, 1962.

Kraus, Sidney, Reuben Mehling, and Elaine El-Assal. "Mass Media and the Fallout Controversy." *Public Opinion Quarterly* 27, no. 2 (Summer 1963): 191–205.

McAuliffe, Mary S., ed. *CIA Documents on the Cuban Missile Crisis.* Washington: Central Intelligence Agency History Staff, 1962.

McNamara, Robert S. *In Retrospect: The Tragedy and Lessons of Vietnam.* New York: Random House, 1995.

Mandelbaum, Michael. *The Nuclear Question.* Cambridge: Cambridge University Press, 1979.

——. *The Nuclear Revolution: International Politics Before and After Hiroshima.* Cambridge: Cambridge University Press, 1981.

May, Elaine Tyler. *Homeward Bound: American Families in the Cold War Era.* New York: Basic Books, 1988.

May, Ernest R. and Philip D. Zelikow, eds. *The Kennedy Tapes: Inside the White House During the Cuban Missile Crisis.* Cambridge: Belknap Press, 1997.

Mead, Margaret. *And Keep Your Powder Dry.* New York: William Morrow and Company, 1942.

Myers, Caron. "The Night the Sky Fell." *Our State*, June 2012, 52–5.

National Security Archive. *The Cuban Missile Crisis, 1962: The Documents.* http://www.gwu.edu/~nsarchiv/nsa/cuba_mis_cri/docs.htm.

Neal, Arthur G. *National Trauma and Collective Memory*, 2nd edition. Armonk, NY: M.E. Sharpe, 2005.

Nehnevajsa, Jiri and Morris I. Berkowitz. *The Cuban Crisis: Meaning and Impact.* Pittsburgh: University of Pittsburgh, 1962.

Niebuhr, Reinhold. *The Children of Light and the Children of Darkness*. New York: Charles Scribner's Sons, 1959.

Nitze, Paul, Steven L. Rearden, and Ann M. Smith. *From Hiroshima to Glasnost*. New York: Grove Press, 1989.

Oberdorfer, Dan. "Survival of the Fewest." *Saturday Evening Post*, March 23, 1963, 17–21.

Olson, Nathan and Brian Bascle. *John F. Kennedy: American Visionary*. Mankoto, Minnesota: Capstone Press, 2007.

Paterson, Thomas G. and William J. Brophy. "October Missiles and November Elections: The Cuban Missile Crisis and American Politics, 1962." *Journal of American History* 71, no. 1 (June 1986): 87–119.

Pérez, Louis A. Jr. *Cuba In the American Imagination: Metaphor and Imperial Ethos*. Chapel Hill: University of North Carolina Press, 2008.

Pollard, Robert A. "The Cuban Missile Crisis: Legacy and Lessons." *Wilson Quarterly* 6, no. 4 (Autumn 1982): 148–58.

Preparedness Investigating Subcommittee of the Committee on Armed Services, U.S. Senate, *Investigations of the Preparedness Program: Interim Report*. Washington: Government Printing Office, 1963.

Rasenberger, Jim. *Brilliant Disaster: JFK, Castro and America's Doomed Invasion of Cuba's Bay of Pigs*. New York: Scribner, 2011.

Reeves, Richard. *President Kennedy: Profile in Power*. New York: Simon & Schuster, 1993.

Relin, David Oliver. "The Era of Fear." *Scholastic Update*, September 7, 1990, 11.

Rose, Kenneth C. *One Nation Underground*. New York: New York University Press, 2001.

Rose, Lisle A. *The Cold War Comes to Main Street*. Lawrence: University Press of Kansas, 1999.

Sagan, Scott D. *The Limits of Safety*. Princeton: Princeton University Press, 1993.

Schlesinger, Arthur M. Jr. *A Thousand Days*. Boston: Houghton-Mifflin Company, 1965.

——. *Journals, 1952–2000*. New York: Penguin, 2007.

Select Committee to Study Governmental Operations, U.S. Senate, 94th Congress. "Alleged Assassination Plots Involving Foreign Leaders," November 20, 1975, http://history-matters.com/archive/contents/church/contents_church_reports_ir.htm.

Shriver, Maria. *One Minute to Midnight: The Real Story of the Cuban Missile Crisis*. NBC, October 23, 1992.

Shute, Nevil. *On the Beach*. London: Heinemann, 1957.

Sorensen, Theodore C. *Counselor: A Life at the Edge of History*. New York: Harper, 2008.

——. *Kennedy*. New York: Harper & Row, 1965.

Steinberg, Blema S. "Shame and Humiliation in the Cuban Missile Crisis: A Psychoanalytic Perspective." *Political Psychology* 12, no. 4 (December 1991): 653–90.

Stern, Sheldon. *The Week the World Stood Still.* Stanford: Stanford University Press, 2005.

Sulzberger, C.L. *Last of the Giants.* New York: MacMillan, 1970.

Trachtenberg, Marc, "The Influence of Nuclear Weapons in the Cuban Missile Crisis," *International Security* 10, no.1 (Summer 1985): 137–63.

Utz, Curtis A. *Cordon of Steel: The U.S. Navy and the Cuban Missile Crisis.* Washington: Naval Historical Center, 1993.

Walsh, William G. ed. *Children Write About John F. Kennedy.* Brownsville, Texas: Springman-King Publishing Company, 1964.

Weart, Spencer R. *Nuclear Fear: A History of Images.* Cambridge: Harvard University Press, 1988.

White, Mark J., ed. *The Kennedys and Cuba: The Declassified Documentary History.* Chicago: Ivan R. Dee, 1999.

Wigner, Eugene P. ed. *Survival and the Bomb.* Bloomington: Indiana University Press, 1969.

——. *Who Speaks for Civil Defense?* New York: Scribner, 1968.

Young, Major John M. Young. *When the Russians Blinked: The U.S. Maritime Response to the Cuban Missile Crisis.* Washington: History and Museums Division Headquarters, U.S. Marine Corps, 1990.

Index